Palgrave Macmillan Studies in Banking and Financial Institutions

Series Editor: Professor **Philip Molyneux**

The Palgrave Macmillan Studies in Banking and Financial Institutions are international in orientation and include studies of banking within particular countries or regions, and studies of particular themes such as Corporate Banking, Risk Management, Mergers and Acquisitions, etc. The books' focus is on research and practice, and they include up-to-date and innovative studies on contemporary topics in banking that will have global impact and influence.

Titles include:

Mario Anolli, Elena Beccalli and Tommaso Giordani (*editors*)
RETAIL CREDIT RISK MANAGEMENT

Seth Apati
THE NIGERIAN BANKING SECTOR REFORMS
Power and Politics

Caner Bakir
BANK BEHAVIOUR AND RESILIENCE
The Effect of Structures, Institutions and Agents

Alessandro Carretta and Gianluca Mattarocci (*editors*)
ASSET PRICING, REAL ESTATE AND PUBLIC FINANCE OVER THE CRISIS.

Dimitris N. Chorafas
BASEL III, THE DEVIL AND GLOBAL BANKING

Dimitris N. Chorafas
HOUSEHOLD FINANCE
Adrift in a Sea of Red Ink

Dimitris N. Chorafas
SOVEREIGN DEBT CRISIS
The New Normal and the Newly Poor

Stefano Cosma and Elisabetta Gualandri (*editors*)
THE ITALIAN BANKING SYSTEM
Impact of the Crisis and Future Perspectives

Juan Fernández de Guevara Radoselovics and José Pastor Monsálvez (*editors*)
CRISIS, RISK AND STABILITY IN FINANCIAL MARKETS

Juan Fernández de Guevara Radoselovics and José Pastor Monsálvez (*editors*)
MODERN BANK BEHAVIOUR

Franco Fiordelisi and Ornella Ricci (*editors*)
BANCASSURANCE IN EUROPE
Past, Present and Future

Josanco Floreani and Maurizio Polato
THE ECONOMICS OF THE GLOBAL STOCK EXCHANGE INDUSTRY

Jill M. Hendrickson
FINANCIAL CRISIS
The United States in the Early Twenty-First Century

Otto Hieronymi and Constantine Stephanou (*editors*)
INTERNATIONAL DEBT
Economic, Financial, Monetary, Political and Regulatory Aspects

Paola Leone and Gianfranco A. Vento (*editors*)
CREDIT GUARANTEE INSTITUTIONS AND SME FINANCE

Philip Molyneux (*editor*)
BANK PERFORMANCE, RISK AND FIRM FINANCING

Philip Molyneux (*editor*)
BANK STRATEGY, GOVERNANCE AND RATINGS

Victor Murinde (editor)
BANK REGULATORY REFORMS IN AFRICA

Bernardo Nicoletti
CLOUD COMPUTING IN FINANCIAL SERVICES

Özlem Olgu
EUROPEAN BANKING
Enlargement, Structural Changes and Recent Developments

Fotios Pasiouras
GREEK BANKING
From the Pre-Euro Reforms to the Financial Crisis and Beyond

Daniela Pîrvu
CORPORATE INCOME TAX HARMONIZATION IN THE EUROPEAN UNION

Ramkishen S. Rajan
EMERGING ASIA
Essays on Crises, Capital Flows, FDI and Exchange Rate

Allesandro Roselli
FINANCIAL STRUCTURES AND REGULATION: A COMPARISON OF CRISES IN THE UK, USA AND ITALY

Yasushi Suzuki
JAPAN'S FINANCIAL SLUMP
Collapse of the Monitoring System under Institutional and Transition Failures

Gabriel Tortella and José Luis García Ruiz
SPANISH MONEY AND BANKING
A History

The full list of titles available is on the website: www.palgrave.com/finance/sbfi.asp

---

Palgrave Macmillan Studies in Banking and Financial Institutions
Series Standing Order ISBN 978-1-403-94872-4

You can receive future titles in this series as they are published by placing a standing order. Please contact your bookseller or, in case of difficulty, write to us at the address below with your name and address, the title of the series and the ISBN quoted above.

Customer Services Department, Macmillan Distribution Ltd, Houndmills, Basingstoke, Hampshire RG21 6XS, England

---

The Economics of the Global Stock Exchange Industry

Josanco Floreani and Maurizio Polato
Department of Economics, University of Udine, Italy

palgrave
macmillan

First published 2014 by
PALGRAVE MACMILLAN

Palgrave Macmillan in the UK is an imprint of Macmillan Publishers Limited, registered in England, company number 785998, of Houndmills, Basingstoke, Hampshire RG21 6XS.

Palgrave Macmillan in the US is a division of St Martin's Press LLC, 175 Fifth Avenue, New York, NY 10010.

Palgrave Macmillan is the global academic imprint of the above companies and has companies and representatives throughout the world.

Palgrave® and Macmillan® are registered trademarks in the United States, the United Kingdom, Europe and other countries.

ISBN 978–1–137–32182–4

This book is printed on paper suitable for recycling and made from fully managed and sustained forest sources. Logging, pulping and manufacturing processes are expected to conform to the environmental regulations of the country of origin.

A catalogue record for this book is available from the British Library.

A catalog record for this book is available from the Library of Congress.

Typeset by MPS Limited, Chennai, India.

Contents

List of Tables

List of Figures

Preface

This work is the product of detailed research into the organization and economics of the securities and exchange industry. Actually, it is useful to distinguish the *exchange* (or inner) *industry* as a part of the whole securities industry. In this book we focus mainly on the exchange industry, although our analysis will of course consider the exchange as part of a wider industrial structure. We refer to *platform operators* rather than to *exchanges* because of the rapid growth of alternative trading systems. Such systems are stealing considerable amounts of order flow from established exchanges. Their role in the competitive game, therefore, cannot be overlooked.

The academic literature has so far widely studied exchanges as markets for securities trading focusing on microstructural matters. The focus on the market has shadowed the understanding of the organizations running them. A vast body of literature has investigated exchange governance since many exchanges around the world started to demutualize and, successively, to list. Moreover, the growing interest in the consolidation process among exchanges, which has accelerated in recent years, has spurred research into operative performance and value creation in the exchange industry. Such developments require an in-depth analysis of the exchange as a firm.

In our opinion, however, there has been a lack of research that systematically studies the industrial organization of securities trading and its impact on the value drivers of platform operators. Our purpose is to bridge the gap in the literature. Assuming an industrial organization perspective, we first provide a broad picture of how the industry has changed over the years. We adopt the value chain conceptual framework to define value generating activities in the exchange industry. The industrial dimension has, obviously, a significant impact on exchanges' strategic decision making and performances.

The central idea of our work is that all of the transformations that have concurred to substantially change the industry's structure raise strategic implications for established exchanges and, more generally, for platform operators.

The main forces driving the change can be identified *as technological developments*, increasing *consolidation, regulatory reforms* and *governance* transformations.

The IT revolution heavily impacted on the production technology of platform operators, eased access to trading platforms and spurred competition. The most relevant dimension is that of potential competition, as rivals may easily access the market for order flow and steal liquidity from established exchanges. Efficient trading platforms become the most relevant asset for platform operators, requiring them to make higher investments in IT solutions. This has had a great impact on the cost function and the production levels that exchanges and other platforms may achieve.

Governance arrangements have radically changed over time. There has been ample debate on the rationale of exchanges abandoning their traditional mutual status to become private, for-profit entities. And at the same time, the reasons prompting major exchanges around the word to list have been widely investigated. An interesting feature of exchange governance which, to our knowledge, has not received attention is the institutionalization of ownership and the increasing links among exchanges. Figures show that major groups are largely owned by institutional investors. Moreover, a few large investors hold multiple ownership in the largest exchanges. What is emerging, therefore, is a network of increasingly interconnected exchanges.

At the same time, interconnections have been reinforced by a significant wave of mergers which gave rise to the formation of large groups on a transatlantic scale operating highly diversified business models. Consolidation, moreover, started to occur among electronic communication networks (ECNs).

Finally, regulatory reforms have significantly contributed to change the landscape and affect the competitive behaviour of platform operators. Recent pieces of regulation both in Europe and the US were aimed at fostering competition among market centres, favouring the rise of new rivals. In light of the financial crisis, regulation was increasingly entrusted with the responsibility of ensuring financial stability. Regulatory reforms in this area (specifically, the mandated central counterparty clearing for certain over-the-counter (OTC) derivatives transactions) are expected to sharply impact on competition within the industry.

On balance, the very significant changes in the securities industry landscape have hugely affected the way in which securities exchanges and other trading platforms compete. These developments are expected to mostly affect three areas; namely, strategic decision making, risk and performance measurement and governance arrangements, the latter in particular with reference to external governance.

The main contribution of our work is that we provide a wide insight into the exchange's management and governance investigating the links between the industry structure, exchange behaviour and performance. In particular, analysing strategic behaviour and addressing performance issues requires that we adopt a formalized microeconomic approach entrusted with the representation of the utility and production functions of platform operators. In the meanwhile, increasing competition exposes them to increasing risks. Strategic management, moreover, requires a conceptual framework which, after mapping the relevant risks, defines a model for managing them. The most relevant issues here are strategic capital allocation at corporate level and across business units, the construction of appropriated risk-adjusted performance measures and pricing, which should cover the cost of risk. These issues have so far been neglected in studies of the exchange industry.

The book is organized as follows. First we outline the main features of the exchange industry, defining the operators, the outputs and the relevant market. After that we shed light on the current structure of the industry and discuss how regulation may affect it. Then we deal with the governance arrangements of platform operators showing their evolutionary paths. A detailed analysis of the microeconomics of platform operators is then carried out. Here, in particular, we characterize the production function of operators alongside their revenue and cost function and discuss their maximization problem. After modelling the strategic behaviour of exchanges, we turn to discuss the issue of value measurement, introducing, in particular, a risk-adjusted performance metric. Finally, we conduct an empirical analysis of the performance of various exchanges. Building on data referred to the listed exchanges we investigate, in particular, financial performances and share returns.

Acknowledgements

The authors would like to thank colleagues and doctoral students at the Department of Economics and Statistics, University of Udine, for reviewing parts of the book. Discussions were very helpful in improving our focus on the relevant topics. Special thanks to Professor Philip Molyneux for his helpful comments and suggestions.

1
Securities Industry and Exchange Industry: Organization and Value Chain

1 Introduction

The securities and exchange industry performs an important function within the financial system. By facilitating the execution of orders it enhances the liquidity of securities markets, and therefore allows the efficient allocation of capital flows to investment opportunities.

The exchange industry addresses the demands of two types of customers: issuers seeking finance at a low cost of capital, and investors wishing to trade bearing lower transaction costs and at reliable prices. The utility functions of issuers and traders are tightly linked by cross-externalities which make their relationships resemble a typical feature of two-sided platforms. Although the organizational set-up of the securities industry entails concerns about market microstructure and the quality of securities prices, we do not specifically address these topics in this book, apart from occasional references in this chapter to the relevant literature. Rather, we focus on the organization of the industry, describing the demand side, the supply side and the production process.

Securities exchanges are the main actors moving this process, operating within organizational and governance arrangements which have significantly changed over time. In particular, almost all exchanges have moved from a mutual governance setting to a demutualized status. However, technological development and regulatory advances have also substantially improved competition within the industry, stimulating the entry of new entities; incumbents have reacted by merging, giving rise to a consolidation process leading to the creation of a few large exchanges. Thus, actual competition and potential competition have both contributed to reshape the basic structure of the industry.

In this chapter our purpose is to sketch the main features of the securities and exchange industry, paying particular attention to its main functions and the features of the production process; we go on to develop the various introductory points we make here in more detail throughout the book. The chapter is organized as follows: section 2 clarifies the concept of the exchange industry and identifies its constituent parts. In particular, we provide a representation of the securities industry's value chain, identifying its main functions and the linkages between them. In section 3 we analyse the demand and supply side of the industry, while in section 4 we explore exchanges' functions in light of the two-sided platform literature. In section 5 we discuss the public-interest feature of the exchange production, and in section 6 we outline the relations between competition, market microstructure and industry organization. In section 7 we outline the main issues surrounding the identification of the relevant market within the industry. In section 8 we offer some conclusions.

2 The *securities* and *exchange* industry

It is not easy to define the securities and exchange industry due to the considerable flexibility which characterizes it. Assuming a retrospective approach and, in particular, looking back at the last two decades, it should be immediately clear that the securities and exchange industry has showed a high degree of sensitivity to changes in both the economic and competitive landscape. These changes triggered impressive transformations in the morphology of the industry. We will have occasion later to extensively discuss the forces driving changes in the industry, since the topic is central to our analysis, but for the moment it is sufficient to draw attention to the fact that the borders of the industry have been widely expanding during the last few years as a by-product of both financial innovation and technological advances; the array of products and services offered has increased, and access by new market operators has been encouraged.

Despite the foregoing note of caution, we may define the securities and exchange industry by adopting an industrial organization approach, thereby clarifying the main concerns of industrial organization. Broadly speaking, it is well known that the study of industrial organization deals with the functioning of markets and industries and, in particular, the way firms compete with each other. More precisely, the field is concerned with how production is harmonized with the demand for goods and services through an organizational system, and how imperfections occurring in this mechanism may affect the optimal allocation of resources.[1] Although the organizing mechanisms may vary from a traditional to a central planning or a free market approach, industrial organization primarily deals with the market system setting. But the field of industrial organization is not just restricted to the study of how markets work; it also embraces a far larger perspective that sheds light on firms' strategies and market interactions. Industrial organization studies are, therefore, concerned with topics such as price competition, product positioning, product differentiation, research and development and so on.

When it comes to addressing the notion of industrial organization in a more systematic way, one should tackle a number of issues which are centred on the concept of market power. This poses some relevant questions about how firms acquire and maintain market power, the implications of market power and the role of public policies in addressing the adverse effects of that power.

The aforementioned features of industrial organization apply to any kind of industry, each, however, having its own set of distinctive features. The exchange industry should be defined and analysed within the same framework. From this perspective we shall define which goods or services are exchanged in the industry (the production), the nature of the firms involved and their competitive strategies, the very distinctive features of the market as an organizational mechanism, and the role of regulators which extends far beyond mere antitrust policies.

Before proceeding with the analysis, we have to remark that this methodological approach is somewhat unusual in the field of securities industry studies, despite almost all of the relevant research being obviously interconnected with industrial organization matters. Dealing with efficiency matters, or examining the economics of regulation, is a means of shedding light upon very challenging issues which are integral to the industry's structure. The changing nature of competition and falling barriers to entry affect the strategies of financial firms and market operators, and have implications for the functioning of securities markets and, at the same time, their regulators. There is a reciprocal effect as well, since firms' behaviour drives change that affects the industry's structure. The concept of securities trading as an industry triggering efficiency and regulatory implications is well grounded.[2] Moreover, the fact that barriers of any kind – a central topic in the industrial organization approach – may undermine the efficiency of securities markets is also well known.[3] What is still lacking in the literature is a systematic in-depth analysis of the constituent parts of the industry's structure and organization and their links with the strategic behaviour of firms: these are precisely the topics that we are going to address in the following pages.

Starting with a definition of production we have to bear some caveats in mind. First of all, production in the securities and exchange industry is multi-faceted, comprising as it does a wide array of goods and services which are complementary. While the securities industry is mainly involved in the provision of investment services (the core services), financial firms provide a great variety of complementary services. The latter are intended to increase the utility deriving from the consumption of the core services. Finally, the services provided may entail a high degree of customization and may be produced according to a variety of organizational settings.

Bearing these premises in mind, it may be said that the securities and exchange industry is primarily concerned with the exchange of securities. More precisely, production comprises services that are aimed at ameliorating the exchange of securities. While intuitively sketching the features of the production process, this definition still suffers from an excessive degree of generality. Rather, it is convenient to distinguish between those services which are strictly essential for the exchange (*trading*)[4] of securities to materialize and which define the so called *exchange industry* (or *inner industry*), and an ample array of services complementing them. The latter comprise the broader *securities industry*. Therefore, the functions of the securities industry may be summarized as follows:

a) Realization and organization of securities trading (exchange industry or inner industry).
b) Elimination or reduction of information asymmetries between the buyer and seller of securities.
c) Reconciliation of the diverging preferences and different attitudes of the parties involved, thus increasing the willingness to trade.
d) Provision of a wide scope of advisory services (for example, supporting investment decisions, asset allocation and issuance of securities).
e) Portfolio management.

We can, therefore, think of the exchange industry as the central nucleus of the securities industry. The production (that is *origination*) of the goods which are traded (the securities) should not, in fact, be regarded as part of the securities industry. However, the securities and exchange industry is directly involved in facilitating both the origination of securities and their distribution in the primary market.[5] Throughout this work we will be dealing mainly with the exchange industry. In order to gain a better understanding of the functioning of the exchange industry we should take care with the terminology and definitions employed, and describe the main activities involved in the provision of investment services. For a refined representation of the industry it would be useful to apply the *value chain* approach, identifying the *demand side*, the *supply side* comprising both *main activities* and *supporting activities* or functions, and the *output*. This approach is unusual in our field of study. However, it would be very useful for the purposes of this work which is centred on the industrial organization of exchange trading. Figure 1.1 depicts the basic constituents of the industry, and the links between each stage that give shape to the value chain.

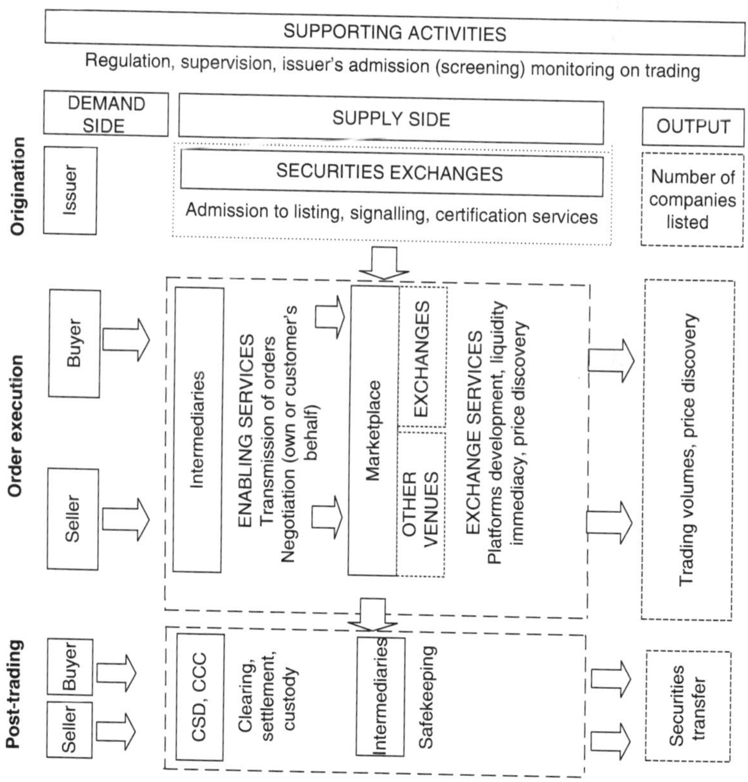

Figure 1.1 The exchange industry value chain

The main (or base) functions shaping the value chain are concerned with *origination, trading* (order matching and execution) and *post-trading.* Origination refers to the admission of issuers to listing; trading refers to the process through which buyers and sellers of securities find (and agree upon) feasible contracts. Post-trading refers to the process through which market participants clear and settle their own obligations. Base functions are concerned with the implementation of platforms and all the relevant organizational arrangements. In order to permit the smooth functioning of its main activities and the linkages between them, the exchange industry provides a complex superstructure comprising supporting activities in which there are regulatory and supervisory activities that are performed by both regulators and market operators.

Platforms perform an important function throughout the entire economy by reducing transaction costs that may arise in matching the needs of entities that would benefit from interacting. Indeed, several industries are populated by businesses presenting this very feature. Examples have been provided in the relevant literature, but here we develop the topic with reference to platforms that bridge the needs of typical customers within the exchange industry, namely issuers and buyers and sellers of securities. In today's exchange industry trading occurs on electronic platforms that define a virtual marketplace for buyers and sellers getting together. Moreover, investments in platforms define the competitive space among providers and are one of the most important value drivers. Service providers in the exchange industry do not just engage in implementing trading platforms. Rather, they arrange all the organizational settings which comprise rules and procedures for admission to listing, trading and post-trading activities and *market surveillance*. Both platforms and organizational arrangements give shape to what we may define as market infrastructures.

3 The demand and the supply side

The *demand side* of the exchange industry combines the demands of two different kinds of customers, namely issuers of securities on the primary market, and buyers and sellers on the secondary market. Since securities exchanges put together two parties (issuers on the one hand and buyers and sellers on the other) they should be regarded as two-sided markets with the relevant implication that their strategic behaviour, along with interdependencies between the two parties, needs to be carefully analysed.

The first side of market demand comprises *issuers* (corporate, sovereign and others) seeking admission to list their securities. Basically, the issuer, in exchange for a fee, requires scrutiny by the entity responsible for the admission to listing, which could be a securities exchange or a supervisor. The decision to admit its securities to listing would imply that the issuer has been deemed trustworthy by the market. When listing its securities an issuer seeks access to finance on convenient terms. To this end, we may think of the cost of capital as being a decreasing function of the credibility of the certification process and complying with standards which follow the admission to listing.[6]

Moreover, by applying for admission to listing the issuer expresses a demand for liquidity on its securities, provided that the greater the liquidity the greater the appetite of investors for those securities, and thus the easier it is for the issuer to raise new finance. The other side of market demand comprises buyers and sellers of securities who require services in order to facilitate their negotiation. The utility function of the two parties is rather complex, with two kinds of services entering it.

First of all, they require *exchange services*, as it would not be feasible or might prove too costly due to market imperfections to find autonomously a suitable counterparty. To this end, buyer and seller agree to make use of the services and facilities provided by a market operator, which would improve the investor's utility by permitting him to find a counterparty in as short a time as possible and at reasonable costs.

Therefore, what we simply label as exchange services need, properly, to be seen as a bulk of different services each adding to the investor's overall utility. In particular, we should refer to *liquidity services*, *immediacy services* and *price discovery*. Investors need liquidity in order to trade at low costs and without suffering losses. A liquid market enables buyers and sellers to exchange securities with immediacy and without causing significant movements in their prices. Finally, the market is organized in such a way as to discover and disclose the price at which buyers and sellers may complete the trade. There is, therefore, a clear relation between the utility functions of issuers and buyers and sellers on the secondary market. Increases in market liquidity will attract even more issuers demanding admission to listing. In turn, increases in the number of companies listed will result in spillovers on the investor side.

Moreover, investors' needs comprise *intermediation services* which are intended to make the trade smoother and more efficient. In this sense, intermediation services are a true complement of exchange services since the efficiency of intermediation (intended in a broader way to comprise economic efficiency, professionalism and loyalty by the intermediary) would raise the utility of exchange services. Here, the involvement of the financial firm may range from the simplest (and, in a certain sense, mechanical) services, such as the transmission of orders to the marketplace or negotiation on behalf of the customer, to services that add more value, such as advice on portfolio management. As will become clear, analysing the utility function of investors is a far from easy task. A great deal, in particular, is involved in understanding the interactions between intermediation services and exchange services. The interplay of these two kinds of services is conditioned by a variety of factors such as the market structure on the supply side of the exchange services and, perhaps most important, the loyalty of intermediaries.

Looking at the exchange industry value chain, we now introduce the *supply side* of the market, defining the nature and functions of the firms (or other entities) populating the exchange industry. We have to distinguish different types of suppliers which may be engaged both in main activities and supporting activities. Their productive processes are strictly interrelated, and indicate complex coordination among suppliers along the value chain. We may describe this coordination as a process where the services each supplier provides increase the utility of services provided by other suppliers.

The main actors within the supply side are the *market service providers*, entities that operate trading platforms enabling the matching of buying and selling orders (traditional securities exchanges and new competitors), intermediaries and regulators. As we will point out later, the role of regulators is interesting because alongside providing supporting activities they may also be entrusted with undertaking main functions.

When we refer to market service providers in the context of the exchange industry we primarily refer to the securities exchanges as operators of the platforms enabling issuers and investors to come together. But before moving forward with the analysis it would be useful to clarify some terminology we are going to use, which centres around the concepts of *market* and *exchange*.

We generally think of the market as a space (physical or virtual) where demand and supply converge and clear according to certain procedures and rules. Within the context of the exchange industry, *security exchanges* define the marketplaces where securities are traded.[7] The functioning of a securities exchange according to a well-defined organizational setting implies the existence of a subject entitled to decide upon the specific rules and procedures.

The term exchange may, therefore, entail some ambiguity since it can refer to either the marketplace (the so-called *market view*) or the firm operating and regulating it (the *firm view*). For the sake of clarity, one could be tempted to argue that the distinction does not matter since the two approaches refer to two sides of the same coin. However, referring to the exchange as the firm running the market has substantial implications since it permits the adoption of a microeconomic approach in analysing it, allowing the focus to fall on the services and relations that the firm provides, its competitive strategies and governance arrangements. We may also think of the exchange using a third approach, viewing it as a broker dealer, thus stressing its function of intermediary among intermediaries. While this view has received some support (Domowitz, 1996) and could be deemed as useful because it stresses the functions of exchanges, we feel that for our purposes the firm view fits better. Most exchanges are involved along the entire value chain of the exchange industry, starting from *origination* to *post-trading* services.

It should be noted, however, that the emergence of rivals (labelled as alternative trading systems, or electronic communication networks) competing with traditional exchanges makes references to the *exchange* obsolete. Rather, it is more useful to refer to the *trading venues* that comprise different types of platform-running entities and which may strategically choose to engage in different stages of the value chain.

Origination is the first stage of the value chain, being concerned with the *admission to listing*.[8] At this stage the production process consists of defining the rules and standards that issuers are required to comply with. Upon receipt of the issuer's application for listing, the competent body (which could be the exchange or a supervisory authority) assesses the compliance with admission rules and decides upon the admission request. The provision of admission to listing relies upon an organizational structure (implementation is part of the supporting activities) comprising human resources and functions dedicated to ascertaining the suitability of an applicant to access the market. It is important to note that not all platform operators are engaged in this particular function. While traditional exchanges generally bear the admission to listing within their business model, other platforms, such as alternative trading systems, do not provide this function. Therefore, they have a cost advantage over exchanges since they do not bear the costs (mainly fixed) related to the implementation of the organizational arrangements. Output is measured in terms of the number of companies listed during a certain time frame.

The second stage of the value chain (*order execution*) is primarily related to building up the mechanism for matching buying and selling orders for securities admitted to trading, described in the relevant literature on the topic as a *market microstructure*. At this stage of the value chain the base activities entail investments in trading platforms, design and implementation of the market microstructure, rule setting as regards trading activity and obligations binding market participants. The trading process occurs under tight market surveillance, targeted to ensure a fair market and prevent price manipulations. It should be noted that in implementing the infrastructure for market surveillance, exchanges cooperate with supervisory authorities, thus sharing important tasks and functions with them.

The exact nature of production at this stage of the value chain is questionable, with the definition varying according to how we consider securities exchanges. Viewing the exchange as the operator of the trading system entails focusing on the production of trading services and on information on prices and quotes as a by-product. Output could be measured in different ways, for example, the number of trades (contracts), the trading value or average trading value over a certain period. Actually, statistical releases either by exchanges or securities exchanges' associations place great emphasis on market volumes. There is no doubt that the magnitude of trading activity reflects the ability of exchanges to attract liquidity and, therefore, may underpin the importance of the exchange in capturing international capital flows.

However, a more refined approach would be to consider exchanges (trading venues) as information producers and suppliers. According to this view we see information on *prices* of securities traded as the most relevant output of order matching given the paramount economic relevance of *price discovery*. We think that prices are not just a simple by-product of trading activity. Since market prices are the key coordinating devices when it comes to investment decisions and allocation strategies, it is important to consider them as the main output of exchanges' production, bearing in mind that price formation is not just a matter of market microstructure. In fact, the strategic policies that exchanges considered as firms choose (for example, choices regarding the competitive arena, the markets to serve and so on) should be deemed to have a relevant impact on price discovery. When assuming an economic perspective, however, it is not easy to split costs between the production of trading services and the production of information (Lee, 1995).

The last stage of the exchange industry's value chain comprises post-trading activities, which come up with a bulk of services that are, namely, *clearing* (which is concerned with ascertaining the respective obligations of counterparties), *settlement* (comprising the transfer of securities from the seller to the buyer, and the reverse for the cash leg) and custody. From an industrial point of view, the provision of post-trading services could be organized in different ways involving both central securities depositories (CSDs) and central counterparties. The former are normally involved in settlement and custody services whereas the latter specialize in risk management services. Again, from an industrial point of view, an interesting case is the vertical integration between trading venues and post-trading operators, something which has important economic and competitive implications. We will explain in more detail when we consider this topic in Chapters 3 and 4.

Intermediaries provide services along the different stages of the exchange industry value chain, making it easier for both issuers and investors to access the market. The cornerstone of the literature on financial intermediation points to market imperfections (either in the form of information asymmetries or transaction costs) to justify the role and scope of financial firms (intermediaries). Therefore, the market system as an organizational structure presupposes that the intervention of intermediaries is necessary for the exchange to occur. Intermediaries provide those facilitating services which permit the market to clear; otherwise the supply and demand for securities would not meet due to incompatibility between respective preferences.

At the origination stage intermediaries bring issuers to the market, and provide a wide array of valuable services spanning due diligence to the discovery of the offering's price. By providing sponsoring services the intermediary certifies that the issuer complies with the exchange's admission standards and is suitable to have its securities listed.

The credibility of the sponsor is crucial for soliciting investors' interest over the business case. When securities are traded on the market the intervention of intermediaries is targeted to smooth the trading process by transmitting the buying–selling orders placed by investors or providing liquidity for the securities traded (in the latter case they operate on their own account as specialists or market makers). The services provided at this stage are far from a pure mechanical transmission. Rather, as the same security could be traded on multiple trading venues, the transmission service is expected to bear valuable economic content with the intermediary charged with the duty of selecting the venue that grants the customer the best execution. At least for small stocks, intermediaries provide stabilization services on the primary market and liquidity services on the secondary market.

Finally, we have to point out that the distinction between markets and institutions (the financial firms) has progressively blurred. As we will have occasion to clarify, this convergence is mainly grounded either on technological developments or regulatory changes. As a result, markets and institutions no longer constitute two parallel, albeit interconnected, worlds; rather, they now tend to overlap to a considerable degree. In fact, nowadays intermediaries are permitted (and have the financial and technical resources) to develop their own order-matching platforms or to internalize customers' orders. When they do so, they operate as markets.

This development is not specific to the securities industry since almost the whole of the financial system is developing along a path of greater convergence between markets and institutions. However, this overlapping bears very specific implications within the sphere of the securities industry and poses a number of challenging issues for investors, financial firms, regulators and, more generally, all the relevant stakeholders involved in the industry. These issues encompass the economics of the securities industry, in other words how value is created and how it is distributed to (and appropriated by) the various stakeholders. In that sense there is an obvious problem of governance as well. In fact, from an industrial organization point of view, what differentiates the exchange industry is the fact that the end users (mainly the intermediaries) may have a stake in the exchange's ownership as well. The utility function of the intermediary is, therefore, multi-faceted. Previously, an intermediary simply enjoying membership of the exchange sought a convenient transaction environment (low execution fees); this was particularly the case when exchanges were run as mutual organizations. By contrast, an intermediary holding shares in one of today's for-profit exchanges would seek maximization of profits. Should that intermediary also run a proprietary trading venue competing for order flow with the exchange its profit maximization objective would come into conflict with the exchange he or she owns.

4 Two-sided platforms

During the last decade a prolific field of research in economics has been flourishing which is related to so-called *two-sided platforms* (also known as *two-sided markets*). The literature on the topic refers to the contributions of the pioneering work of Rochet and Tirole (2001) and subsequent works by Evans (2003) and Evans and Schmalensee (2007).

Two-sided platforms are a feature of many industries. Some examples would be payment card systems, software platforms and magazines, but many others have been detected by researchers. The exchange industry should be deemed as much a two-sided platforms industry as those we have just mentioned. The concept will become clearer by recalling the definition of a two-sided platform.

Rochet and Tirole (2006) laid down the basic features of such industries.[9] According to them, two-sided markets refer to situations in which firms target two interdependent groups of customers which need each other in order to achieve externalities that otherwise they cannot sort out for themselves; essentially, 'the platform can affect the volume of transactions by charging more to one side of the market and reducing the price paid by the other side by an equal amount'.

This definition stresses a central point for the theoretical construction that is being built over it. Providing a common marketplace where two groups of customers can easily interact is a necessary but insufficient condition for two-sided platforms to emerge. Rather, the relevant conditions for such platforms to emerge are dependent on the relationship that links transaction volumes and the price structure; it is the structure, and not just the overall level of fees charged to each party, that affects volumes. As structure matters, strategic pricing across groups is allowed for exploiting cross-externalities, bringing as many members as possible on board and raising the platform's profits.

For businesses operating two-sided platforms the externalities stemming from interactions between members belonging to different groups are expected to change the pricing policy of the firm. Given the profit maximization objective, the outcome no longer derives from simply selecting the quantity at which marginal revenue equals marginal cost, and then choosing the corresponding price on the demand curve. Instead, there are more complex relations between price and cost, and the optimal pricing schedule should be a function of marginal cost, the elasticity of demand on each side and the magnitude of cross-externalities. For either group the optimal price could fall below marginal cost or be negative (Evans and Schmalensee, 2007).

Agents' utility and the structure of platforms' fees and costs, however, depend on the specification and design of the benefits which each part may reap from joining the platform. Theoretically, benefits may arise from interacting with agents on the other side (which gives rise to *usage externalities*) or may be enjoyed by using the platform (that is, each member gains *membership externalities*).[10] The structure of prices in equilibrium may be substantially different, allowing pure usage externalities (Rochet and Tirole, 2001), pure membership externalities (Armstrong, 2004) or integrating usage and membership externalities (Rochet and Tirole, 2006). The structure of fees is not neutral, and a fixed fees or a variable fees structure may affect the magnitude of externalities (Armstrong, 2004).

Having this in mind we may immediately detect the typical features of two-sided platforms in securities exchanges (Evans and Schmalensee, 2007; Cantillon and Yin, 2010). However, there has been no scholarly contribution so far that examines in any great detail the features and implications of two-sidedness in the exchange industry. Along the exchange industry's value chain we find a network of relations between end-users which presents the features of two-sidedness spreading from origination to trade execution and ending with post-trading.

An investment bank engaging in initial public offerings (IPOs) serves the needs of issuers and investors, the former willing to raise capital selling securities and the latter in search of valuable business cases. The more investors the investment bank is able to address, the greater the issuer's utility. On the other hand, the bank's reputation in servicing valuable firms benefits investors. Far from being neutral, the fee's structure plays an important role in determining the outcome. For example, if we assume that issues through an underwriter serve as a signal of the issuer's quality, we may see fees paid by issuers as a reward for certifications services. Higher fees would discriminate among issuers, ensuring that the most valuable join the platform and bringing more investors on board who could then be rewarded with lower prices.

Both order execution and post-trading constitute two-sided industries. The former by means of the network externalities arising between buyers and sellers of securities using exchanges' platforms in order to agree upon feasible contracts. In a post-trading business the relevant groups are exchanges seeking access to clearing and settlement services in order to settle trades occurring on their platforms, and market participants (the intermediaries executing trades and settling them on behalf of their customers).

In this work we are mainly concerned with two-sidedness at the execution stage of the value chain. Focusing on securities exchanges and looking at how they function we actually see the features of multi- rather than two-sided markets. In fact, in order to ensure a proper functioning of the markets they manage the exchanges need to take on board different groups of customers, issuers, traders and liquidity providers, all of which may give rise to multiple interactions. The nature of interactions is quite different according to the groups which are involved. Thus, the issuer–trader interaction is different from the trader–liquidity provider interaction.

The relationship between issuer and trader taking place on the exchange's platforms is not a buyer–seller interaction since negotiations occur among traders, one willing to buy the security and the other willing to go short. Notwithstanding this, each of them derives a utility which depends upon how well the platform performs in attracting customers from the other group. The aim of the issuer is to attract trades to its securities. Traders, on the other hand, benefit from having access to a wide pool of securities on which to transact. The trader–liquidity provider relationship, by contrast, is a buyer–seller interaction as the latter commits to transact (either on the buyer or seller side) with the trader.

As exchanges provide marketplaces where issuers can raise capital by listing their securities and investors can negotiate and exchange them, they target two groups of customers which need each other in some way. In fact, the interaction between the two groups of customers gives rise to externalities that are beneficial to both. More precisely, we may detect two kinds of externalities.

Direct externalities, within each group, arise because issuers will be more willing to list on an exchange the more other companies also decide to list on it. In the meanwhile, more participants are likely to join the exchange as the participation base widens. Each group's member, in fact, benefits from liquidity improvements that follow from the widening of participation within it.

Cross-externalities derive from interactions between issuers and traders. The value for an issuer to list on the exchange increases with the number of trading participants because the interest in the issuer's case would rise (more investors potentially demanding that stock) along with liquidity (Economides, 1993; Domowitz, 1995), and this will, eventually, drive reductions in the cost of capital. Traders, on the other hand, will benefit if the number of listed companies increases.

Alongside the effects on liquidity, the literature on externalities applied to exchanges has extensively investigated the implications for competitiveness. It has been argued that increasing network externalities encourages mergers between exchanges (Domowitz, 1995) seeking to increase liquidity flows.[11]

Given the liquidity externalities across groups, the exchange may attempt to strategically define the fees structure to attract as many issuers and traders as possible. The fees schedule of a typical exchange resembles those prevailing in many businesses operating two-sided platforms. Alongside *transaction-independent fees* charged to both parties, the exchange charges *usage fees* for both issuers and traders. The setting of fees should be viewed in strict relation to the exchange's cost structure. Exchanges, in fact, operate with substantially fixed costs that are related to the implementation of platforms and the organizational structure needed to promote its main functions, while the marginal cost of performing a further transaction is negligible.

Transaction-independent fees are paid by issuers on the occasion of an IPO, and by market participants on an annual basis; they may be assimilated to membership fees. A participant's membership fees represent fixed costs, and are related to the fixed costs that exchanges bear for the structure.

Usage fees, by contrast, are charged when the agent decides to use the platform's facilities. Traders, therefore, pay trading fees whenever they execute a trade, which, in many exchanges, are a function of the execution value. Annual fees paid by issuers may be seen as usage fees as well. We may think of these fees as the cost of using the platform as a mechanism to attract and mediate liquidity on the issuer's securities (and, thus, benefiting him or her the more liquidity the platform is able to gather), discovering the price and permitting the issuer to raise new capital through secondary offers.

Due to their cost structure exchanges can suffer competition from new venues which operate with simplified organizational arrangements and thus can support lower fees. Usually these systems tend not to charge fixed fees, rather foreseeing only transaction based fees.

The pricing schedules adopted by certain exchanges, at least with reference to trading activity, entail a choice between pricing schemes which may differ according to the relative portion of both fixed and variables items. Thus, alongside variable-fee pricing schemes members may opt for a pricing line with prevailing fixed costs and lower variable costs (sometimes decreasing according to different buckets of volume traded). As for annual listing fees, exchanges usually set them as a direct function of market capitalization, which, at least to some extent, depends on the trader's perception of the business case.

The standard literature on two-sided platforms assumes simplified settings where both membership and usage fees do not allow for options and, generally, do not vary according to the levels of utilization. By introducing flexible structures the exchange allows for different outcomes in terms of profits, agents will benefit from using the platform and there may be competitive implications.

Giving a market participant the option to choose the preferred line according to its convenience – which depends both on the number of contracts executed and the average trading volume – means providing an incentive to actively use the exchanges' platforms. From an industrial point of view, this makes sense because it tends to favour participants frequently trading on the market, thus rewarding them for their contribution to overall liquidity. Moreover, we might expect such contributions to liquidity to accrue benefits to the issuers as well as reduce the indirect costs of going public.

A specific pricing structure results in shaping the competitive field among the exchange industry. This is particularly important in a context in which potentially different trading venues compete for order flow. We may think, theoretically, of exchanges competing either on the listing or the trading sides. As exchanges try to reward participants that bring liquidity to the market they primarily focus on competition on the trading side, trying to counteract pressure stemming from high-efficiency alternative platforms. If costs on the listing side remain low – so issuers are willing to list – indirect liquidity externalities outweigh compliance costs and the exchange would succeed in bringing the other side on board. The exploitation of cross-externalities involving the two sides of the market, however, is dependent on the structure of the industry. As competitive pressures change on both the listing and trading side, the interaction between the two sides of the market (listed companies and traders) might turn out to be substantially altered with relevant impacts on the equilibrium fees' structure.

5 Exchange's services, property rights and regulatory implications

The firm view of exchanges (or, more generally, *trading venues*), leads us to devote close attention to the nature of production and the *rights* of trading venues over the results of their production process. Both listing services and the exchange of securities, especially price discovery, have implications for market efficiency, and thus entail a substantial public interest, although their assimilation to *public goods* is in our view questionable. As is well known, the term public goods refers to goods that are non-excludable and non-rivalrous in the sense that individual usage does not reduce their availability for others. Often, public goods entail problems related with *free riding*. While free riding is deemed to be present in an exchange's business, the non-rivalry is debateable, since exchanges have always been able to restrict access to their facilities (in particular, prices).

We are not aware of any studies that directly treat the output of trading venues as public goods, although some financial literature focuses on the general public interest in having capital markets that function well. Our purpose here is to briefly outline the public goods feature of the exchange industry's services for their regulatory implications and the incentives in production stemming from a more competitive framework.

While representing sources of revenues for private for-profit entities, origination and trading services impact on the quality of capital markets. Listing services mirror the ability of exchanges to select and list valuable issuers and thus efficiently channel the allocation of funds to profitable investment projects. By doing so, exchanges provide a *certification service* (signals) which is available to all investors, that may each use that signal in its decision making process. Price discovery mirrors the information efficiency of markets and is a function of both the trading rules and the prevailing organization structure within the industry. Again, prices are observable and available to all participants in their decision-making process provided a tight and cost-efficient transparency mechanism is in operation. In our view, this makes the microstructure approach and the industry organization approach complementary. Moreover, given the relevance of prices in driving and coordinating allocation decisions, the trading venue producing high quality prices may be deemed to exert some form of control over the allocation process.

There is, therefore, a strong case for regulation (and supervision) to pay particular attention to the production process of trading venues. At the same time, the economic analysis of organizations will provide regulators with a useful framework for exercising the duties they are entrusted with. Both origination and price discovery in advanced capital markets came under close scrutiny by regulators seeking to determine the level of effort which platforms could be expected to exert in order to ensure the orderly functioning of markets and the promotion of efficient governance structure for investor protection. In doing this, exchanges and other trading venues have been operating as *self-regulatory organizations* (SROs) under the regulator's supervision, adopting their own rule books and setting conduct rules for both issuers and market participants, and then monitoring compliance with these rules. Focusing on trading venues, the regulatory intervention implies compliance costs which constitute a constraint for profit-maximization to platform operators.

Theoretically, venues may be tempted to lessen their efforts when screening issuers and monitoring trading on their platforms due both to the cost burdens and relevant *free-riding* problems potentially connected with their production process. However, it transpires that in an environment of segmented markets and exchanges operating as natural monopolies free riding is not a problem. Growing competition in the industry and certain competitive policies adopted by rivals, however, entail risks for established exchanges, potentially impairing their incentive to produce efficient levels of output. Obviously, such an incentive should be evaluated in light of the benefits (for example, in terms of reputational capital) the exchange may extract from producing costly goods on which others may free ride. As benefits outweigh the production risks exchanges would continue to devote efforts to developing fair market places. But the reality is that the balance is difficult to achieve as the competitive fields between incumbents and rivals are expanding.

When an issuer obtains an admission to listing for its securities, especially in a primary market in terms of transparency standards, a rival may decide, focusing on just a specific stage of the value chain (order matching and execution), to provide a market place for such securities. In that case, the competing trading platform leverages on the goods produced by others (the signal over the issuer's quality) and captures part of the order flow on that security.

It is clear that the exchange should be rewarded for producing that good; in other words, it should be granted a *property right* on the output produced.[12] At the origination stage of the value chain, fees paid by issuers primarily represent remuneration for using the exchange's platform, which allows us to see these revenues as a reward for the contribution to fair and orderly markets. However, since an issuer lists its shares in order to raise capital, even with successive offers, we may see the property right on the listed securities as the right to attract any successive secondary offers that the issuer plans. In other words, the right to future streams of liquidity that secondary offerings would produce.

It could be argued, however, that the main concerns are related to the price discovery function as it entails substantial costs and investments, and this represents the area in which the most relevant free-riding risks hide. With multiple trading venues, each makes a contribution to the price discovery process, which is directly related to the liquidity that the particular venue manages to attract. Provided that price transparency regulations are well designed, as for mandatory disclosure and waivers, the efficiency of the overall price discovery mechanism would not be impaired. At a microeconomic level the competitive mechanism between price-discovering venues would reward those venues that provide the most valuable contribution (those whose prices capture wider information content and thus are most reliable) in a way that they would be able to attract an increasing order flow.

Execution mechanisms which match orders at prices which have been discovered by other venues, rather than providing any valuable contribution to price discovery, pose challenges. They may, for example, potentially hamper the willingness of trading venues to devote efforts to efficient price discovery. It could be the case of intermediaries crossing, on an over-the-counter basis, the orders of their customers, or perhaps other organized market centres taking prices from outside. Such venues appropriate a good that other firms produce without paying for it (or at a little cost) and sell it for a fee (trading fees) to third parties (the traders whose orders are crossed). In turn, this may undermine market transparency and the quality of price discovery.

Protecting property rights on prices, therefore, becomes particularly compelling for the purposes of efficient market design. However, achieving a feasible protection mechanism – that is, one that protects the investments made by exchanges in the resources required to arrive at accurate prices, while ensuring the investor's right to take informed decisions – is complicated. It encompasses industrial arguments, competitive concerns and microstructural matters, and we can immediately see the conflict that may arise between competition and property rights.

If we view a financial exchange (the same may be applied to other trading venues) as firms producing and supplying information, creating property rights on it should provide the incentives to promote industrial investment in information rather than just protecting a monopoly power.[13] On the other hand, it could be argued that some regulatory intervention, targeted to promote competition between trading venues while providing investors with a unique strand of information, may, somewhat, weaken property rights (Cunningham, 1994). Putting the problem in this way would legitimate the question about who owns the information: does the exchange through which the information has been produced own it, or can it be characterized as public property?

The balance between competitive needs, protection of proprietary rights and investor protection may give rise to a variety of different solutions. Provided that competition for order capture and execution is desirable, the above-mentioned balance may be attained by allowing a variety of venues to compete for orders while centralizing price information, or otherwise by allowing for competition in both execution and dissemination of information. The former course has been the solution adopted by the US Securities and Exchange Commission (SEC) since the introduction of the National Market System (NMS). Here, every venue has to report information on trades to a network which produces a consolidated stream of information on a particular security that is then sold to multiple buyers. While the SEC's intention is to provide a setting for unrestricted public access to consolidated market data, the solution has been criticized for attenuating exchanges' property rights on price information, for treating provision of information as a natural monopoly and for creating inefficiencies in the management of the network. In turn, it is argued, this results in substituting imperfect markets with imperfect regulation (Brown-Hruska and Ellig, 2000).

Theoretically, technological developments which reduce the costs of acquiring information, the possibility of arbitrages between different venues and the contestability among venues, would make feasible a competitive solution for the problem of price dissemination in which a trading venue reports by itself its trading data without mandatory consolidation through a network. This appears to have been adopted in Europe, where the Market in Financial Instruments Directive (MiFID) does not mandate a specific consolidation mechanism. It is worth saying that information dissemination could hardly, in today's capital markets, be deemed a natural monopoly. Moreover, the debate over property rights on prices would be misleading if it were not embedded in a more comprehensive analysis that jointly considers the overall cost and revenue structure of exchanges, something that we explore in the next chapter.

6 Competition and *market microstructure*. Why study the organization of the securities industry?

So far we have presented the main constituents of the securities industry. How the industry is organized, and its changing shape and morphology, play an important role in understanding efficiency in the industry's production process; our main concern is with *price discovery*.

As is well known, prices in the exchange market are the result of a matching process between *buying* and *selling* orders which occurs according to a specified set of rules and procedures defining the so-called *market microstructure*. In general terms, market microstructure is a branch of economics and finance which studies how exchange takes place in markets. It is, in particular, concerned with the interplay between market participants, trading mechanisms and the behaviour of prices in the presence of market frictions (mainly due to *information asymmetries* and *transaction costs*).

There is a huge body of academic research dealing with how the functioning of markets affects price formation, trading costs, volumes and trading strategies. The case for studying market microstructure is based on contesting the *frictionless trading process hypothesis*. Admitting the existence of market frictions implies that prices in securities markets are not set according to a process resembling the classic Walrasian auction. Instead, it claims for specifically modelling frictions in order to gain an insight into how they cause market prices to deviate from an equilibrium price.

Within this conceptual framework, an interesting topic relates to the growing competition in exchange markets which confirms the suggestion of new trading systems jostling for order flow with established regulated exchanges. These rivals could be organized (although not regulated), multilateral trading systems or financial institutions trading against customers' orders. The spread of advanced technological solutions is primarily responsible for creating a more competitive environment, although regulation itself also played (and continues to play) a relevant role in promoting competition. Since the 1970s the debate in the US has continued over promoting greater competition in the market for order execution, in particular following the earliest attempts of the SEC to permit brokers to promote off-exchange markets to trade certain stocks.[14] In comparison, the European securities industry has been behind in improving competition in the market for order flow. However, the most recent regulation – MiFID and Reg. NMS – poses significant challenges for both market operators and supervisors.

So far, academic and industry research has produced plenty of work that measures the magnitude of competition in securities markets by estimating the reduction in primary exchanges' market share to the benefit of alternative trading systems. Although different studies have come up with results that vary according to differences in data sets, overall the results are quite straightforward to interpret and testify to an impressive acceleration in the spillover effect during the last few years. According to Gomber and Pierron (2010), primary exchanges still enjoyed a 100 per cent market share in Eurostoxx 50 stocks at the beginning of 2008, but this had fallen sharply to 78 per cent by the end of 2009.

The aforementioned studies chart an intense struggle for the capture of traders' orders in which established exchanges appear to be quite disarmed in their attempt to retain market activity.

Those making policy choices at this level are faced with the trade-off between the potential benefits for traders, attributable to greater competition (that is, the opportunity to choose the trading venue on which to place the order according to the level and cost of service among different alternative platforms), and the potential adverse effects on the quality of prices, should more competition induce greater fragmentation.[15]

Theoretically, competitive markets, according to the classical price theory, would lead to securities prices behaving like prices stemming from a Walrasian auction, provided that the markets are frictionless.

However, fragmentation in the securities industry causes some concerns as to the quality of price discovery. Apart from the impact on the economics of exchanges, an issue to which we will turn later, relaxing entry barriers implies a radical change in the structure of the industry affecting the interplay between market participants and trading mechanisms and altering the way in which the latter operate. The main concern here is the functioning of the basic rules of order execution.

The consolidation/fragmentation debate centres around several issues affected by the nature and design of market competition: there is the maintenance of priority criteria (in particular, price priority and secondary priority rules), the consolidation of information on order flow, the public-good nature of prices alongside other relevant services provided by exchanges, fairness in order execution and servicing the specific needs of a variety of investors.

Whether fragmentation is desirable or not depends on its effects on market quality. In the first instance, the main threats to price discovery are associated with the potential loss of price priority. Cohen et al. (1985) formally demonstrate that the violation of such a rule negatively affects the overall market quality. The authors model the effects of fragmentation as resulting in longer attendance periods for limit orders before finding execution, thinner markets as investors prefer to withhold their orders which cannot find prompt execution, wider spreads and increasing price volatility.

Similarly, secondary priority rules raise concerns as well. Among the possible different designs that such rules may present the most common is the *time priority rule*, which states that incoming orders bearing the same price are executed according to the time of their arrival, with the earliest orders being rewarded with priority over later orders. While it is acknowledged that time priority is at least as desirable as price priority, fragmentation of order flow may impair the ability of trading venues to reward the first movers. Theoretically, a centralized trading system, to which the overall order flow would be conveyed and which could deal with the time priority, would be the solution. In fact, in this case the ranking of orders according to different criteria (price, time of arrival and so on) would run smoothly. With fragmented markets the operation of time priority, although desirable, may be difficult to enforce. Due to differences in liquidity among the trading venues offering execution services on a particular stock, investors may be tempted to convey orders to a system which does not run a complete time priority.

Apart from the potential to impede the proper working of priority rules, fragmentation alters the interplay between trading venues and market participants. Actually, from a welfare perspective it is not necessarily true that the relationship between exchanges and market participants in fragmented markets results in adverse effects for the latter. The established exchanges will obviously suffer, but the users of platforms would be better off due to a more competitive environment in the provision of exchanges services.

By allowing rivals to enter the market and threaten the oligopolistic position of exchanges, the supply side changes radically and raises corporate strategy to the forefront of exchange industry studies. The competitive policies of the various trading venues unwind along a vector of different strategic options including, for example, the stocks to admit to trading, the type and level of service to be offered to customers and the nature of competition. Thus, different trading venues may decide to trade only certain kinds of stocks identified according to specific selection criteria (for example, high capitalization stocks, small stocks), focus on certain trades (block trades) or grant access only to a limited array of investors (such as institutional investors). The customer base itself is conditioned by the strategic choices made by the trading venue. Other trading venues may decide to compete on *prices*, or behave according to *non-price* competition strategies (for instance, distinguishing on the grounds of admission standards for both issuers and financial firms, which accrue the reputational capital of the trading venue).

Should the interaction between trading venues develop along a *genuine* competitive path, the outcome would lead to a *profit sharing* among venues and other stakeholders. As it reduces the oligopolistic power of price-setting agents (the *trading venues*), increased competition would result in better execution and prices for traders. At the very least it dampens the ability of established exchanges to extract rents to the detriment of traders and listed companies. And on the other hand, it may force the incumbents to raise their regulatory standards in an attempt to retain customers by offering prime quality admission and supervisory services, and thereby improving the value of the certification they release to the market.

Concerns arise when the diversion of orders from an established exchange to another trading venue takes place not just on a purely competitive basis, with the latter trying to selectively attract a specific portion of the order book. For instance, this could be the case of *purchased order flow* where the distribution of orders among trading venues does not occur randomly, the selection being, in most cases, based on the information content of the orders. Rival markets may also attempt to divert uninformed traders from exchanges simply by adopting a *derivative pricing* strategy (that is, matching the bid–ask quotation observed in the primary markets) instead of pricing inside the spread. Such a strategy would permit rival markets to extract rents by getting transactions from less sophisticated retail customers; the latter will, of course, lose price improvement opportunities (McInish and Wood, 1996).

Easley et al. (1996), in studying the effects of purchased order flow, account for a relevant information effect of competition among trading centres, with a high probability of the diverted orders reflecting small, retail trades. The greater the proportion of liquidity trades diverted, the greater the probability that only informed trades remain on the exchange, thus entailing an adverse selection in the primary market. This sort of order selection constitutes the dark side of fragmentation insofar as it undermines the working of markets and the quality of price discovery.

Similarly, the *cream-skimming* effect in financial markets has been recently analysed by Bolton et al. (2011); although they address a very different issue, the authors come to conclusions that, at least to some extent, resemble those of Easley. Assuming a financial industry setting where competition takes place between two types of markets – regulated transparent exchanges and opaque over-the-counter (OTC) markets, respectively – they model the interaction between the real sector with entrepreneurs wishing to sell assets and financial markets. They argue that entrepreneurs with valuable assets will prefer to sell in the OTC market due to the greater valuation skills of informed dealers who themselves, therefore, may extract informational rents from entrepreneurs. The main topic of Bolton's paper is the excessive high rents in the financial industry and the potential attraction of young talent. However, the cream-skimming effect they account for implies an adverse selection process in organized markets, and a negative price externality since investors know that they will find on these markets only poor assets.

What may be expected from the overall economic effects of inter-market competition is difficult to foresee. One should certainly distinguish between the possible effects on the customer, and broker or dealer side respectively, but the exchanges may be affected as well. While it is uncertain if customers would actually benefit from diversion, at least to the extent that forgone price improvements outweigh any fee benefit (Fialkowski and Petersen, 1992), dealers would definitely be better off. This is particularly true if they succeed in attracting rents by dealing with small, uninformed traders. Exchanges obviously suffer from being under the threat of losing trading volumes. However, there may be considerable *side effects* directly related to an adverse selection process to the extent that the alteration of the customer base (for instance, the diversion of uninformed traders that would leave on the exchanges only informed traders) would force the exchange to modify its fees' schedule.

7 Competition between trading venues: the relevant market

So far we have widely explored the likely effects of the substantial changes that have occurred in the industry's structure, but have paid relatively little attention to exchanges' strategies and their implications for the economics of exchanges. It is to this that we now turn.

As a result of increasing competition among trading venues a market for order flow has been growing and flourishing, where the venues involved jostle to attract greater portions of market activity – here defined as the liquidity in both primary and secondary markets. A more refined approach of industrial organization requires, however, to define closely the relevant market. As usual in industrial organization studies, we must define the relevant market with reference to the concept of *substitutability*. To the extent that two (or more) trading venues offer products and services with a high degree of *substitutability* we can say that these venues insist on the same market and, therefore, are expected to be competitors. When different venues do not address the same type of orders or traders they are not direct competitors and so do not belong to the same market.

As a basic premise, we have to point out that it is rather difficult to define the relevant market when looking at the exchange industry for at least two reasons. First, it is theoretically feasible for trading venues to differentiate according to a wide vector of parameter and criteria, taking into account the location, the securities traded, the intermediaries admitted to trading and the market model.

Secondly, the traditional segmentation criteria (that grounded on geographical location) is no longer appropriate to uniquely define the market. For a long time securities exchanges operated as natural monopolies within their home jurisdictions and they were, therefore, largely shielded from international competition. The exchange's relevant market was confined, to a great extent, within the boundaries of the home country. Advances in technology, however, virtually abolished the exchanges' dependency on physical location, opening them suddenly to cross-border competition and leading to the emergence of new competitors.

Falling geographical barriers and the growth of new ventures, however, do not necessarily imply that trading venues become direct competitors. Competitive strategies may lead them to insist, totally or partially, on the same market segment, or indeed to serve wholly different markets.

Broadly speaking, the *type of venue* criteria is not suitable for segmenting the relevant markets; in other words, different types of venues do not necessarily mark different markets, although we may find some types of venues serving the needs of a restricted portion of homogeneous customers or capturing only certain types of trades. In most cases, different trading venues share, at least to some extent, the same base of traders and traded securities. The relevant market, therefore, may part overlap and part differ across venues (inter-type differentiation). Of course, we may have same-type trading venues serving different markets (intra-type segmentation).

When defining the relevant market for the purposes of addressing the competitive issue among venues one should keep in mind the typical services falling within the sphere of the exchange industry. As the main functions of the industry are related to both origination and management of trading platforms, the competitive arena spans issuer services to trading services, although we should have two caveats in mind. First, listing and trading services are strictly related, due to the well known externality effects. Second, the entry of new rivals implies changes in the competitive space since these venues generally restrict their business model to trading services.

When focusing on a two-sided platform as a traditional exchange serving both issuers and traders, the relevant cross-externalities deriving from the conjunction of the two business lines make the strategic interaction between platform operators multi-faceted. More precisely, gaining a comprehensive understanding of the nature of competition requires that we should give an insight into the relations linking issuer and trading services. The greater the sensitivity of the trading value in relation to changes in the number of listed companies (and the reverse), the greater the cross-effects between business lines. This implies that the exchange is not competing in two separate markets. By admitting an issuer to listing the exchange becomes the primary market for its securities, and arguably gains market power on the streams of liquidity and acts as a reference centre for successive issues. Due to these cross-effects, we may argue that by choosing the competitive arena for listing services the exchange conditions the outcome on the trading side. In the meanwhile, due to rivals trying to free ride on listing, it determines the degree of substitutability with new venues.

Given the centrality of origination in shaping the competitive environment it is worth drawing out a few considerations that relate to the forces that drive competition on listings. Substitutability in the market for listings depends to a large extent on the preferences of issuers (something upon which, however, the exchange can exert some influence) and the structure of market participants. At this stage, two venues are substitutes from an issuer's point of view if he or she seeks to derive the same utility by listing in one or the other. This is a challenging point for exchanges seeking to expand their listings over foreign companies, and is related to the so-called *home country bias*.

On the listing side, *home country bias* is intended to mark the preference of issuers for their home market, something which may be due to a variety of reasons such as, for instance, the consuetude with domestic legal arrangements and praxis, the information closeness with the domestic exchange or the preference schedule of investors. The bias is then, reinforced by investors' preferences. Research provides evidence that investors mainly tilt portfolios toward domestic securities. The relevant studies by French and Poterba (1991) and Tesar and Werner (1995) were among the first to document the preference of investors for domestic securities accounting, in particular for a suboptimal allocation of their wealth. That is, they tend to allocate too much of their investing portfolio to domestic equities and too little a fraction to foreign equities. The literature on the topic has not yet led to a definitive answer as to why investors do not hold larger shares of their portfolio in foreign stocks, although different possible explanations have been provided, many focusing on the costs related to foreign investments (mainly due to information acquisition), regulatory restrictions or uncertainties in estimations.[16] Another stream of research has documented what has been called the *home bias at home* (Coval and Moskovitz, 1999; Huberman, 2001; Huberman and Sengmuller, 2002), what may be discerned as the investor's preference for firms with local headquarters, or the habit of employees who prefer to invest a large portion of their retirement plans in their own company stocks.

The existence of such biases may contribute to some forms of spatial segmentation surviving despite falling of barriers across countries. As the bias relaxes, issuers would considering a listing abroad and, therefore, exchanges located in different jurisdictions would insist on the same market for listings.

There are, however, reasons for maintaining that the attitude toward foreign listing differs across issuers. The forces driving an issuer to consider listing abroad may be diverse and may not just be limited to large companies. For example, it could be the case of an export-orientated firm seeking a listing on the market where its major customers are located, or perhaps a firm operating in a particular sector (for instance, new technologies) which is considering listing in a financial centre where there is a widespread interest in that sector.[17] A measure of openness in the market for listings could be derived from the statistics on the number of foreign companies listed (see Chapter 2).

Apart from subjective preference schedules and attitudes, listing decisions depend on exchanges' endogenous choices about standards and exogenous factors such as regulatory compliance requirements.[18] However, it becomes ever more difficult for exchanges to retain market shares in trading activity on the stocks they admit to listing. In this sense, technological development acts in two directions. First of all, it is easier for exchanges to reach international traders by integrating on their platforms trading activity in international blue-chips. But at the same time it reduces the costs for new rivals to emerge, raising the contestability of markets. The degree of substitutability across trading venues is high, making the relevant market potentially cross-border, at least for large liquid securities.

The competitive game within the exchange industry is complex, and is essentially driven by two forces moving in opposite directions. On the one hand, exchanges and other venues may seek *compatibility*, but on the other hand, they may seek to segment the markets they serve. We can identify a competitive space on a tri-dimensional scale (see Figure 1.2) which captures the product mix ranging from trading services (Ts) to trading combined with origination (O) and other services (S), the type diversification identifying the type of venue (low indicates homogeneous venues comprising traditional exchanges whereas high means a very heterogeneous trading environment comprising exchanges, alternative systems and OTC trades) and the degree of compatibility. As for the latter, *low* indicates trading venues that try to differentiate and *high* indicates trading venues that insist on the same markets.

Different combinations of these dimensions may give rise to different industry settings. So far, the industrial organization has been moving from a low type-diversification setting, in which traditional exchanges running core business activities (origination and trading services) were linked by low degrees of compatibility, to more diversified settings. For example, we may now design industry settings with different types of venues engaged in largely diversified business models which, according to the competitive strategies employed, may exploit compatibility, or otherwise seek differentiation.

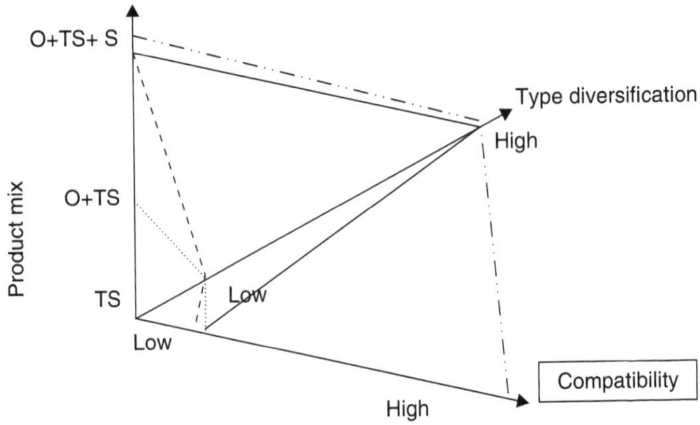

Figure 1.2 The competitive space

Compatibility can have an ambiguous meaning and, therefore, it should be defined. Moreover, it could be exploited both to dampen or raise competition. Traditionally, compatibility in the exchange industry is regarded as a strategic choice made by two or more exchanges to share their platforms, adopt a common one or permit mutual access to respective members of each other's platform. In this case it is realized through actual mergers, implicit mergers or other forms of alliance, and it is intended to dampen competition. Indeed the most common way to realize compatibility is through mergers; the last decade has witnessed a widespread process of consolidation within the industry (some movement was also observed during the 1990s), leading to large conglomerate exchanges extending their operations over different national jurisdictions. The largest groups (for example, NYSE Euronext, NASDAQ OMX and the Deutsche Börse Group) operate at a transatlantic level. Mergers result in the exchanges involved adopting a single platform and acting as different access points to a single liquidity pool. By contrast, the traditional segmentation across countries produced a low-compatibility environment where competition was prevented by geographical boundaries.

Compatibility may result from a unilateral choice made by a venue to offer execution services over securities admitted to trading on other venues. In that case, compatibility is not realized at a production process or technological level; rather it reflects the unilateral choice of the venue to provide substitutability for trading on securities admitted in other platforms. The outcome is an increase in competition in the exchange industry. There could be cases of alternative trading systems which decide to admit to trading securities listed on primary markets, leveraging on the efficiency (in terms of costs and speed) of their platforms. Here, the increase in a trader's utility would rest on lower trading costs and the possibility of fast or *strategic execution*. But it could also be the case of traditional exchanges extending their platforms to meet the demand of international traders for highly liquid international securities. The role of alternative systems poses a challenge to traditional securities exchanges for both strategic reasons and matters of governance. In the offering catalogue of these systems one may find different kinds of securities, ranging across exchange-listed securities, unlisted securities,and securities with a diffuse presence on investors' holdings although not listed.

To the extent that alternative systems provide trading services on listed securities they overrun the playing field of exchanges by piggybacking on the functions that exchanges perform. In our view, these considerations are crucial because they imply a reconsideration of the way in which we address substitutability and market segmentation in the securities industry. It could be argued that traditional exchanges are facing a puzzle directly related to their supervision of issuers and trading activity.

Basically, at the same time as the exchange sets its listing policies it defines its own competitive arena (that is, its relevant market). The exchange needs to invest in monitoring standards given the centrality of the listing function for the externalities implied on the trading side of the market and the implications in terms of its reputational capital. Simultaneously, setting premium standards for listings may succeed in attracting further listings if other issuers perceive high levels of scrutiny as a guarantee of efficient and orderly markets, potentially leading to cuts in the cost of capital.

Yet by trying to target certain types of issuers, for example, large firms or firms operating in new technologies, the exchange is exposed to competition on the trading side moved by other players (alternative systems or exchanges running trading platforms on international stocks) which may decide to exploit the scrutiny and monitoring functions of the primary market to provide compatibility (substitutability) with those securities. We find that large alternative systems admit to trading securities in the main market indexes. For example, Instinet has adopted an admissions policy of automatically admitting to trading any security as soon as it enters one of the top indexes, piggybacking on the listing scrutiny performed by the exchange and, therefore, sharing the relevant market with it. It is noteworthy that alternative systems enjoy a competitive advantage over exchanges since they do not have to build up and sustain the implied costs of the organizational arrangements (the infrastructure) for performing the listing function. As a result they may be able to afford the provision of trading services at far lower costs than exchanges, beyond relying on high efficiency trading platforms. For example, such systems do not foresee, in their pricing schedules, fixed costs, as happens in traditional exchanges; rather they charge only low and variable fees on the volumes traded. The competitive fight between trading venues bears, moreover, relevant governance implications. In fact, alternative platforms are generally operated by large intermediaries, which, in turn, are members of exchanges as well. This posits interesting questions as to the overall industry's governance, since the strategic interaction between exchanges, alternative platforms and intermediaries–owners may potentially alter capital flows among jurisdictions. We explore this point in more detail in Chapter 4.

We now briefly turn to discuss how trading venues may act to segment markets, creating niches within which they may establish some form of market power. Assuming a very rough approach we can say in the first instance that markets may segment according to the type of traded securities or the characteristics of market participants. While the pure combination of market participants and traded securities has never been an accurate criteria for delimiting the competitive field, in today's exchange industry this inconsistency is even more apparent.

Integration, growing complexity of trading mechanisms and strategic policies of exchanges require that we define more precisely which factors may drive segmentations. To this end, we identify as relevant factors *information, liquidity, market segmentation,*[19] the *market model* and *business diversification.*

We discussed in the previous section the role of *information.* It will be recalled that according to the information they possess we may distinguish informed traders from uninformed ones. It could be interesting for a trading value to compete on a certain type of traders, especially the uninformed one, rather than to strive for market share on particular securities. In particular, a venue which shares the same market with other trading facilities may choose to strategically reduce substitutability against competitors, thereby diverting the most valuable traders. It could be the case of an OTC platform which at a first stage observes the information content of prices forming on a primary market and then tries to pick up uninformed traders by simply matching the best quotes prevailing on that market.[20] Closely linked to the role of information is that of *liquidity*. Due to externality effects we may think that the most liquid market centres will exert a centripetal force over issuers and traders. Moreover, the information content of their prices would be more valuable for customers bearing different implications: it could drive a trader's preferences to the extent that they put a predominant importance on prices, but it could be possible to design price consolidation mechanisms that better reward those market centres contributing with more reliable prices.

Market segmentation is, then, a policy widely used by exchanges which insulate a particular segment within the markets they run to try and target a certain type of issuer. Segmentation criteria are generally based on very simplified rules for accessing the segment. For example, many exchanges design special segments for the admission of small–medium enterprises or issuers that satisfy high governance standards.

Generally, market segmentation is accompanied by some form of differentiation in the market model; that is, the exchange fits the organization (for example, the design of auctions) and the mechanics of trading (the market microstructure) to the features (essentially, in terms of liquidity) of the securities admitted to the segment.

Although the creation of particular market segments is targeted to develop a well-suited environment for issuers that otherwise may find it difficult to access the main market, it does not, however, shield the exchange from potential competition. In fact, it is possible for other financial centres to create segments targeting the same type of issuers. In the European segment of small and medium-sized enterprises (SMEs), for example, exchanges' market segments are facing the strong competition of the London Stock Exchange which attracts a huge number of SMEs from around Europe.

Trading venues may also try to differentiate themselves by investing in advanced trading platforms that allow investors complex investment strategies which rely on algorithms and enable the execution of orders at best prices across markets; this strategy minimizes market impact and transaction costs.

Finally, exchanges may try to differentiate by diversifying their business model into trading-related activities such as selling market data and post-trading services. The rationale here is to raise the utility of customers using the exchange's platform by offering a unique bundle of complementary services. Through product diversification the exchange may try to bind the customer into a long-term relationship. In turn, the exchange may exploit cross-selling opportunities, such as those entailed by the conjunction of cash and derivatives trading. An interesting case is presented by exchanges which integrate trading and post-trading, trying to lock the customer into a relationship alongside the value chain (for example, by inducing him or her to buy from the exchange a bundle of services located at different stages of the chain). Recent regulatory advances, however, prevent exchanges from exploiting anti-competitive behaviours on these grounds. However, we think that business diversification still permits exchanges to make their overall services in some ways unique.

8 Conclusions

The literature on the exchange industry has been widely concerned with microstructural matters. The interest in studying how trading rules affect price discovery has mirrored the implications of the overall quality of prices for the allocation role that capital markets are entrusted with.

But it is necessary to add that exchanges traditionally operated as public entities. The subsequent corporatization and listing of exchanges requires that we gain a better understanding of the functioning of securities exchanges. This perspective requires us to regard exchanges according to the *firm view*. This chapter has laid down the conceptual framework on which we will build throughout this book. In particular, we provide the basic concepts for analysing the strategic decision-making process.

We have employed an interdisciplinary approach, but industrial organization is the main field on which we draw. The securities industry's value chain is the basic framework for understanding competitive strategies and representing value-generating activities. The firm view requires an analysis of the demand and supply side of the industry. Whilst such an approach has already been developed in the securities industry literature, we elicit new developments in light of recent transformations. In particular, increasing competition and mergers among exchanges (and other platforms) have changed the competitive landscape. Exchanges no longer operate as natural monopolies in their local markets. Rather, they have widened their competitive space, and these developments require that we carefully define the relevant market. They lead us to consider factors such as *information, liquidity, market segmentation,* the *market model* (which have traditionally been regarded as attributes of market quality impacting on the price discovery mechanism) along with *business diversification* as relevant drivers of market segmentation and strategic competition.

2
The Exchange Industry: An Overview

1 Introduction

The exchange industry has been rapidly evolving over the last decade at least, with the main drivers being the demutualization of securities exchanges (and, sometimes, their listing) and a widespread consolidation process, which has speeded up during the last few years. In the meanwhile, through successive waves of consolidation, both on a regional and transatlantic level, the morphology of the industry has substantially changed: a few large cross-border groups now dominate trading across the world.

Mergers among exchanges were primarily targeted to pursue business diversification strategies and counteract the centrifugal forces that were leading to trading fragmentation, a process that was directly related to the growth of new competitors. Increasing competition, in fact, prompted exchanges to expand their liquidity pools and find new sources of revenues as exchange trading fees came under downward pressure in the jostle with more cost-efficient rivals. Since exchanges are deemed to operate with a fixed-cost structure, they are concerned with increasing their trading volumes in order to reduce average costs.

The competitive battle between incumbents and rivals has several interesting strategic implications. Alongside the mergers among traditional securities exchanges, the reaction to the changing competitive landscape has led exchanges to attempt to take over their new rivals, stimulated mergers between alternative trading systems and induced the exchanges themselves to set up their own alternative trading systems.

The aim of this chapter is to sketch the main features of the exchange industry as they have evolved over the last decade. We assume an evolutionary perspective and describe the main changes occurring within the industry and outline the major challenges. This chapter should be read as a precursor to Chapter 5, which analyses the economics of securities exchanges.

The chapter is organized as follows. Section 2 provides an overview of the consolidation process which has led to the rise of large conglomerate exchanges. Section 3 sketches the exchange industry's structure that underpins developments of market activity across major areas; here, we take into consideration the main variables such as number of companies listed, market capitalization and trading volumes. In section 4 we sketch the basic framework for measuring exchange value, while in section 5 we discuss industry-specific sources of value. In section 6 we analyse the cost and revenue structures for exchanges, building on industry-wide aggregate data. Section 7 provides an overview of exchanges' business models. Section 8 discusses the role of alternative trading venues and their relations with traditional securities exchanges. Finally, section 9 draws some conclusions which will be useful for subsequent discussions throughout the rest of the book.

2 The consolidation process and the rise of conglomerate exchanges

Following the demutualization and subsequent listing of major exchanges, a widespread consolidation process took place within the exchange industry spurring the creation of a few large conglomerates. Although some consolidation took place in the late 1990s and early 2000s, it was in the years immediately preceding the financial crisis that the phenomena assumed a paramount relevance. The purpose here is to provide an overview of the main mergers that took place. Alongside the industrial implications of the consolidation process, for the purposes of this work relevant matter is represented by values recognized in the main deals. Chapter 7 contains an in-depth analysis of the multiples at which such mergers were settled (Polato and Floreani, 2010 and 2012).

In Europe the most relevant deals were those involving the creation of Eurex, the largest European derivatives market in Europe,[1] and the Euronext Group as a result of the merger between the exchanges of Paris, Amsterdam, Brussels and Lisbon and the subsequent acquisition of the London-based Liffe. Other important deals were those involving the Nordic exchanges: in 1998 the OM AB futures exchange launched a takeover of the Stockholm Stock Exchange. Subsequently, in 2003, the group merged with the Helsinki Stock Exchange to become first OM HEX, and then OMX, which forms the European leg of the current NASDAQ OMX Group.

However, the most significant mergers are those that have taken place rather more recently: they have involved the largest stock exchanges in the world, and have linked American and European finance which has resulted in new regulations and a system of mutual recognition (Tafara and Peterson, 2007). Finally, the main stock exchanges are increasingly changing their ownership structure, with groups of purely financial investors (institutional investors, hedge funds, etc.) holding even larger stakes than previously. The principal objective of these investors is to maximize profit, but often they also seek the power to direct the strategic choices of stock exchanges.

In most cases mergers have taken place between stock exchanges with similar business models and forms of ownership. It is also evident that the strategy of the largest stock exchanges has been to take advantage of mergers in order to widen their product range, thus extending trading services to derivatives and other instruments; they have also sought to gain control of processes along the production chain. In the latter case, mergers are conceived to pursue vertical integration strategies.

The largest mergers were accomplished in successive stages of integration and included:

a) The merger between the NYSE and Euronext, which was announced in 2006 and completed in April 2007 with the start of trading of the new holding's stocks in Paris and New York. The NYSE Group itself had originated from a merger between NYSE and Archipelago in 2006.
b) The merger between the London Stock Exchange and Borsa Italiana, which took place between June and October 2007 and gave rise to the London Stock Exchange Group (LSEG).
c) The merger between NASDAQ and OMX, which resulted in the establishment of the NASDAQ OMX Group in February 2008.
d) The acquisition of ISE, an American options exchange, by Deutsche Börse in 2007.

Despite leading to large conglomerate groups the scope for potential consolidation was far from exhausted by the aforementioned deals. In 2011 the struggle for control of the largest marketplaces restarted when the bid of the LSEG for the Canadian TMX Group was declined, and the battle between Deutsche Börse and the NASDAQ OMX Group–ISE partnership for the control of NYSE Euronext, with the latter finally accepting the Deutsche Börse offer (which was then blocked by European authorities for antitrust reasons). In 2012, however, NYSE Euronext accepted the ISE offer, which is expected to give rise to a large conglomerate with a dominant position in US equities and derivatives trading, alongside a powerful position in European markets.

On balance, mergers can be seen as a response to pressures from new rivals offering cheaper services. Despite being an obvious way to cut costs, we would suggest that mergers (at least those occurring on the largest scale) may have major shortcomings. In particular, they might turn out to weaken the financial position of large conglomerates – as we discuss in Chapter 7 – and introduce risks to the viability of the business on an ongoing basis. However, it seems that mergers will continue for the time being, through regional deals (we note the merger, completed in 2012, of the Tokyo and Osaka stock exchanges), or for strategic purposes (for example, the LSEG plans to complete the acquisition of LCH. Clearnet in order to leverage on regulatory changes that mandate the clearing of complex derivatives).

3 The exchange industry: some figures

In this section we describe the main features of the worldwide exchange industry by analysing developments in market activity. The major variables which we use to represent the dimensions of the industry are market capitalization, number of companies listed and trading volumes. Trading volumes are generally reported in terms of the trading value for cash markets and as number of contracts traded with reference to the derivatives market.

Taken together these variables help to define the overall liquidity of a particular exchange. The trend in listings can be assumed to be a good indicator of the competitiveness of exchanges; the greater the number of listings the greater the attractiveness of the marketplace for traders. In today's competitive environment the major attribute of listings is, in particular, the number of foreign listings, as this better mirrors the attractiveness of exchanges in the competitive arena. On the secondary market, by combining market capitalization and trading value, we may derive the turnover velocity, which can be taken as a good proxy of the liquidity of the exchange.

Overall market activity is, however, affected by trends in the real economy. Intuitively, during periods of expansion reflected by increases in GDP and earnings we expect the appetite for risk – among both issuers and investors – to rise, resulting in an increase in listings, trading values and market prices; we might expect the reverse during periods of economic downturn. However, the magnitude of the response is not easy to capture as arguably market activity is affected, at least to some extent, by country-specific attributes (such as, for example, institutional arrangements and productive structure).

Moreover, by combining measures of market activity with measures of economic development, we may assess the significance of the exchange industry in channelling savings to investments and, therefore, the depth of capital market penetration in the financial system's allocation function.

In primary markets securities exchanges experienced growth in the number of companies listed during the time frame 2003–8, although a slowing down has occurred over the last few years (Table 2.1). The evidence is, however, mixed and, in fact, breaking down the date range 2003–11 by macro-regions we observe an overall decline for American exchanges whereas the Asia–Pacific region and the Europe–Africa–Middle East region experienced growth in the number of companies listed. The Asia–Pacific region, in particular, has experienced a continuing positive trend in the growth of companies listed even after 2008.

However, even the trend within American exchanges is mixed: NASDAQ OMX, NYSE Euronext and the Canadian TMX count for more than 84 per cent of total listings in the region. And, while NASDAQ OMX and NYSE Euronext have experienced sharp declines since the beginning of 2008, the Canadian Exchange has been quite successful in retaining its listings. The attractiveness of listings depends, however, on a broad variety of factors that includes the positioning of the exchange on the worldwide capital market, its structure, organization and governance, and the institutional and legal arrangements of its national jurisdiction. The balance between legal protection and compliance costs may have a great impact on listing choices. So while a well-designed legal system may improve investor protection and raise the quality of capital markets, the compliance costs may alter the incentives of listing firms, especially in a very competitive landscape between market centres. The introduction of the Sarbanes–Oxley Act in the US has been blamed for lessening the attractiveness of the NYSE in the face of foreign investors.

Table 2.1 Number of companies listed

	2003	2004	2005	2006	2007	2008	2009	2010	2011	CAGR
America	33021	32954	33532	33736	34133	32479	31209	31026	31611	−0.5%
Asia–Pacific	53593	52482	56620	58178	58549	62487	62534	63884	65850	2.6%
Europe–Africa–Middle East	35395	25630	26170	32785	41096	41220	40987	40118	40844	1.8%

Source: Our elaborations on WFE statistics.

Table 2.2 Primary market turnover

	2003	2004	2005	2006	2007	2008	2009	2010	2011
America	−4.34%	1.88%	1.75%	1.18%	0.69%	−0.57%	3.37%	−0.42%	1.62%
Asia–Pacific	1.12%	−1.96%	2.85%	2.60%	4.03%	1.06%	2.00%	3.32%	2.97%
EAME	−2.11%	2.44%	2.64%	0.20%	4.72%	−2.40%	−3.58%	−0.47%	−0.33%

Source: Our elaborations on WFE statistics.

A more appropriate representation of the attractiveness of an area or exchange for issuers is, however, one based on flows rather than on stocks. The yearly balance between new companies listed and de-listings provides a more precise picture of the turnover on primary markets.

Over the last decade American exchanges have experienced, in aggregate, a lower turnover (computed as the ratio of the net new listed companies during the year and the stock of listed companies at the end of the year) on the primary market than the other macro-regions (Table 2.2).

Exchanges in the Asia–Pacific macro-region proved to be, in aggregate, more dynamic in attracting issuers. The greatest exchanges in the region (namely Singapore and Hong Kong) present the highest rates of primary market turnover during the crisis period, whereas other exchanges around the world experienced difficulties in preserving turnover rates on the primary market.

We now turn to analyse the dynamics in foreign listings, and to that end we build on figures from the World Federation of Exchanges (WFE). We analyse, in particular, the magnitude of the phenomena across world exchanges showing how the relative weight of foreign listings over total listing has been evolving over time and deriving a measure of concentration of the market for foreign companies. We take into consideration the flows of newly listed companies over the timeframe 2003–11, and focus on 53 WFE members. Table 2.3 summarizes the distribution of foreign listings across exchanges.

Over the last few years, and especially since 2006, the number of foreign listings among total listings has been growing remarkably, despite slowing down in 2010 as a result of the financial crisis. The average number of foreign companies listed has also been growing. When looking at the twenty-fifth and seventy-fifth percentiles we observe a widening of the distribution to the right side. This is symptomatic of the increasing attractiveness of exchanges to foreign companies and marks, to some extent, the intensification of cross-border competition in attracting issuers. However, the market for foreign listings is highly

Table 2.3 The distribution of foreign listings

	2003	2004	2005	2006	2007	2008	2009	2010	2011
%Tot. listings	11.0%	9.4%	8.0%	11.1%	16.1%	17.2%	17.3%	15.4%	17.8%
Mean	4	5	4.46	6.06	12.08	7.69	4.77	8.06	8.67
Median	0	0	0	1	1.5	0	0.5	1	0
P25%	0	0	0	0	0	0	0	0	0
P75%	2	4	2	6	6.5	4.25	5	6.25	5
Outliers	11	10	11	11	12	12	10	12	11
Market share outliers	94.4%	91.1%	94.2%	90.6%	92.6%	95.7%	86.5%	89.9%	93.7%

Source: Our elaborations on WFE statistics.

concentrated, with those exchanges falling within the last twenty-fifth percentile of the distribution controlling roughly 90 per cent of total foreign listings.

Breaking the data down by macro-region, we find that Deutsche Börse and the LSEG account for roughly 64 per cent of total foreign listings within the Europe–Middle East region. In the Asia–Pacific region three exchanges (the Australian Securities Exchange, the Singapore Stock Exchange and the Taiwan Stock Exchange) control roughly 74 per cent of foreign listings. Within the Americas, NYSE Euronext and NASDAQ OMX control 58.2 per cent of foreign listings in the region.[2] The attractiveness of the above mentioned exchanges to foreign companies is arguably due either to their prestige as international financial centres (LSEG and NYSE), their particular suitability for certain sectors (NASDAQ OMX, Singapore and Taiwan) or because of their strategic locations (for example, the clear role of Deutsche Börse in attracting firms from central Eastern Europe).

The attributes of capital markets may then, be measured in terms of capital market deepening and market liquidity. Market deepening measures the relative importance of capital markets in financing economic activities, and it can be expressed in terms of market capitalization on domestic GDP. The latter may be defined in different ways, but here we use a measure based on the concept of turnover velocity meant as value of trading on market capitalization.

Market capitalization grew at a very fast rate up to mid-2007, together with the turnover velocity. In four years the dimensions of the exchange industry increased roughly three times, before falling in concomitance with the crisis. Figure 2.1 describes the trends in market capitalization, trading value and turnover velocity across the 53 WFE exchanges since 2003. The data are reported on a quarterly basis.

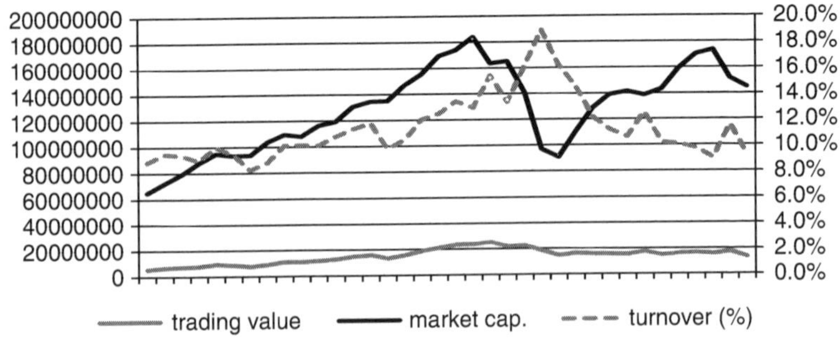

Figure 2.1 Market capitalization, trading value and turnover velocity
Source: Our elaborations on WFE statistics. On the left: market capitalization and trading value in million $. On the right: turnover velocity (%).

Up to 2007 turnover velocity increased with market capitalization with a correlation coefficient of above 90 per cent, marking an improvement in overall market liquidity. These results would suggest that the size of the market, measured in terms of market capitalization, have a strong effect in attracting flows of liquidity and, therefore, they account for positive network externalities.

However, the divarication between the two series that we note starting from 2009 has been reversing the relation. The recovery in market values was accompanied by a sharp decrease in turnover velocity, dampening down the correlation between the two series. Looking at the broad picture, the explicative power of the market dimension over turnover velocity has sharply weakend.

While it is not easy to determine to what extent the contraction is attributable to the crisis (which may have produced a reduction in the appetite for risk) or to the magnitude of competition,[3] there is no doubt that a decrease in turnover velocity poses significant concerns for exchanges since their revenues are a function of trading values.

The trends in turnover velocity may be seen as a proxy of the main business risk faced by exchanges (that is, the risk of losing market activity). American exchanges are, seemingly, more volatile in market turnover in comparison with their European counterparts. During the timeframe under consideration American exchanges operated with an average turnover velocity of 14.6 per cent and a standard deviation of 4.4 per cent; by contrast, European exchanges operated with a lower average velocity (8 per cent), and a lower standard deviation as well (1.5 per cent).

We now compare the main exchanges within the three WFE macro-regions in terms of both capital market deepening and turnover velocity.

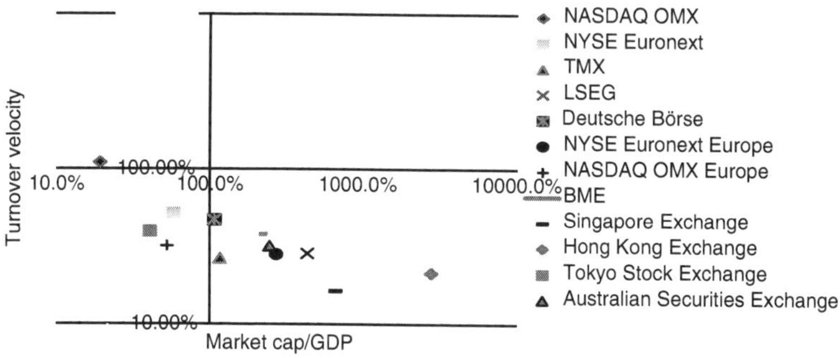

Figure 2.2 Market capitilization on GDP
Source: WFE statistics for market capitalization and turnover velocity and Thomson Reuters Datastream for domestic GDP. Values are exposed in logarithmic scale.

Capital markets in the Asia–Pacific region have been deepening their penetration within their economies. Looking at the ratio of market capitalization to GDP, Asia–Pacific exchanges present (with the exception of the Tokyo Stock Exchange) higher ratios than in other countries (Figure 2.2).

Due to the huge dimensions of their capital markets compared with domestic GDP, the ratios of trading values on market capitalization are generally lower for Asia–Pacific exchanges. However, and this is particularly true for the Hong Kong Stock Exchange, the incidence of values of share trading on GDP is noticeably high.

The above mentioned figures suggest swift trading flows across the regions and, viewed in perspective, they may have strategic implications for the reorganization of the whole exchange industry. To date the most important aggregations between exchanges have occurred within Europe and the US, and also on a transatlantic scale. Looking forward, we suggest that the dynamics which now characterize the industry may open room for a broader restructuring involving Western and Asian exchanges, the development of which follows that of their economies.[4]

We shall deal in more detail with the issue of market concentration. The polarization of the industry has led to a few groups controlling the vast majority of trading across almost all asset classes. We should, however, keep two caveats in mind.

In equity markets this is a flourishing era of new players; they are diverting large flows of orders from traditional exchanges and are making a significant contribution to the radical changes that are occurring in the morphology of equity trading, where, if compared with the recent past, it used to be traditional exchanges, at least in Europe, that attracted the largest part of trading activity.

In derivatives markets, the situation is substantially different, with the great majority of activity being dispersed across a wide stream of off-exchange deals. However, if we concentrate only on exchange transactions the concentration is far greater than in equity markets (Table 2.4).

There emerge huge differences across geographical areas and asset classes. Equity trading on US markets is concentrated in the two biggest exchanges, which together account for more than 90 per cent of trading, whereas in Europe and the Asia–Pacific regions trading is less condensed. However, the four main exchanges in Europe still account for more than 60 per cent of trading volumes. By contrast, the dominant equity exchanges generally have far lower market shares (these are sometimes negligible) with the exception of the LSEG and the Spanish Exchange. In derivatives trading the picture is rather more complex since the vast majority of trading occurs over the counter. Therefore, the market share of each exchange of total exchange trading could be misleading if it is used to define exchanges' penetration of derivatives markets. Far from being neutral, the issue may have practical relevance, above all when defining the market in mergers. Moreover, derivatives markets comprise a wide array of underlying assets and the involvement of exchanges is not the same across all of them. Globally, Deutsche Börse and NYSE Euronext have roughly a 70 per cent market share in European derivatives which, for certain underlings, becomes much more. The diversion of order flow from exchanges by new venues has widely impacted, as we have noted, on trading volumes; therefore, one should expect turnover velocity to be affected in some way as well.

4 A framework for understanding value creation

Before delving in more detail into the issue of measuring exchanges' economic performances, we wish to lay down in this section a general framework for the reasoning that we will develop throughout the book. Broadly speaking, exchange profitability is driven by a combination of four forces which we may label as *strategy, regulation, risk management* and *corporate governance*.

The concept of strategy is central in our analysis. It encompasses a full understanding of the interactions of the exchange industry with the surrounding economic space, the identification of the levers of value and the definition of competitive policies. The latter assists in defining

Table 2.4 Concentration of trading across asset classes and geographical areas

	Europe			America			Asia–Pacific		
	Equities	Bonds	Derivatives	Equities	Bonds	Derivatives	Equities	Bonds	Derivatives
NASDAQ OMX	7%	8.8%	2.5%	38%		13%			
NYSE Euronext	18%	0.04%	24%	54%		12.5%			
TMX				4.6%	0.5%				
LSEG	24%	17.8%							
Deutsche Börse	14.8%	0.2%	44%						
BME	10.3%	57%	1.4%						
Singapore Stock Exchange							1.6%		1.2%
Hong Kong Stock Exchange							8.1%		2.4%
Tokyo Stock Exchange							22%	0.3%	0.4%
Australian Exchange							6.7%	0.1%	2.3%

Source: WFE statistics.

the relative positioning of the exchange against its competitors. Within this general framework a proper perception of the industry-specific value drivers, and their sensitivity to developments in macroeconomic variables, is crucial for the exploitation of the growth options available to the exchange coherent with its desired risk exposure.

Following identification of the main value drivers management should be able to take proper decisions regarding the geographical extension of the business, appropriate activities to engage in and the strategies to control risk exposure. According to the prospects for each macro-region and different market segments, coherent decisions should be possible that maximize value while containing risk to the corporate profile. Moreover, the contextualization of the industry within the macroeconomic landscape should help the management to identify correlations and synergies among different geographical jurisdictions and business units. Moving along a common evolutionary path, global exchanges pursue business diversification strategies that may be horizontal (product and geographical diversification) or vertical – they occasionally pursue both simultaneously – as a means of sustaining revenues and margins and reinforcing their franchises.

Strategic choices regarding the business model and geographical extension define the *risk exposure* of the exchange, something that is exacerbated by increasing competitive strains. A still open question relates to the impact of governance reforms on the risk attitude of securities exchanges: it has been argued that corporatization entails significant incentives for excessive risk taking, although the existing research does not account for substantial changes in risk attitude according to the governance structure.

Governance, however, remains an important pillar in the overall exchange's value proposition. The rapid changes that are currently reshaping the industry's structure require quick reactions from platform operators. As we discuss in Chapter 3, ownership structure is the most relevant attribute of corporate governance since it conditions the ability of the exchanges to catch valuable growth options thorough mergers, alliances or other forms of networks.

In any case, it is a fact that risk management is assuming an even more strategic importance for securities exchanges and should be grounded on appropriate risk-adjusted performance measures. Events that were unpredicted may cause exchanges' earnings to drop, adversely affecting shareholder value. While the diversification of the business model entails new profit centres, it also brings, at the same time, new sources of risk within the exchange. What emerges, therefore, is the need to properly measure performances and risks across different business units. Assuming a managerial perspective, a risk-based framework for measuring performances would be useful for managers seeking to assess the contribution of each unit to corporate value and drive the strategic decision-making process; it might also help them design an efficient system of performance-based rewards. More precisely, risk mapping and risk management are expected to become an ever more important part of the overall governance architecture, especially within the new institutional and regulatory framework that is emerging in the wake of the crisis and which contains tighter requirements for platform operators.

In the following pages we analyse the industry-specific sources of value, while particularly in Chapters 3 and 4 we turn in more detail to the analysis of corporate strategies, governance implications and the impact of industry regulation on value creation.

5 Industry-specific sources of value

Securities exchanges satisfy the demands of two types of customers: companies applying to have their securities listed, and traders demanding an efficient and reliable marketplace. In order to perform their duty of satisfying the needs of their customers, exchanges provide a highly liquid market for securities where issuers can raise finance at a lower cost of capital and traders can negotiate with lower transaction costs. As stressed, liquidity is the main attribute of securities exchanges to the extent that it affects the efficiency of price discovery. For user–owners at least, it is the most valuable attribute for maximizing their utility function. By contrast, for publicly owned exchanges it is questionable if liquidity itself is sufficient to maximize shareholder value.

We expect liquidity to have a positive impact on an exchange's valuation for at least two reasons. First, we expect highly liquid exchanges to attract more customers (both listed companies and traders) due to well known externality effects. Moreover, since an exchange's trading revenues are a function of trading values, the higher the turnover the higher the trading revenues should be. The volumes that exchanges are able to attract have, obviously, an impact on their revenues.

When analysing the perspectives of exchanges and, more generally, of the exchange industry, investors (here assumed to be those investing in the shares of the company managing the market), financial analysts and rating agencies put the relationship between customers' demands and the macroeconomic environment at the forefront of their calculations.[5] Managing securities exchanges is a substantially cyclical business, at least on cash markets, and thus when addressing the economics of exchanges we should have a framework which represents the drivers of market demand.

As a starting point, it is reasonable to assume customer demands being affected by a combination of economic and financial variables. Indeed, in section 3 we outlined the dynamics in the value of share trading and observed how turnover velocity declined during the financial crisis.

But economic growth affects both issuers' and investors' decisions. The former seeks equity or debt financing when they have viable investment projects to support. Traders' market activity, on the other hand, is mainly driven by their risk attitude. During periods of high market volatility and uncertainty trading volumes flatten. Obviously, the economic cycle is not the only driver of market activity; at a micro-economic level the ability to attract either issuers or traders depends on a number of factors such as the exchange's reputation, its competitive positioning, the efficiency of trading platforms and the design of the price schedule.

At an industry level the characteristic features of the businesses involved make volumes naturally sensitive to the cycle. While for cash markets the cyclicality of volumes has been widely recognized and indeed confirmed by the evidence, the behaviour of derivatives trading is deemed to be quite different. Both exchanges and rating institutions, and financial analysts in general, have long supported the case of integration between cash and derivatives markets in order to smooth and stabilize exchanges' performances. In fact, while cash trading closely follows the fluctuations of the cycle, derivatives are seen as a countercyclical business. Trading volumes on derivatives markets (generally measured in terms of number of contracts traded) has actually been rapidly growing during the past few years, at least within the major exchanges. There are a variety of reasons why derivatives behave in a countercyclical manner, most being related to their flexibility and the multitude of uses to which they may be devoted. Actually, derivatives may serve as a useful tool for taking direction on the market or to hedge positions on the underlying assets, especially during cyclical downturns when risks and uncertainty arise.

With reference to other business lines in which securities exchanges may be involved, sensitivity to the cycle may be deemed strictly related to the behaviour of trading activity. Therefore, post-trading activities manage volumes which are obviously dependent on trading volumes on the reference markets. Vertically integrated exchanges which present highly cyclical business on trading markets would, therefore, be subject to the propagation of downward swings in the value chain. Data dissemination business segments are, to the same extent, correlated to trading activity in both cash and derivatives products.

The macroeconomic environment is then, related to the dynamics of interest rates. We expect the yield curve to affect an exchange's valuation through the standard impact on discounted cash flows and its relationship to the economic cycle. For example, an inverted yield curve is generally associated with expectations of an economic downturn which, in turn, would have a negative impact on an exchange's turnover and, therefore, on expected revenues; the evidence does indeed show just this effect.

To start with, we test the sensitivity of cash trading to both the economic cycle (captured by the GDP growth rate, and other variables which may serve as good barometers of economic conditions, such as the price-to-earnings ratio) and the dynamics in the yield curve. We then describe the yield curve as the difference between ten-year and two-year yields.

To this end, we compare different exchanges belonging to different macro-areas. We refer to the timeframe 2003–11 and employ quarterly data. This timeframe spans an entire economic cycle and, therefore, we suggest that it adequately captures tendencies in trading markets. Table 2.5 summarizes the correlations between exchanges' trading volumes listed companies (L) and economic indicators across exchanges for the specified

Table 2.5 Trading volumes, GDP, yield curve and price-to-earnings ratio

Exchange	Variables	TV	L	GDP	10y2y	P/E
NASDAQ	TV	1				
	L	0.6236	1			
	GDP	0.6446	0.5859	1		
	10y2y	0.0337	0.1986	−0.0629	1	
	P/E	−0.0362	0.1750	0.2186	0.4625	1
NYSE		TV	L	GDP	10y2y	P/E
Euronext	TV	1				
(US markets)	L	0.3842	1			
	GDP	0.5666	0.8376	1		
	10y2y	−0.4995	0.3944	0.0720	1	
	P/E	−0.2122	0.3011	0.1042	0.3838	1
TMX		TV	L	GDP	10y2y	P/E
	TV	1				
	L	0.8052	1			
	GDP	0.8968	0.7192	1		
	10y2y	−0.4061	−0.5629	−0.2431	1	
	P/E	−0.3955	−0.4089	−0.4175	0.3527	1

(continued)

Table 2.5 Continued

Exchange	Variables	TV	L	GDP	10y2y	P/E
LSEG		TV	L	GDP	10y2y	P/E
	TV	1				
	L	0.8739	1			
	GDP	0.9196	0.8100	1		
	10y2y	−0.0779	−0.2780	0.0130	1	
	P/E	−0.5407	−0.5967	−0.6613	−0.0930	1
Deutsche Börse		TV	L	GDP	10y2y	P/E
	TV	1				
	L	−0.0274	1			
	GDP	0.5671	−0.4605	1		
	10y2y	−0.7162	0.0811	−0.1243	1	
	P/E	−0.0195	−0.1535	0.2071	0.3903	1
NYSE Euronext (European Markets)		TV	L	GDP	10y2y	P/E
	TV	1				
	L	−0.5869	1			
	GDP	0.2963	−0.5064	1		
	10y2y	−0.6568	0.5610	−0.0773	1	
	P/E	−0.0879	0.2690	−0.1593	0.3024	1
BME		TV	L	GDP	10y2y	P/E
	TV	1				
	L	0.3788	1			
	GDP	0.1882	0.3198	1		
	10y2y	−0.6762	−0.2198	0.1498	1	
	P/E	0.4401	−0.1654	−0.7311	−0.6818	1
Hong Kong Exchanges and Clearing Houses		TV	L	GDP	10y2y	P/E
	TV	1				
	L	0.6778	1			
	GDP	0.7609	0.9431	1		
	10y2y	−0.2536	−0.1364	−0.2559	1	
	P/E	0.0589	−0.4085	−0.3614	0.2778	1
Singapore Securities Exchange		TV	L	GDP	10y2y	P/E
	TV	1				
	L	−0.3655	1			
	GDP	0.4186	0.1637	1		
	10y2y	−0.0389	0.7742	0.2911	1	
	P/E	0.5576	−0.4392	0.3763	−0.2385	1
Australian Securities Exchange		TV	L	GDP	10y2y	P/E
	TV	1				
	L	0.7066	1			
	GDP	0.5403	0.9397	1		
	10y2y	−0.4744	0.0983	0.2605	1	
	P/E	−0.2519	−0.1090	−0.0589	0.5776	1

Source: Our elaborations on Datastream data (GDP, yield curve and price-to-earnings ratio) and WFE statistics (trading volumes).

timeframe. The P/E ratio is that of the shares comprised in the main exchange indexes.

As argued above, market activity expressed as the volumes managed (that is, trading volumes and number of companies listed) by exchanges is closely connected to the dynamics of GDP. The degree of correlation between both value of share trading and the GDP growth rate is markedly high across almost all market centres (with the exception of the Spanish Exchange and the European activities of NYSE Euronext, where the relationship is noticeably weaker). There is also a positive relationship between listed companies and GDP, except for the German Exchange and NYSE Euronext European markets.

By contrast, market volumes and GDP generally show (with a few exceptions) a negative correlation with the differential between ten-year and two-year government bonds rates, which we assume as a proxy of the yield curve. Indeed, during downturns short-term yields are generally bound at low levels while higher rates on the long-term spectrum of the curve could be regarded as expressive of expectations of recovery in the economic cycle. Therefore, a negative relation between trading volumes and the slope of the yield curve seemingly makes sense and is something that we might reasonably expect.

Finally, results in Table 2.5 show a negative correlation between the value of share trading and the *price-to-earnings* ratio (with the exceptions of Deutsche Börse, Hong Kong Exchanges and Clearing Houses and the Singapore Securities Exchange). It would indicate that with increasing trading volumes earnings increase relative to share prices. From another perspective, the sign of the correlation suggests that as trading volumes increase exchanges' shares tend to behave as *value stocks*.

On balance, the figures we have produced are supportive of our suggestion of a tight relationship between trading activity and the macroeconomic cycle. In that sense they provide a general framework for contextualizing the economic performance of exchanges. The relationships that we have uncovered are of paramount importance in properly assessing the risks that exchanges are exposed to.

6 The economics of the exchange industry

The industrial organization approach for studying security exchanges and other platforms, claims to provide an overview of the economics of the industry. The following discussion is intended to provide a broad picture of cost, revenues and profitability at an industry level and their trends over the last decade. We base our arguments on data provided by

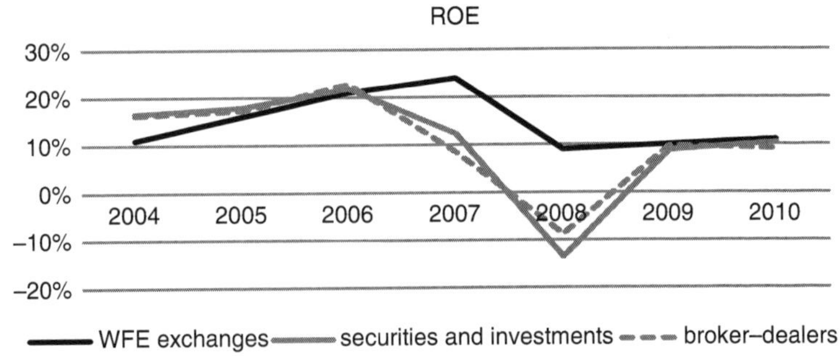

Figure 2.3 Return on equity
Source: Our elaboration on WFE's 2010 Cost & Revenue Survey and SNL Financial.

the WFE. In Chapter 5 we analyse in greater detail the cost and revenue functions of exchanges, while in Chapter 7 we provide an empirical investigation with reference to listed exchanges.

We start by comparing the performances of security exchanges over the last eight years with those of the wider financial industry. We focus, in particular, on the return on Equity (ROE) trends. We took as reference the aggregate performances of the exchanges affiliated to the WFE, and assume as the reference term for the comparison the *broker–dealer* financial sector[6] and the securities and investments sector (Figure 2.3).

As Figure 2.3 shows, during the four years from 2004 to 2007 the profitability of exchanges rapidly increased, catching up in a few years with the average profitability of the financial sectors that we have taken for the purposes of reference. This trend should be interpreted in light of the movements occurring around the exchange industry in that period, in short, the speeding up of the consolidation processes that we have already touched upon. Those years were particularly fertile for mergers with the finalization of the most important deals involving the largest Western exchanges.[7] Growing profitability was reflected in steep increases in the share values of major listed exchanges, mirroring expectations of high-growth profits for the near future. During the financial crisis the decline in profitability was less pronounced than in the financial sectors used by us for reference. However, the consolidation process was stopped until 2011 when another round of mergers was put on stage, the most noteworthy being an ambitious merger agreement between NYSE Euronext and Deutsche Börse which would have resulted in a dominant transatlantic market centre (at least in the derivatives business); for that reason the deal was blocked by the European authorities.

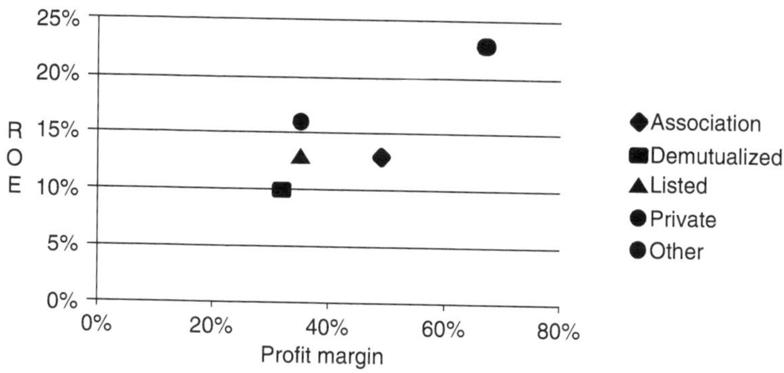

Figure 2.4 ROE and profit margin breakdown by legal status
Source: Our elaboration on WFE's 2011 Cost & Revenue Survey.

However, when breaking down profitability by legal status (see Figure 2.4) the results which emerge are noticeably heterogeneous.

What may be surprising are the lower figures for listed exchanges compared with other legal statuses. Both in terms of ROE and profit margin (expressed as net income on total revenues) economic performance for these exchanges appears quite subdued when compared to other statuses. While having roughly the same ROE, exchanges incorporated as associations fare better in terms of profit margin. Private exchanges are better off than listed exchanges as well. Demutualized but unlisted exchanges have the lowest returns. The residual category (other exchanges) achieved the best performances.

These results seem to contradict the widely held belief that for-profit listed exchanges have a strong focus on profit maximization; indeed the results may be even more surprising when the widespread presence of institutional investors in the ownership structure is recalled. We may invoke three plausible explanations for what appears at first sight to be a puzzle.

First of all, the category of listed exchanges comprises those exchanges that were mainly involved in the consolidation process; merger expenses may have, to some extent, affected performances. When we consider those exchanges' annual reports which account for relevant merging costs (for example, NYSE Euronext), this certainly appears to be plausible.

Another possible explanation lies with the competitive pressures which are, supposedly, greater for listed exchanges. As the large listed exchanges make a greater contribution to the major blue-chip indexes they, arguably, should suffer most from competition created by certain global alternative trading values focusing on those shares. Chi-X Europe offers market participants trading in stocks listed in 15 European markets and has gained, over time, increasing market shares in the main blue-chip indexes: a 27.8 per cent market share in the STOXX Europe 50 index and 22.7 per cent in the EURO STOXX 50 index, along with more than a 25 per cent market share in the FTSE 100, the CAC 40 and DAX indexes. The downward pressures on exchanges' fees may act as relevant factors in subduing economic performances in comparison with other legal statuses.

A third explanation for lower profitability ratios for listed exchanges emerges if we adopt a governance approach. As listed exchanges mainly present a substantially dispersed ownership structure one could be tempted to invoke the separation between ownership and control to justify lower performances; this assertion certainly appears in the literature on management incentives.[8] Admitting such an explanation would imply that shareholders exert a weak monitoring over managers who, therefore, would be able to consume perquisites or engage in low-profit investment projects. Despite being run as public companies, we have identified a group of institutional investors holding relevant stakes in major exchanges, and we find it implausible that such shareholders would not exert strong control over managers.

Whatever the exact explanation is, it would hardly explain the high profitability ratios of exchanges incorporated as associations or other legal statuses. In fact, their member–owners are supposedly guided by objectives related to the efficiency of trading platforms rather than a pure profit-maximizing goal. Otherwise, such exchanges might have some public influence, again causing a deviation from a pure profit-maximizing objective.

Moreover, in the last few years share prices have continued to drop across listed exchanges despite the fact that market activity, as reflected by trading volumes trends (especially in derivatives), has somewhat recovered. Notwithstanding this, the industry remains concerned with the sustainability of previous high-growth profit rates. In this regard, the crisis may be seen as an event amplifying pressures on revenues and margins stemming from increased competition.

During the period 2004–11 the aggregate revenues of the exchanges affiliated to the WFE showed a 15 per cent compound annual growth rate (CAGR) against a 8.6 per cent compound annual growth rate in costs. However, when restricting the analysis to the sub-period 2007–11 we compute a revenue's CAGR of just 5.8 per cent against a cost's CAGR of 6.6 per cent. Therefore, whereas market trends lead to a huge drop in revenues' growth rates, exchanges were not able to carry on relevant cost efficiencies, despite their focus on cost synergies during the last few years. One explanation may be related to the consolidation process, which could have resulted in increased burdens on the exchanges' cost structures, at least in the short term. The fact that only in 2011, as reported by the WFE 'Cost & Revenue Survey', was there a reduction in overall costs may provide some support for this view.[9]

We now move on to analyse the relationship between costs and revenues on the one hand and the value of share trading on the other. As we have just pointed out, exchanges run a transaction-based business that charges fees based on the trading activity of market participants. However, exchanges are also deemed to operate with a (at least partially) fixed-cost structure reflecting investments in technology (trading platforms) and other organizational arrangements; the marginal cost of an additional unit of trading, once all the organization has been set up, is negligible. Figure 2.5 relates costs and revenues with share trading value.

Whereas trading revenues grow with the value of share trading and the relationship appears to be significant, the cost function appears to be flatter with a higher constant factor. These results provide some evidence that costs for securities exchanges are mainly fixed. They also have implications in light of the competitive struggles that exchanges are facing in the new landscape. Cost efficiency requires exchanges to expand trading volumes in order to reduce average costs; this is the main force moving exchanges forward with sizeable acquisitions. Despite being

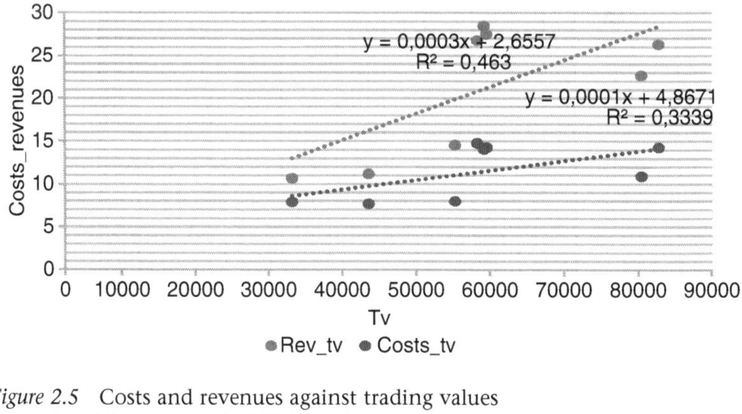

Figure 2.5 Costs and revenues against trading values
Source: Our elaboration on the WFE 2011 Cost & Revenue Survey.

targeted to exploit both cost and revenue synergies, mergers between exchanges are primarily focused on cost efficiencies, seen as an essential outcome to cope with highly efficient alternative platforms.

As we have explained, exchanges run platform businesses that entail a complex infrastructure built up with organizational arrangements and technological premises which are deemed to count for a large portion of fixed costs. Notwithstanding this, however, exchanges may also bear transaction-related costs which, in many cases, mirror the rewards for liquidity providers or other cost items (such as routing or clearing fees); such costs are essentially variable.

However, a proper understanding of the main trends requires an in-depth analysis of security exchanges' cost structures. As a basic premise, it should be noted that cost structures vary somewhat across different exchanges. Putting it in general terms, the main categories of costs comprise personnel costs, administrative expenses, IT costs, depreciation and amortization. There are, however, certain cost items that, although representing a small portion of the aggregate costs, for some exchanges assume a great relevance. For example, *regulatory costs*, which generally represent fees paid by the exchange to the supervisors, in some jurisdictions may be particularly relevant.[10] Other cost items may comprise *liquidity payments*, representing retrocessions that the exchange awards to broker-dealers, or routing and clearing fees; these costs vary considerably across exchanges.

When examining cost structure, moreover, it should be recalled that not all cost items affect an exchange's economic performance since certain categories may be neutral. For example, regulatory costs are generally matched by a corresponding item on the revenue side. That is certainly the case of NYSE Euronext which covers such costs by charging *activity assessments fees* to market participants.

Looking in more detail to the cost structure of exchanges, we observe that personnel costs far exceed the other cost items (Table 2.6).

As will be seen, the main cost items (personnel, IT and administration) show a moderate growth rate over the last four years and they may be deemed as mainly fixed. They account for roughly 50 per cent of total costs. Depreciation and amortization, by contrast, show a high compound annual growth rate during the period which, however, is mainly attributable to the high levels observed during the period 2008–10. Arguably, this trend is related to the crisis and the consolidation process that was occurring in the industry at that time. In fact, exchanges moving forward with sizeable acquisitions report high levels of goodwill which, during the crisis, was subject to significant

Table 2.6 Costs breakdown (million US$)

	2007	2008	2009	2010	2011	CAGR
Salaries and benefits	3755.7	3668	4015	4143	4237	3.1%
IT	1177	1092	1060	1308	1378	4%
Administration	1369.6	1414	1505	1268	1392	0.4%
Depreciation and amortization	941.6	2993	2401	2096	1491	12.2%
Marketing	353.1	162	297	118	169	−16.8%
Cost of regulation	930.9	633	862	701	656	−8.4%
Other costs	2172.1	3534	3922	3586	3840	15.3%

Source: WFE Cost & Revenue Survey 2007–11.

impairments. Other relevant costs are those labelled as 'other costs', which, as mentioned, comprise certain items – such as liquidity rebates – that are dependent on trading volumes and are, therefore, mainly variable. According to WFE figures these costs account, in aggregate, for less than 30 per cent of total costs.

7 Exchange business models: an overview

The various exchange business models may be analysed according to the degree of *product differentiation* and *business integration* that they display. Mapping the prevailing business models is relevant in that the models reflect the competitive strategies of exchanges and, supposedly, affect their economic performances while hardly impacting on the industry's structure.

For the sake of simplicity, we may identify three main business models which we summarize as follows:

a) A *narrow* business model, where the exchange engages in listing and trading in cash markets with the focus being on a narrow array of asset classes (for example, equities or bonds). Within the narrow business model we may include pure derivatives exchanges as well, although they may run marketplaces in derivative contracts written on different asset classes.
b) A *diversified* business model. Under this cluster we may include exchanges that engage in trading in a great variety of products ranging from equities to bonds and derivatives or other products (such as exchange-traded funds (ETFs), which are becoming an important product for a lot of exchanges). Many exchanges have expanded

their business models recently to incorporate multiple asset classes through a process of *horizontal integration*, which entailed the merger between exchanges specializing (or having a strong competitive position) in different products.[11]

c) A *vertical integrated* business model, which arises as a result of exchanges developing or acquiring post-trading operators (CSDs or Clearing Houses). By running trading and post-trading services, the exchange controls the entire value chain of securities trading. The vertical integrated model, then, may combine with a narrow business model or with a diversified business model. The latter example identifies those that we may label conglomerate exchanges.

Before moving on, we believe that it would be useful to clarify two relevant points. When looking at financial accounts we find that almost all exchanges report income from information services. This source of revenue is related to the selling of market data, mainly prices and quotations. However, it does not constitute a specific business model. In fact, the production of market information is inherent to (and constitutes an essential part of) the exchange business. More precisely, both narrow and multi-product exchanges (comprised vertically integrated exchanges) are involved in information services, although income generation from this business line may assume a different magnitude across exchanges.

Moreover, despite the fact that all exchanges are engaged in different business lines, many of them derive the great majority of their revenues from only one line – or at most a few lines – or asset classes. Therefore, some caution must be used when classifying an exchange as a multi-business exchange. When formally vested with a diversified business model, it may be, de facto, a mono-product exchange when both market activity and revenues derived from the other business lines are negligible in comparison to the main one.

Bearing these caveats in mind, we provide a summary of how business models have been evolving over time. We build again on the figures reported by the WFE and then focus on the main listed exchanges. Table 2.7 summarizes the breakdown of WFE members by product.

The figures show the increasing attempts of exchanges to become global players, engaged in multi-product (services) businesses. The great majority of exchanges operate in all segments of trading, ranging from equities and bonds to derivatives products. The narrow business model has characterized only a few exchanges in the past few years, with the proportion of cash-equity-only exchanges sharply declining in the last few years. There are a few derivatives-only exchanges as well, but it

Table 2.7 WFE exchanges by product

	Cash equities only	Cash equities, bonds	Cash equities, derivatives	Cash equities, bonds, derivatives	Derivatives only	Post-trading
2007	8%	33%	10%	47%	2%	68%
2008	11%	24%	11%	49%	5%	73%
2009	13%	21%	11%	51%	4%	74%
2010	2%	26%	8%	60%	4%	74%
2011	2%	27%	4%	61%	6%	75%

Source: WFE Cost & Revenue Surveys 2007–11.

is worth noting that this category includes the three large American pure derivatives exchanges (the Chicago Mercantile Exchange (CME), the Chicago Board Options Exchange (CBOE) and the Intercontinental Exchange) which accounts for a high proportion of aggregate WFE revenues. Breaking down by revenues, the narrow exchanges count for 23 per cent of aggregate WFE revenues with the figure comprising the 15 per cent weight of pure derivative exchanges, whereas cash and derivatives exchanges enjoy 77 per cent of total revenues. Finally, exchanges integrating post-trading activities count for 88 per cent of aggregate revenues.

At the same time, the proportion of exchanges engaged in post-trading services has widened and now covers two-thirds of total member exchanges. Putting these figures together, what emerges is a widely diversified and vertically integrated business model: a combination of models *b)* and *c)*.

As for the profitability of exchanges by business model (ROE and profit margin) WFE figures only sketch the breakdown between exchanges engaging in post-trading activities and other exchanges; nevertheless it may be interesting to note how the former are less profitable than the latter. In fact, exchanges with post-trading activities report, in aggregate, a 29 per cent profit margin and a 10 per cent ROE against profitability ratios of 45 per cent and 20 per cent for other exchanges. One of the rationales that has always been recognized behind business diversification is the search for new sources of revenues and high margins. To this end, certain activities such as derivatives trading and post-trading are traditionally seen as highly profitable. The above mentioned figures may, therefore, appear somewhat surprising, although it should be observed that the category of no post-trading exchanges is rather limited and comprises two big Chinese exchanges. In the literature, however, we find some contributions that have analysed the efficiency implications of business diversification for securities exchanges. The results are interesting, and give no support to the efficiency hypothesis for diversified exchanges. Schmiedel (2001) assessed the conditions of economic efficiency in European stock exchanges between 1985 and 1999, while a year later the same author (Schmiedel, 2002) examined gains in the productivity between 1993 and 1999 of both stock exchanges that focused on their core business and those that also operated in derivatives and post-trading activities. On the contrary, Serifsoy (2007)[12] adopted Farrell's notion of technical efficiency and applied his analysis to a sample of 28 stock exchanges.[13] The study used a non-parametric approach based on Data Envelopment Analysis and his findings showed that diversified stock exchanges were less efficient than exchanges focused on the conventional cash market. It is important to note, however, that all the studies dealing with this subject deliver results which are highly dependent on the particular notion of efficiency that is employed. Nevertheless, the results seem to converge, and this may cast some doubts on the effectiveness of the competitive strategies that exchanges are ever more extensively pursuing. Besides this, they posit some doubts as for future strategies.

We now take into consideration the most relevant listed exchanges and map their prevailing business models, breaking down the data by cash market trading (both on equities and bonds), derivatives trading and post-trading involvement. Table 2.8 provides the broad picture.

Among the major listed exchanges, only three adopt a narrow business model focused on derivatives; the others operate with widely diversified business models, at least with reference to the trading side ranging from

Table 2.8 Major listed exchanges: a map of business models

	Equities	Bonds	Derivatives	Post-trading
NYSE Euronext	✓	✓	✓	
NASDAQ OMX	✓	✓	✓	
CME			✓	
CBOE			✓	
ICE			✓	
LSEG	✓	✓	✓	✓
Deutsche Börse	✓	✓	✓	✓
TMX Group	✓	✓	✓	
BME	✓	✓	✓	✓

Source: Exchange websites and annual reports.

cash to derivatives products. A few incorporate post-trading activities; however, the relevance of post-trading business on total revenues considerably varies across exchanges. Most diversification arose as a result of mergers among exchanges, but the degree of diversification greatly varies, and in some cases it is possible to identify a business area which is dominant and accounts for the majority of revenues produced by the exchange. In cases such as this, we can hardly maintain that the exchange operates with a diversified business model.

Figure 2.6 plots the revenues breakdown with reference to the exchanges operating with a diversified business model. We break the data down, in particular, by cash market revenues, derivatives market revenues and post-trading revenues, and represent the weight of each source on total revenues. Here we do not report other service revenues such as *market information* revenues since, as previously noted, we do not consider their magnitude to be a contribution to business diversification.

Reading the figures in Figure 2.6 provides mixed evidence as to the degree of business diversification. Deutsche Börse appears as the exchange with the most balanced business model, with derivatives and post-trading counting for more than 30 per cent each of total revenues, while the contribution of equity markets (in terms of both listing and trading revenues) is quite small, just exceeding 10 per cent. Market information services, however, make an appreciable contribution as well. Other exchanges, despite undergoing important aggregations targeted at finding new sources of revenues along with cost efficiencies,

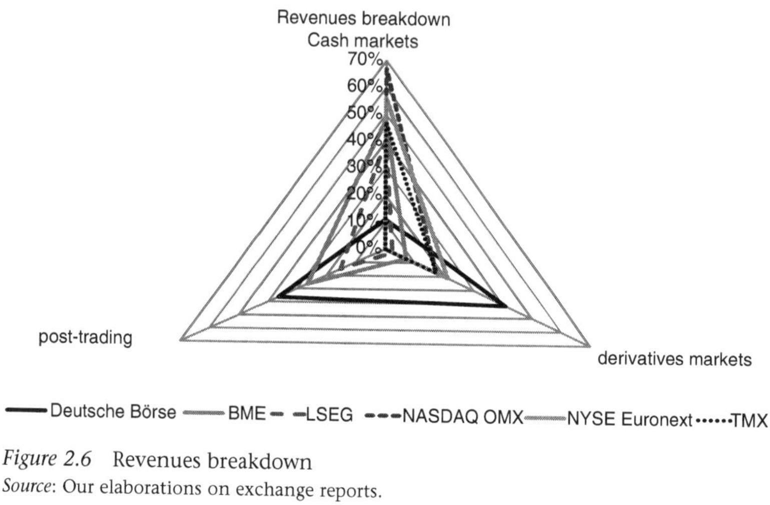

Figure 2.6 Revenues breakdown
Source: Our elaborations on exchange reports.

continue to operate with a concentrated business model. By merging with Borsa Italiana the London Stock Exchange sought access to the derivatives and post-trading activities of the Italian Exchange. Nevertheless, the resulting Group's contribution to total revenues continued to be focused on cash markets. Apart from a significant contribution of post-trading, derivatives are negligible whereas a notable fraction of revenues is due to market information services which, to an extent, can be considered as cash market products. By contrast, the American exchanges, NYSE and Euronext, continue to derive far above 50 per cent of their revenues from cash markets. This is, however, not surprising since NASDAQ and NYSE are by far the most liquid cash markets, greatly exceeding other exchanges in terms of annual turnover. Equity markets, therefore, naturally dominate other business lines. For NYSE Euronext, however, derivatives constitute a relevant part of the exchange's business. In the US market it has a relevant market share, at least in certain underlying assets. In the European derivatives market it shares an oligopolistic position with the Eurex Exchange.

8 Securities exchanges and alternative systems: an evolving relationship

As previously noted, the morphology of the industry has been reshaped by the emergence of new trading venues that have challenged established securities exchanges in attracting liquidity. At least in those countries which had adopted a *concentration rule*, exchanges were challenging low competitive threats. Some competition took place between exchanges whenever the relevant markets were overlapping. The operation of other platforms was limited and restricted to bonds and derivatives.[14] However, as soon as regulation was changed, allowing and indeed promoting competition in the market for order execution, new venues appeared and immediately started to erode the high volumes of exchanges' market activity.

According to statistics from the Federation of European Securities Exchanges (FESE) multilateral trading facilities account for some 26 per cent of aggregate European electronic order book trading.

These systems caused competition in the securities industry to move a step forward and are assuming great importance for at least two reasons.

First of all, they are clearly successful in stealing large order flows from securities exchanges. The potential fragmentation that arises may undermine the efficiency of price discovery, and that is enough to inspire the stringent transparency standards adopted by regulators. In equity

Table 2.9 Multilateral Trading Facilities' market share in Europe

	2008	2009	2010	2011
Exchanges	94.3%	83.1%	76.5%	73.3%
MTFs	5.7%	16.9%	23.5%	26.7%

Source: FESE statistics.

trading followers in many cases soon began to adopt a compatibility strategy, admitting to trading securities listed on the main market. The forces driving the competition between venues are complex and are developing along several dimensions.

Commentators view a growing number of mergers among exchanges as an immediate response to the changing landscape and, in particular, an attempt to reinforce their market share of trading activity. However, exchanges were developing competitive strategies for international securities long before mergers started to speed up by adapting their respective market models. In particular, the segmentation of markets was designed in order to carve out segments tailored to the trading of securities listed on foreign markets, and to respond to the needs of investors interested in buying and selling the most liquid international stocks. By designing dedicated segments to foreign securities, exchanges actually did what alternative multilateral trading platforms are now doing in seeking to gain coverage over a multitude of countries.

On the other hand, following the increasing success of their rivals, exchanges moved forward in coping with fierce competition by launching their own MTFs or acquiring already established operators. The genesis of MTFs is quite different in the two cases. The earliest MTFs were established by large international banks and investment firms trading on exchanges. For the latter, therefore, new multilateral facilities represented a threat from their customers, who were attempting to create a cheaper (and, sometimes, more flexible) way of trading securities. Therefore, exchanges taking over existing MTFs represented an attempt to recapture an order flow which had drifted away. Other exchange-operated MTFs were targeted to create a dedicated marketplace for certain kinds of issuers who did not comply with the standards for admission to the primary market. This is the case of the markets for small and medium enterprises, the constitution of which was not actually prompted by the need to recapture orders that had flowed away; rather they aimed to attract firms that traditionally sought access to finance outside the capital markets.

According to the MiFID database there are currently 149 multilateral trading facilities operating. Table 2.10 provides a summary of exchange-operated MTFs.

The competition between exchanges and other multilateral platforms is evolving downwards alongside the exchange's industry value chain, and is resulting in competition between post-trading operators. From an industrial organization perspective these movements are rapidly changing the entire system of relations between market platforms.

Traditionally, the links between exchanges and post-trading platforms were simple, with the former designating a single clearing and settlement operator, either belonging to the exchange's group or independent platforms; multiple designations were unusual. The landscape started to change as a result of recent regulation, and the initiatives of various representative bodies targeted at improving interoperability among platforms; a growing network of links among platforms emerged, with some exchanges designating more than one post-trading platform to process their trades.

The growth of new trading venues has furthered the process of changing relations among platforms. Major multilateral trading facilities clear their trades in newly created post-trading architectures. In 2007 the European Multilateral Clearing Facility (EMCF) was set up by major investment banks to serve as a central counterparty for trades occurring on multilateral trading facilities. Following this, the EuroCCP was

Table 2.10 The MTFs of European exchanges

	MTF	**Strategy**
LSEG	Turquoise	Acquisition
NYSE Euronext	NYSE Arca Europe	Own MTF
NASDAQ OMX	NASDAQ OMX Europe INET First North	Acquisition
Nordic Growth Market	Nordic MTF	Own MTF
Luxembourg Stock Exchange	Euro MTF	Own MTF
Deutsche Börse Group	Tradegate	Acquisition
Bolsa de Madrid (BME Group)	Latibex	Own MTF
Börse Berlin	Equiduct	Own MTF
Athens Exchange	Alternative market	Own MTF

established as a subsidiary of the American Depository Trust and Clearing Corporation (DTCC).

These new post-trading architectures have implications for the overall prospects for the exchange industry. Such platforms offer clearing solutions to MTFs in multiple markets[15] and, therefore, seem to be ahead in realizing what has long been an aim of European authorities, namely the creation of a pan-European infrastructure at central counterparty (CCP) level to overcome fragmentation in the market. While post-trading costs have been recognized as accounting for a relevant fraction of total trading costs for some time, there is a huge difference in clearing and settling cross-border transactions compared with domestic ones, the former spanning all the stages of post-trading activities (custodian services, clearing and settlement, custody and safe keeping and CCP services).[16] These differences are mainly due to the traditional segmentation across countries at post-trading level which are mainly attributable to the costs of establishing links and interoperability restrictions. While important progress has been made in these areas as a result of industry level initiatives, the problem of fragmentation has not yet been fully addressed.

What is happening, in our view, is a consolidation of the industry, at least for equity trading, along two dimensions encompassing both trading and post-trading activities; we may summarize the situation as follows.

At trading level the industry is developing into a form of oligopolistic competition where two main blocks are facing each other. On the one side, large coalitions of exchanges that span different jurisdictions are emerging as a result of mergers; on the other side, multiple-market, flexible MTFs contest for supremacy with exchanges in securities trading. The idea of block competition captures the fact that the big struggle is between traditional exchanges, which seem to prefer to ally than compete, and new platforms. Moreover, some form of consolidation is taking place among MTFs as well. We may recall the merger between BATS and Chi-X Europe, but also the closure of NASDAQ OMX Europe once it failed to achieve the targeted level of market activity – scale is clearly relevant for alternative platforms as well. Among European MTFs, on the other hand, two platforms (BATS Europe and Chi-X) retain a 23 per cent market share of overall European electronic order book trading.

Besides this, at post-trading level the jostle between global exchanges and multi-market alternative platforms may lead to some form of consolidation as well. It could be questioned if the operation of multiple post-trading platforms, although linked together on an interoperability basis, would actually fit the needs of global trading systems. Moreover, MTFs capturing large flows of orders may represent a competitive threat to vertical integrated exchanges on both trading and post-trading level: at a trading level when they divert relevant flows of liquidity from exchanges, and at a post-trading level when they design their own post-trading entities (or, more generally, post-trading operators not controlled by exchanges) to process their trades.

9 Conclusions

Following the demutualization and subsequent listing of major exchanges a widespread consolidation process took place within the exchange industry spurring the creation of a few large conglomerates; in the years immediately preceding the financial crisis the phenomena assumed a paramount relevance. Major deals involving important Western exchanges were struck, while certain Western financial centres (NASDAQ and LSEG) established tight links with certain Arab markets (in particular, the Dubai financial centre). And some consolidation has recently started to occur in the Asia–Pacific area.

Mergers among exchanges contributed to the polarization of trading, with a few large groups coming to account for the great majority of trading values. In the meanwhile, the integration of capital markets around the world has increased as well. A particularly useful measure of integration is the number of foreign listings: figures confirm a huge increase of foreign listings during the last few years, although market shares are highly concentrated. Overall, the Asia–Pacific macro-area is growing fastest. Variables measuring market activity (market capitalization, trading values and listed companies) are of great importance since they represent the main value drivers of securities exchanges. Our findings show that these variables are correlated with macroeconomic and financial variables.

In the final analysis, a very significant issue is that of the relationship between performance and legal status. Exchanges largely demutualized, and subsequently became public, in order to endow themselves with the flexibility required to challenge increasing competition. Observing aggregate data from the WFE, however, we note that listed exchanges have fared somewhat worse than not-for-profit exchanges, something which at first might seem hard to explain. Listed exchanges are, however, those suffering most from the competitive threats posed by large electronic communication networks (ECNs). The appearance of ECNs is significant since it stimulated the reaction of established exchanges. The latter, more precisely, tend to counteract increasing competition by acquiring their main competitors, or by constituting their own ECNs. These trends are interesting in that they trace a new path in the convergence among trading platforms.

3

Securities Industry Regulation. Implications for Exchanges' Performances

1 Introduction

It is well known that the regulatory framework has paramount importance for the efficient functioning of the finance industry. The rationale behind financial regulation is to prevent market failures which would hamper the flow of funds to the most efficient investment opportunities. Nearly all actors in the financial industry (institutions, markets and issuers) are subject to regulation.

Rules for financial institutions protect customers who, by their nature, need particular care. Legislative bodies and supervisory authorities intervene with the aim of setting fair conduct-of-business rules and transparency requirements for the provision of financial services to customers. The ultimate goal is to enable customers to take informed decisions and to prevent miss-selling practices.

Over the years financial regulation has rapidly evolved, imposing tighter requirements on financial institutions and raising concerns about the cost of compliance and, ultimately, the cost burden on customers. These concerns are shared by institutions.

More recently, regulators have intervened heavily in the structure of the exchange industry as well. Regulation in this field is far from recent, but in the era when exchanges were public entities and natural monopolies, the regulation of exchanges and platforms was considered merely as a means of preserving the integrity of the price discovery process and to ensure adequate levels of transparency. The corporatization of exchanges led to innovation in the regulatory field. The transformation of exchanges into profit-oriented entities led to an evolution of regulation. In today's securities industry, regulators are even more interested in how exchanges (as firms) are managed rather than just focusing on the markets they run.

Initially, the regulation of exchanges was based on a pro-competitive approach, giving rise to a framework in which competition between exchanges was stimulated. This framework was the direct consequence of conceiving of exchanges as corporations. It stimulated a shift from competition between orders to competition between market centres, forcing exchanges to innovate, to further strategic competition and, eventually, to engage in risk taking. The most obvious outcome of this transformation was consolidation in the industry, and a jostling for the control of platforms.

Consequently, regulation needed to move on from firms and markets to platforms, where the rationale is mainly concerned to regulate access rights – something which involves access to all the services in the industry, not just to orders.

Section 2 in this chapter examines the rationale of exchange industry regulation and provides an overview of how it has evolved over time. Section 3 compares the European and American regulatory systems and discusses repercussions in terms of competitive pressures. Section 4 deals with the principles of regulating access rights. Section 5 focuses on the economic and industrial implications of exchange industry regulation. Section 6 concludes.

2 The rationale of exchange industry regulation

The basic rationale of exchange industry regulations is the need to preserve the integrity of capital markets, and to provide investors with marketplaces where trades can occur with the lowest possible transaction costs.

The literature abounds in discussions of the integrity of capital markets, their transparency and the monitoring of both issuers and traders, and although we make some reference to prominent works on these topics they are not the main concern of this book. Rather, and since the aim of our work is to investigate exchanges as firms, we mainly focus on the economic and industrial implications of regulation. We are, in particular, interested in how new regulations may impact on competition.

One discussion bridging the debates on the integrity of capital markets and on competition concerns the virtues of *consolidation* and *fragmentation* of capital markets. Microstructure theory has widely advocated the benefits of highly consolidated and transparent capital markets. They are said to benefit both investors and issuers by magnifying network externalities through a large pool of liquidity and better price discovery. Ultimately, both transaction costs and information asymmetries are reduced.

Therefore, it is argued, investors and issuers choose a single highly liquid and transparent market governed by prime monitoring and disclosure requirements. According to the bonding hypothesis[1] traders benefit through lower transaction costs. For issuers, better investor protection provides an environment for prime corporate governance entailing lower expropriation risks. Sound governance requirements, therefore, constitute the prerequisite for lowering the cost of capital when seeking external finance. According to some financial theorists, traders also prefer highly transparent capital markets (Huddart, Hughes and Brunnermeier, 1999). For as long as liquidity traders have a clear incentive to opt for high-disclosure markets, informed traders will follow them. Highly liquid markets will permit the latter to disguise their non-public information.

The implications of the bonding hypothesis constitute the rationale for consolidation in the exchange industry by means of mergers and other forms of alliance. Once the lowering of barriers to cross-border capital flows and the availability of instantaneous information due to technological innovation became feasible, these new forms of competition started to occur. Now we can see that this mode of competition is resulting in the formation of large conglomerates. However, it is unclear where this process is going to end and what regulatory changes can be expected. Roughly ten years ago, before the widespread wave of mergers, some commentators argued that those players offering wider liquidity pools and lower transaction costs, alongside better technologies, would be the winners in this process, eventually giving rise to a winner-takes-all contest with only a few large players in major financial centres surviving.[2]

The merits of consolidation would lead to the affirmation of a large super-exchange naturally eroding the space of small market centres. Currently, competition is leading to increasing consolidation among stock exchanges – giving rise to a polarization of trading – yet rivals are still emerging and establishing themselves as viable.

Thus, there appear to be strong economic reasons for fragmentation in the exchange industry, reasons that may be detected in the heterogeneous preferences of both traders and issuers. A variety of markets could match the different preferences of a set of non-homogeneous customers (Seppi, 1997). Differences in utility functions argue for the existence of diverse players addressing the specific needs and preferences of a particular category of customers.

With reference to issuers, differences in ownership structures have different governance implications and may entail diverging behaviours.

Concentrated rather than dispersed ownership is expected to sharply influence the choice of the exchange for listing, with issuers with a dispersed ownership preferring high-disclosure exchanges in order to gain better protection against the risk of expropriation, while concentrated ownership induces a listing in more opaque exchanges. In the latter case, the controlling shareholders are subject to a lower level of monitoring.

Information asymmetries give rise to a *cream skimming* effect, with uninformed traders preferring large liquid markets and informed ones preferring more opaque market centres. There are implications about immediacy as well; due to the types of traders operating in less regulated and more opaque markets, immediacy becomes the main feature there.

Fragmentation may benefit market operators by providing trading environments that fit a variety of preferences in terms of transaction costs, immediacy and so on. In such an environment, traders may resort to the market that best fits their preference in terms of transaction costs, immediacy and transparency.

Regulators around the world (in particular, in Europe with the MiFID and in the US with NMS regulation) promote competition among markets thereby encouraging potential fragmentation. According to economic theory, transaction costs (at least those that are explicit, such as commissions) should be lower in fragmented markets due to competition for orders. However, for the other aspects of transaction costs (spreads[3] or market impact), fragmentation is particularly concerning since it can impact on the efficiency of price discovery and the ability of the market to find an equilibrium price.

Today's exchange industry is evolving towards a situation where there is a balance between competition among major financial centres on a cross-border basis and segmentation with the rise of new trading venues addressing different types of demand. While the mobility of issuers and liquidity characterizes the exchange industry, greater attention could be paid to the consequences of new forms of competition on corporate governance and their possible effects on the international regulation of the industry.

Industrial competition may be accompanied by regulatory competition, as has been amply shown by the literature. Coffee (2002) suggests that regulatory competition is inherent in cross-border competition involving securities markets operating under different regulatory regimes. Therefore, regulatory competition is something that is endogenous to a model of competition among exchanges subject to different regulatory regimes.[4] Specifically, he argues that this competition counteracts the forces of centralization that some commentators and theoreticians suggest lead to the oligopoly of a small number of exchanges, dominating de facto all trading. Coffee also suggests that competition provides improved investor protection.

Regulatory competition may have two different outcomes, one undesirable and the other beneficial. The former involves a sort of regulatory arbitrage[5] lowering standards; the latter goes in the opposite direction, towards tighter and tighter requirements, forcing exchanges to raise admission standards and monitoring practices in order to attract issuers and traders based on their high reputations. As Coffee points out, regulatory competition does not actually work as envisaged by the proponents of *issuer choice*; issuers are able to escape their home jurisdiction and their supposedly more stringent legal standards. In contrast, cross-listing, or foreign listing[6] systems which lead to jostling between international market centres for high-quality issuers, leads the issuers to seek high legal standards as a means of signalling their quality to the market. Choosing a deep and liquid market is, therefore, inconsistent with opting for a poor jurisdiction in terms of the legal and regulatory apparatus.

The bonding hypothesis, and the form of regulatory competition envisaged for example by Coffee, provides a strong incentive for exchanges to improve their standards. The polarization of trading which has resulted from recent mergers will, arguably, reinforce this incentive; above all, a 'race to the top' is expected to become a strategic lever against the increasing competitive threats coming from new rivals. However, regional exchanges are also subject to regulatory competition in the sense that they too are exposed to the risk of losing issuers and traders.

We may see market segmentation (that is, the tendency of exchanges to create prime segments as regards governance requirements) as a strategic choice. To be more precise, they seek strategies to create market segments which have tight admission requirements in terms of governance, as they can then address high-quality firms. On the other hand, high-quality firms are expected to be willing to commit to high governance rules (by seeking access to those segments) as they would be able to attract investors. Should this race to the top work properly, it would contribute to solving an inherent conflict of interests between exchanges (particularly listed ones) and their customers. Specifically, it would enable high-quality exchanges to succeed in attracting liquidity while offering issuers the ability to raise finance at a lower capital cost and providing traders with an environment where trades could occur at (implicitly or explicitly) lower transaction costs.

In light of the developments which have contributed to reshaping the industry's structure, it could be questioned if competition is the sole force influencing the regulatory strategies of exchanges. Ten years ago theorists and practitioners predicted a straightforward speeding up of the consolidation process and its consequences (in essence the formation of a few super-exchanges dominating trading and acting as virtual oligopolies in almost all asset classes), but they underestimated the network-like effect that consolidation has actually produced.

It could be questioned if regulatory competition is the only likely outcome of consolidation or whether convergence among exchanges (or other trading platforms) might stimulate convergence between-regulatory regimes. Theoretically, it could be argued that links between the owners of exchanges will lead to harmonization of their regulatory standards: significant common shareholders[7] in large exchanges may be tempted to cooperate on, for example, strategy, product innovation, governance and regulatory arrangements.

Arguably, clustering can be expected to give rise to a mix of competition between clusters and convergence or coordination within each. But currently it is difficult to predict where and when regulatory competition and convergence will reach a balance.

The challenges for legislative bodies as regulators include the need to combine and harmonize different interests. While promoting differentiation in services and incentives to innovate (for example, in technological endowments, which is the main contribution of ECNs) regulation should promote investor protection, market integrity and risk reduction.[8] Balancing different needs is particularly problematic: on the one hand it requires a continuous effort to keep up to date (regulations need to be adjusted promptly to respond to rapid changes in the exchange industry), whilst – on the other hand – conferring a particular and enduring nature to exchange regulation.

Exchanges are *self-regulatory organizations* (SROs) in that they manage markets and their functioning. As SROs they potentially enter into a wide network of conflicting interests with intermediaries and issuers, one of the most significant of which is related to listed exchanges which set the standards of governance for listed issuers. It could be argued that SROs have been operating under a regime of *soft regulation* where they define the rules governing the markets in which they operate, a set of general normative principles aimed at ensuring the fair functioning of capital markets and promoting non-discriminatory competitive behaviour. An important part of regulation for platform operators comprises codes of conduct stipulated at the level of the associations of which they are members.

The rationale of regulation has developed in three steps: the first enshrined regulatory principles specifically designed to improve the competitiveness of capital markets. In Europe, over the last two decades, financial market regulation has responded to the policy goal of creating a single integrated capital market to enable the free movement of capital. Examples are the Investment Services Directive (ISD) adopted in 1992, and MiFID in 2004, which replaced it. The US followed a similar path with the introduction of the Regulation National Market System (Reg. NMS).[9]

A second step in regulatory progress took place as capital markets became more integrated and competition intensified among trading venues; a new field of regulatory activity emerged, specifically targeted at regulating access to trading and post-trading platforms. *Access rights* are a challenge to regulatory action, impacting on overall market quality and comprising the obvious complement to competitive policies. However, the concept of *access rights* has broadened over the years, becoming somewhat multidimensional.

In the first instance, the concept refers to *access to order flow* and information on prices and quotations. Access to order flow is a matter directly related to competition between markets. It is an essential part of regulation in an environment in which fragmentation counterbalances the forces for consolidation. Access rights should be designed in a way that ensures coordination between market centres – or *market fragmentation* – does not turn into *economic fragmentation*. Each market participant expects to have free access to the best prices or quotations wherever they are, accompanied by all the significant information.

Integration among trading platforms has strengthened the concept of access rights, including access to full platform services. Indeed, competition among trading centres takes place not only in terms of execution quality; it includes the entire trading process, including complementary services such as post-trading. The competitive position of trading platforms depends partly on clearing and settlement efficiency, both through direct ownership of post-trading operators and through the clearing agreements with such operators. In this context, regulation has become even more sensitive to ensure traders non-restricted access to all the significant services for the functioning of the exchange industry. Such regulation encompasses, at most, transparency issues on prices for each service at various stages of the value chain and requirements for greater interoperability between platforms. To overcome fragmentation in the provision of vital services for competing trades, codes of conduct have been implemented alongside industry-wide initiatives promoted by supervisors.[10] On balance, access rights are mostly regulated through industry-level initiatives, albeit supported by financial supervisors. This, essentially, is what is meant by soft regulation.

Finally, a third stage of exchange regulation is now emerging as a by-product of the financial crisis; this is focused on financial stability, with regulators intent on imposing a heavier hand on the exchange industry. Although the new regulations do not substantially modify the regime of soft regulation that governs the functioning of SROs, they may interfere with the free operation of competitive forces and impact, at least to some extent, on the choices of market operators. We go into these points in more detail in the following pages.

In an environment in which centrifugal forces counteract other forces tending towards concentration, leading to the fragmentation of trading, the regulation of access rights is a major topic.

3 New regulatory frameworks in Europe and the United States

This section provides an overview of the evolution of regulation in Europe and the US. New pieces of regulation have been introduced in recent years aimed at increasing the efficiency of markets, improving the price discovery process and investor protection. These new regulations have had significant effects on the organization of the industry and its competitive policies. Instead of providing a mere summary of the contents of the regulations, we focus on their most critical aspects and the likely implications for the functioning of the exchange industry.

These questions are addressed somewhat differently by European and American regulators. We refer here, in particular, to MiFID in Europe and the Reg. NMS in the US. The main purpose of the two regulations is to promote competition in the exchange industry. They envisage a trading environment where formal or informal links between markets provide the opportunity for investors to obtain the best available quotations, wherever they emerge in the system. We return to analyse this point in more detail later on in this chapter.

A central point of the two regulatory frameworks is the attempt to make readily accessible to investors the best prices and quotations. Theoretically, this should stimulate competition between market centres for the provision of efficient price discovery mechanisms as a means of attracting large liquidity streams.[11] In practice, however, these competitive mechanisms only come into play if the best prices and quotations are acknowledged by the market (transparency) and are made available to customers (organization).

The organizational dimension is particularly significant since it has both industrial and legal aspects. From an industrial point of view, accessing better prices and quotations requires setting up linkages between trading venues, so that orders can freely run across the exchange industry; an alternative would be some kind of coordinating mechanism to facilitate the allocation of orders to those venues giving the best result for traders. The legal aspect refers to protection against discriminatory practices when accessing trading and post-trading services of different competing platforms. In Europe, the pre-MiFID exchange industry was characterized by different features in different EU countries, with some regulating for the concentration of trades and others standing more open to competition. Now, the new European regulation recognizes the benefits of competition between markets while inducing potential fragmentation; it better serves investor needs by widening choices and reducing transaction costs.

As is well known, the MiFID framework fosters competition in the exchange industry by envisaging new types of trading venues alongside regulated markets; so-called Multilateral Trading Facilities (MTFs) and 'systematic internalyzers'.[12] The basic point we wish to make is that MiFID rules out the concentration of trading, foreseeing a best-execution duty for intermediaries operating on the customer's behalf. Regulation may impact on the industry by strengthening potential competition from new rivals with excellent technological capabilities; they could enter the market by adopting aggressive pricing policies and attracting large flows of orders from established securities exchanges.

In fact, MiFID has substantially modified the whole nature of competition in the industry, from competition between orders to competition between markets. After the introduction of the the new regulation, new venues sprang up all over Europe. Theoretically, competition between market centres could be expected to affect the industry structure by broadening the scope of competition from prices to a wide array of exchange services. While favouring competition, however, MiFID dictated a set of rules (mainly concerning the conduct of investment firms) devoted to making sure that all market centres comprise a coordinated system of trading venues where competition can take place in various dimensions of order execution, and the investment firm can select the best market centre in the light of customer interests.

From an organizational point of view, therefore, MiFID regulations may potentially create a system of trading venues where the order flow runs from one to another according to their ability to add value for customers, with the coordinating mechanism provided by the behaviour of intermediaries. For this purpose, what ensures accessibility to market prices is the duty of best execution, according to which the investment firm selects (and arranges links to) the platforms where they expect to obtain the best result for the customer according to different execution attributes (best price, trading costs, execution speed and probability of execution). On the one hand, such a system ensures protection for both customers (who would receive best execution) and the platforms offering the best prices and services (which would be included in the execution policies of the investment firms). On the other hand, these arrangements also provide a basis for platform differentiation and the economic rationale for different venues addressing different customers with specific needs. MiFID allows trading venues to offer a variety of options to customers, potentially leading to market segmentation with some venues seeking to attract customers wanting execution certainty (or lower costs), while others compete to provide better services to customers seeking price advantages. Rather than designing a network of technical links between markets, MiFID envisages a market system where coordination is realized through the best duty of execution.

The design of the best duty of execution and the mutual recognition passport reflect a key difference between MiFID and US regulation. Attempting to balance three different goals (protection of SROs, customer protection and greater competition), the US regulatory framework has been criticized as fostering the build-up of barriers. Compared with the European framework, where no registration for trading venues is required (and where mutual recognition is extended to all trading venues, not just exchanges), the need for US exchanges to register with the SEC is a major hindrance to direct competition between exchanges and alternative platforms (Pan, 2007).

It has been said (Pan, 2007) that the SEC goal of increasing competition between trading venues was undermined by the creation of a national market system. Reg. NMS in the US is a set of rules that governs the American market system with the aim of facilitating the trade of stocks through fair price discovery mechanisms and free and unrestricted access to the better quotations.

This set of rules covers four major areas: the *order protection rule*, the *access rule*, the *sub-penny rule* and *market data rules*.

The order protection and access rules, together with the market data rules, are the most challenging regulations for the industry. According to the order protection rule, trading centres are required to 'establish, maintain and enforce written policies' designed to prevent trades occurring at prices that are lower than 'protected quotations', that is, the top-of-the-book quotations displayed by an automated trading centre. Such a rule is the consequence of the proliferation of trading venues, and is a response to SEC concerns that fragmentation may hamper liquidity. To this end, intermediaries admitted to trading on a certain trading venue are not allowed to trade-through better quotations displayed in other venues.

As a complement to the order protection rule, the access rule is designed to protect the best-displayed quotations across the system by allowing brokers to access those quotations under non-discriminatory conditions.[13] The rationale of a (fair) access rule lies in the availability of best-displayed quotations through private linkages among trading venues.

The combination of the two rules is expected to achieve two main goals: incentives for liquidity providers to supply liquidity, and the guarantee that market orders really do receive the best available quotations. The rules are also expected to promote greater competition between venues.

While the goals are clear, some authors have serious doubts about the effectiveness of these rules, arguing that they may actually hamper rather than improve liquidity. The changes that have occurred since the establishment of the NMS have undermined the proper functioning of the system. A comparison between the MiFID and the Reg. NMS based on the protection of best prices highlights two pieces of regulation seemingly inspired by different philosophies as regards the balancing of customer protection and incentives to compete and innovate.

A mandated order protection rule, such as that incorporated in the Reg. NMS, enshrines a more rigid approach than that of the European authorities who allow for a wide range of preferences when executing customer orders. Grounded on the belief that price is the only significant concern, Reg. NMS assumes that the best quotation across all market centres meets the needs of all traders. Considering price as the only significant factor when executing trades potentially reduces incentives for differentiation among venues and hinders the flourishing of a variety of trading venues targeting different kinds of demand. Such a risk may somewhat dampen the innovating nature of alternative systems as they have emerged. ECNs, in particular, enable orders to be executed instantaneously without the need for a specialist to complete the trade. Moreover, the specific motives of traders vary with demand changing and evolving over time, casting further significant doubts on a one-size-fits-all approach to regulation.

O'Hara (2004) argues that Reg. NMS fails to properly take into account the differing needs of traders. As a basic argument, Reg. NMS seemingly focuses on price priority rules which seems inconsistent with a strict price–time priority rule. By simply raising the concern, a market (for example, a large pool) quoting the best price is entitled to receive the order even though it could be executed faster in another market in the system with the inherent risk of prices deteriorating in the meantime. The author maintains that the exceptions[14] put in place by the SEC to overcome these potential drawbacks may have the unintended consequence of causing a dramatic decline in the quality of price discovery. Similarly, Redler (2010) complains that the order protection rule leads to an explosion in high-frequency trades and the drying up of overall market liquidity.

On a similar basis Chung and Chuwonganant (2011) have also investigated the functioning of Reg. NMS. Through empirical analysis they have shown that, contrary to the Commission's belief, SEC rules account for a decline in market depth and an increase in spreads (both quoted and effective ones); the impact on the market has been to slow down the execution of trades. On a comparative basis, they find that the NASDAQ gained substantial market share from NYSE/Amex and other trading venues after the implementation of the regulation.

Both European and US regulatory frameworks include measures to facilitate the integration of different venues within an economically coordinated system. However, increasing coordination on a transatlantic scale reveals a potential weakness in the regulations. While addressing competitive issues within two different macro-regions, they do not entirely eliminate restrictions to mutual access across the regions; certain barriers still exist. For example, for foreign platforms restrictions still remain to open screens in the US. Hence, it is possible that tighter integration among capital markets will require a more efficient mutual recognition system across regions such as the substituted compliance regime advocated by Tafara and Peterson (2007). When extended on a transatlantic scale, such a system would at least facilitate competition between venues across macro-regions and promote more efficient supervision.

Mutual recognition regimes and other protection regulations are not all about promoting fair, efficient and competitive markets. One significant matter is the value of information. Theoretically, market prices convey information, hence price discovery has an obvious commercial dimension – and the sale of market data is a significant business for almost all exchanges – but there is also a systemic relevance since trading venues contribute, by means of prices, to the overall quality of capital markets. Since the contribution to market efficiency is a function of the quality of information that flows from market centres, the information produced by the venues that most frequently produce the best prices or quotations on certain stocks are deemed more valuable than information produced by trading venues that only rarely contribute to the best prices.

In order to ensure efficient competition in an environment with multiple trading venues, it is important to provide the right incentives to engage in efficient price discovery and distribute to the market valuable information on quotations and prices. In a fragmented market two problems arise. The first has organizational implications while the other bears more on conceptual concerns. Specifically:

a) Organizationally, practical problems arise with coordinating the collection of significant information on prices and quotations from each market centre.
b) Conceptually, the main problem is how to design the proper incentives to liquidity providers to contribute to the overall quality of the price discovery process. In practice, that means finding the right formula for rewarding those liquidity providers that continuously contribute to produce top-of-the-book quotations.

For a) two solutions can be envisaged. The first is to allow the market to function, which means either that there is no formal system to receive the data from exchanges and other venues and, subsequently, distribute it to traders, or, alternatively, a private entity should be established to provide this service on a commercial basis. Thus, access to significant information would be coordinated by market forces, although a government entity could also be set up to collect and disseminate the information.

Whereas MiFID does not include a consolidation scheme for gathering information (rather requiring trading venues to ensure fair and non-discriminatory access to their prices), Reg. NMS does include setting up a consolidation mechanism. Currently, there are two consolidation systems. The first is the Consolidated Tape Association (CTA),[15] which is the policymaking and administrative body entrusted with the functions of overseeing the collection, processing and dissemination of market data for exchange-listed securities. More specifically, the CTA comprises two networks: Tape A/Network A for the collection, processing and distribution of market data from all market centres trading NYSE-listed securities; and Tape B/Network B for data consolidation for all other exchange-listed securities. The US consolidation system, moreover, enables quote and trade dissemination for OTC securities through the OTC/Unlisted Trading Privileges (OTC/UTP) plan.

The functioning of consolidated schemes has interesting implications for governance, the pricing of the data feed and the allocation of income. In terms of governance, the CTA is owned by the exchanges and the NASDAQ. It collects and sells data from trading venues and, in turn, provides revenues to the owners. Since these functions are carried out in the interests of the market, a well-designed plan should grant not only fair access to the consolidated data feed but to high-quality data as well. Provided that each participant is entitled to receive a share of the plan's net income, the concrete allocation formula evaluates the contribution by each participant to overall market quality. The US consolidated plans measure the contribution of each participant to market quality (and allocate revenues accordingly) through two parameters capturing respectively the participant's trading and quoting share for a particular security. The former is the percentage of the total trading value of transactions in an eligible security reported by the processor, while the latter is a function of the persistence of a certain participant in providing bid and offer prices that match the best bids and offers provided nationally.

4 Exchange industry services and access rights

In the regulation of *access rights*, access to exchange industry services complements the regulations governing access to the order flow. It aims to ensure the smooth flow of transaction feeds along the value chain. More precisely, it prevents barriers hampering the efficient execution, clearing and settlement of transactions. Conceptually, integration and competition have two dimensions:

a) An *industrial dimension*, where convergence is promoted by the strategic choices of market operators and could be referred to the well known structure-behaviour-performance paradigm.
b) A *regulatory and supervisory dimension*, where in order for competitive forces to work properly arrangements should be put in place to overcome potential distortions in competition.

There is a potential trade-off between the aims pursued at the two stages. While industrial strategies point to platform integration with the aim of delivering the benefits of cost and revenue synergies and liquidity pooling, increasing convergence may raise barriers and impair the free access to exchange services as a whole. In order to achieve a free and fair competitive market, regulatory integration and industrial integration should go side by side.

Within this framework, regulating and supervising capital markets requires the promotion and encouragement of spontaneous competitive strategies whilst preventing unfair and discriminatory behaviours. Potential barriers may arise from a wide array of anti-competitive practices, summarized below.

In the first instance, barriers to access may emerge as the result of particular industrial arrangements. *Vertical integration* is, perhaps, the issue of most concern for both regulators and platform users. While facilitating the flow of transactions from the trading to the post-trading stages of the value chain, it may nonetheless severely hinder access to post-trading services. This may happen whenever an exchange controlling post-trading entities creates impediments (on a contractual or other basis) to other trading platforms wishing to designate its subsidiaries for clearing and settling trades. Such obstacles may derive from price discrimination or other anti-competitive practices. In other ways, vertical integration facilitates the bundling of services: the customer is locked within the group in the sense that by executing orders on a vertically integrated exchange he may be forced to buy the post-trading services offered by the group's clearing and settlement agents even though he or she might find better post-trading services elsewhere in the market. Such a risk may be exacerbated when there is a lack of transparency about the fees charged for each single service at different stages of the value chain. In addition to vertical integration, *property rights* on post-trading platforms may hinder access to post-trading services in the case of *mutual-like ownership* of clearing and settlement operators. This arises when a few trading platforms own significant stakes in a post-trading operator and use their power (for instance, through the exercise of voting rights) to implement and enforce access policies that act as an obstacle to other trading platforms wishing to access that post-trading operator on a fair and competitive basis.

Anti-competitive practices may also arise from poor *governance arrangements*. Here the risk is that audit functions (both internal and external) fail to detect unfair competitive practices. Major challenges are involved in representation on the boards of both exchanges and post-trading operators. Best practice requires a board presence of post-trading operators of independent directors whose main role (especially in an industry context in which platforms become increasingly linked both commercially and in terms of ownership) is, or should be, that of properly monitoring operations with *related parties*. Similarly, independent directors should be recommended for the boards of trading venues.

Finally, major risks to fair access to trading and post-trading services come in the form of *technical barriers*. This concept encompasses a wide array of hurdles to fair access, ranging from huge differences in the standards and protocols used by different platforms to a lack of interoperability between platforms.[16] These risks are exacerbated when there is substantial fragmentation in trading and post-trading markets. Focusing on the European environment, major challenges to the full integration between platforms was, however, related to the lack of common regulations and supervisory practices between countries.

It is important to stress that a single *rulebook* does not ensure fair competitive practices. It is primarily the coordination of supervision which should be designed to prevent disruptions in access rights by promoting the uniform implementation of rules and regulations and the adoption of common standards and protocols. Perhaps the most powerful incentive to overcoming technical barriers derives from consolidation among platforms; although this may create other barriers (for example, customer capture) or pose major risks for financial stability, the latter being a particular concern in relation to integration between post-trading entities (especially central counterparties).

It was particularly challenging for the European authorities to cope with persistent competitive barriers within an institutional framework designed to promote a fully integrated capital market. Despite efforts to further integrate at the trading level, European capital markets have long remained fragmented at the post-trading level, with major concerns related to the smooth flow of transactions along the value chain. In addition to the Giovannini Group Report, other major studies have highlighted the costs of trading on a cross-border basis due to technical inefficiencies caused by fragmented post-trading markets.[17] In the US, in contrast, the Reg. NMS mandated a more integrated capital market more than 30 years ago; at the post-trading level, settlement and clearing systems have a high level of integration.

In today's exchange industry the major risks to efficient and fair capital markets are related to ownership. While consolidation and technological progress arguably smooth out differences in platform efficiency, ownership structures in a widely integrated capital market may incentivize exclusion or discrimination in access rights. It is, at one and the same time, a problem of monitoring shareholdings and supervising governance arrangements.

In recent years increased regulatory convergence has followed the substantial progress achieved in platform integration. A clear path, gradually improving the effectiveness of access regulation, can be traced. Figure 3.1 shows the relationship between integration in the exchange industry and regulatory convergence in Europe.

In the last decade industry integration has been quite rapid, supported by significant innovations at the regulatory level which were introduced in four steps: the introduction of MiFID, the 2006 *European Code of Conduct for Clearing and Settlement* (together with the *Access and Interoperability Guideline* of 2007), the TARGET2-Securities (T2S) project started in 2007 and the European Market Infrastructure Regulation (EMIR) of 2012.

Apart from designating a coordination mechanism among trading venues in Europe, MiFID regulations enshrine the unrestricted flow of orders along the value chain. In particular, MiFID regulates relations between brokers, trading venues and post-trading operators with the aim of lowering competitive barriers within the industry. While reinforcing the principles of free access to exchange industry services, the Directive recognizes the

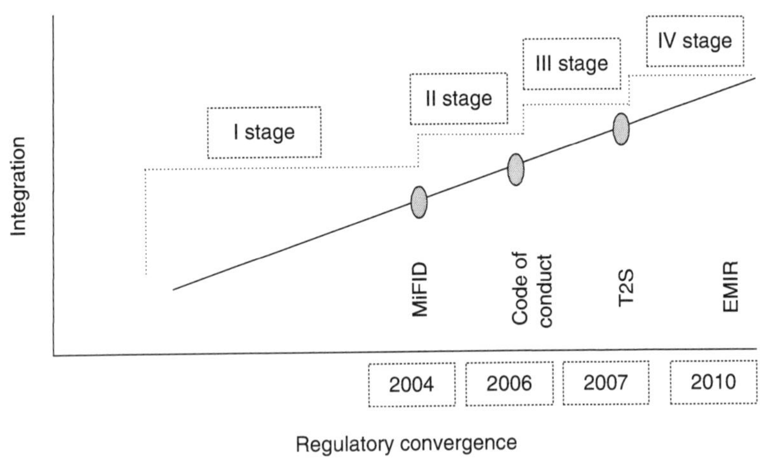

Figure 3.1 Integration and regulatory convergence

risks associated with increasing integration and convergence among platforms. On the one hand, it establishes the right of regulated markets to conclude agreements with post-trading entities of other member states for the clearing and settlement of transactions carried out by their members. And at the same time, members of a regulated market may designate for clearing and settlement operations post-trading systems other than those designated by the market. More generally, it is agreed that a broker should be granted the right to establish remote access agreements with foreign post-trading entities at non-discriminatory conditions compared to those governing the access granted to domestic participants.

In general, MiFID aims to promote integration and efficiency in trading and post-trading markets. Exchanges, therefore, cannot interfere with the right of brokers to freely designate their favourite clearing and settlement systems; at the same time, vertical silos should not be conceived of as a means to restrict access to post-trading services. On the trading side, the rules are expected to lower the overall cost of trading.

Since the proper functioning of competitive forces cannot be ensured by legislation alone, European bodies have promoted an industry-wide approach to access regulation. With the contribution of post-trading operators represented within the Federation of European Securities Exchanges (FESE) and the European Association of Clearing Houses (EACH) the Internal Market Commission pressed for the adoption of a self-regulatory code.[18] Briefly, the *European Code of Conduct for Clearing and Settlement* acts in the following areas:

a) *Price transparency*, seen as an essential prerequisite for the proper integration of European infrastructures. The shared goal of the organizations signing the agreement is to ensure the full understanding of the costs of all the services provided by industry operators and comparability between different operators.
b) *Mutual* access between post-trading entities on a fair and non-discriminatory basis as well as interoperability. The *requesting organization* should be granted free and fair access to the services provided by another post-trading entity (whether incorporated in the same national jurisdiction or in a foreign country). The latter (the *responding organization*) is not allowed to set discriminatory conditions.
c) *Unbundling and transparent accounting practices*. Unbundling is designed to enable customers to complete the trade by resorting to various post-trading providers for specific services. Fair accounting practices are designed to promote the clear reconciliation between costs and services.

In principle, full transparency and comparability may be hindered by certain differences in defining the services provided by various post-trading operators. Moreover, fragmentation across national boundaries is expected to act as a significant burden on total costs. However, integration in European post-trading markets took a step forward with the T2S project, mentioned above. Promoted by the European Central Bank, the project aims to develop a fully integrated European platform for securities settlements through connection to T2S for the settlement of the cash leg of transactions in Euro-denominated securities. On a practical basis, T2S is a settlement platform designed to improve efficiency in cash settlements by overcoming fragmentation; it does not have the characteristic functions of a CSD or related activities. Rather, it is a counterparty to CSDs for the cash settlement of transactions carried out by their members. Legally, CSDs will retain full rights on customer relations with their members.

More recently, EMIR regulations were introduced to promote better risk management within the industry by mandating central counterparty (CCP) clearing for OTC transactions. It also includes regulations on access rights to post-trading entities and the relations between platforms along the value chain. EMIR is expected to have a significant impact on the structure of the exchange industry across Europe.

Arguably, OTC clearing on central counterparties may have the effect of strengthening links between trading venues and between trading venues and post-trading operators; however, prevailing ownership structures may entail substantial risks of unfair competitive policies. Vertical integration is the most worrying issue in this regard, but a situation where large trading companies hold significant stakes in CCPs may also lead to access barriers. There is a risk that a CCP may refuse to clear transactions carried out in certain venues because the former is owned by a competing trading venue (or its major shareholders include brokers who are competitors of the trading firm requesting access), and this requires careful oversight.

In order to avoid competitive distortions, the right of access should be bi-directional, as follows:

a) The duty of a CCP to clear transactions in different trading venues, provided that they comply with the operational and technical standards of the CCP.
b) The duty of a trading venue to grant access to a requesting CCP. This duty applies to industrial arrangements where multiple CCPs are allowed to use the trade feeds of the same trading venue, provided that this does not require interoperability and does not lead to the fragmentation of liquidity.

The conditions for refusing access to a CCP by the trading venue are relevant since they recognize the potential trade-off between the full operation of competitive forces and liquidity fragmentation. The interoperability condition seems to be aimed at preventing mandated integration between a trading venue and a CCP. Refusals based on reasons of liquidity conceal the fear that by granting access to multiple CCPs fragmentation may prevent central counterparties reaching an efficient scale for risk management purposes. Such concerns are significant in that they suggest that the prevailing notion of liquidity fragmentation (both among theorists and industry practitioners) is too narrowly defined since it focuses only on trading-level fragmentation; assuming an industry-wide perspective, post-trading fragmentation is as worrying as trading fragmentation because it may trigger a loss in netting benefits and an increase in systemic risk through greater interconnectedness.[19]

On balance, EMIR promotes greater convergence along the value chain of securities trading by allowing the regulated side of the market to recapture, at a post-trade level, large flows of OTC derivatives trades. EMIR, moreover, prompts greater regulatory convergence between member states, which requires closer cooperation among European supervisors. In our view, the bourgeoning work of regulatory reform of access rights does not substantially alter the architecture of soft regulation. Apart from requesting CCP clearing for certain OTC products, there are no mandated industrial arrangements; as most regulation remains based on principles, and the concrete application of general principles is embodied only at the supervisory level.

Indeed, managing industry-wide access rights goes far beyond the powers and capabilities of national supervisors. Recent reforms of the entire supervisory architecture in Europe provided the European exchange industry with the tools to effectively pursue the integrated supervision of capital markets according to common standards. The European Securities and Markets Authority (ESMA) is the central body coordinating supervision across Europe, but significant powers are given to the Commission as well. Infrastructure regulations entrust the Commission with immediate powers of intervention in order to prevent competitive distortions.

5 Regulation, competition and financial stability

One topic that deserves our attention here is the economic effect of rules and regulations. The considerations discussed above specifically addressed the economic dimension with reference to the conditions under which trades may take place in terms of spreads, market impact and other costs of trading. However, alongside market efficiency there is another significant dimension to consider when analysing the effects of regulation which is centred on the firm running the market rather than the market itself.

Such a microeconomic approach requires an investigation of the impact of regulation on the supply and demand of specific exchange services and the consequences for the economic performance of platform operators. As noted, SROs are characterized by a high degree of flexibility in regulating the markets they operate. Their competitive strategies are subject to a set of soft rules designed to prevent access barriers which may curtail competition within the industry. As we have stated, these regulations include access rights on a non-discriminatory basis. The morphology of the industry, in such a context, arises spontaneously from the competitive choices of platform operators.

Despite this, events following the financial crisis seem to point to a change in regulatory policies with the aim of strengthening control over transaction flows and, arguably, business models. The introduction of new regulations alters the way in which pure competitive forces operate, leading to differences between spontaneous demand and business opportunities determined by regulatory choices. The microeconomic dimension is rather complicated since a number of different aspects need to be factored into the analysis.

In the first instance, regulation may impact on the volatility of revenues, although it is obviously not the only factor which influences revenue volatility. By stimulating competition (for orders, services and market information) revenue generation becomes a struggle to successfully innovate and provide quality services. However, the impact of regulation on revenue volatility is not easy to predict because the combined impact of pro-competitive regulation (which might be expected to increase volatility) needs to be taken into consideration, and the rules are designed to prevent excessive risk exposure within the industry.

Another significant – and related – dimension is the *retention* of customers. As competition increases, and regulators resort to the tighter[20] regulation of access rights, it may become more difficult for trading platforms (and, incidentally, post-trading operators) to lock customers into long-term relationships. Of course, the industry structure significantly affects the behaviour of firms and their attitude to retaining customers. Despite the efforts of regulators to ensure fair and competitive access rights to trading and post-trading platforms, certain organizational arrangements – such as vertical integration – may act as a means to lock customers into stable relationships, thus preventing competition between platforms from properly working.

A further important dimension is related to what we may call *mandated sources of demand*. By this we mean those components of customer demand that, on a purely competitive basis (that is, without binding regulations), would flow outside the regulated spectrum of the exchange industry. Mandated demand is a by-product of *stability regulation*.

Obviously, there are significant interactions among the dimensions of regulatory impact that we outlined above. One by-product of the financial crisis is the repositioning of securities exchange regulation to a new locus at the forefront of financial liberalization. A new balance between competitive policies and stabilizing forces is expected to be achieved with significant implications likely for exchange management.

As a response to the financial crisis regulators across the world have revised significant pieces of existing regulation with the aim of buttressing the resilience of the exchange industry and of preventing contagion in the event of disruptions to large financial institutions and widespread defaults. Focusing on the exchange industry, what caused major concerns to national and multilateral regulators was the opaque side of trading and post-trading activities. In particular, post-trading practices came under the scrutiny of regulators. Regulatory responses at this level are expected to have industry-wide implications, extending to trading venues; arguably, the morphology of the entire exchange industry will be affected.

Financial regulators – in particular those in G-20 countries, and other bodies such as the Financial Stability Board (FSB) – have recommended a broader use of central counterparties for the clearing of transactions in certain derivatives, the source of considerable trouble. Such recommendations are finally entering the new regulatory rulebooks.[21] In certain countries regulators have worked closely with the industry with the aim of substantially standardizing post-trading processes and promoting greater convergence.

Hence regulatory reforms are forcing large flows of financial transactions to return to the regulated side of the exchange industry. Considering the far-reaching extension of OTC transactions the economic benefits for post-trading infrastructures are potentially enormous. Indeed, the crisis may turn out to have been an opportunity for regulated platforms. Almost all post-trading operators are broadening their services to capture new streams of mandated demand. These developments in the regulatory environment may help to explain the renewed interest in post-trading as demonstrated, for example, by the battle for the control of one of the major operators, the London Clearing House (LCH).

However, the mandated centrifugal forces leading to a return of transaction flows to central counterparties may arguably be reinforced by the spontaneous choices of market operators. Market participants wishing to reduce their exposure to counterparty risk may be tempted to increase their recourse to the regulated circuits of the exchange industry. On balance, the dynamics we have accounted for are radically changing the nature of central counterparties and their role within the exchange industry. Initially created with the primary goal of reducing transaction costs by netting counterparty exposures, CCPs are now expanding their role to include greater involvement in the provision of financial stability. They have become a significant part of the overall risk management process and the financial market infrastructure.

On more general grounds, the strategic functions of the exchange industry as a whole are rapidly changing. Alongside its traditional function of providing an efficient marketplace for trading securities, the industry has a new strategic involvement in absorbing shocks. Maybe it is too optimistic to imagine that financial markets will refrain from excessive risk taking. However, a greater sensitivity to reputational capital and the sustainability of growth in financial markets can be expected to prompt business platform operators to refocus on the strategic inclusion of risk mitigation products and services.

Turning to the economic and industrial evaluation of the potential costs and benefits of new platform regulations, an assessment is complicated by the number of factors and variables involved. But broadly speaking, significant impacts are to be expected upon both the demand and the supply side. To recap, the demand side comprises counterparties that trade in OTC instruments (both financial and non-financial counterparties), while the supply side comprises trading and post-trading infrastructures.

On the demand side, major impacts might be expected for non-financial counterparties and the aggregate demand for OTC trades. Arguably, IT investments and additional staff costs may be required for the internal structure of governance (for example, in measuring or keeping track of the types of OTC derivatives and positions) and in implementing monitoring tools to flag derivative trades and monitor related thresholds.[22] On the other hand, counterparties to OTC contracts might also be expected to incur high clearing costs where they are subject to clearing obligations – for example, the cost of providing highly liquid securities or cash for the margins and default, or of guaranteeing the funds required by CCPs, or of transaction fees directly payable to the clearing house.

Increasing transaction fees may be expected at the CCP level due to tighter reporting requirements, the cost of storing data, and the costs incurred to make information accessible. Moreover, new regulations require CCPs to improve transaction and position records: identification of the trading venue, the date and time of interposition of the CCP, a daily calculation of the amount of the position and the calculation of margins must all be logged. In addition to the costs of updating the database, simply collecting the additional data required also has a cost.

Arguably, the most challenging issue is the overall impact on aggregate demand of OTC trades. The question is whether increases in transaction costs will lead to a fall in market activity. While large post-trading entities might be expected to exploit large economies of scale (thus benefitting from relatively lower direct transaction costs), major concerns to them might derive from information requirements. In this regard, the obligation to disclose certain sensitive business information might have a dissuasive effect.

On a commercial basis the offering catalogue of post-trading operators is broadening with major clearing houses (both traditional players and relative newcomers) seizing the opportunity to build up their clearing business.[23] The implications for value creation are rather difficult to predict. On the one hand, mandatory demand is expected to strengthen revenue generation at the post-trading level and, arguably, earnings. Provided that post-trading is, generally, a high-return business, operators at this level of the value chain may largely benefit from any new business opportunities that will be opened up by the most recent regulatory decisions. On the other hand, a new competitive arena is expected to emerge with post-trading operators jostling to capture the flows of financial transactions forced to return to the transparent side of the industry. While the industry as a whole is expected to take advantage of stability regulation, the winners within the industry itself will be those who provide the best solutions. Theoretically, competitive policies at this level may be oriented to substantially retain a traditional business model or, otherwise, to pursue strong product innovation in order to cope with the new regulatory framework that is emerging.

Figure 3.2 below shows the impact of new rules, as embodied in the EMIR on the clearing of derivatives in regulated markets, OTC venues and central counterparties.

The first quadrant shows the demand (ED) captured by the regulated side of the exchange industry, represented as an inverse function of

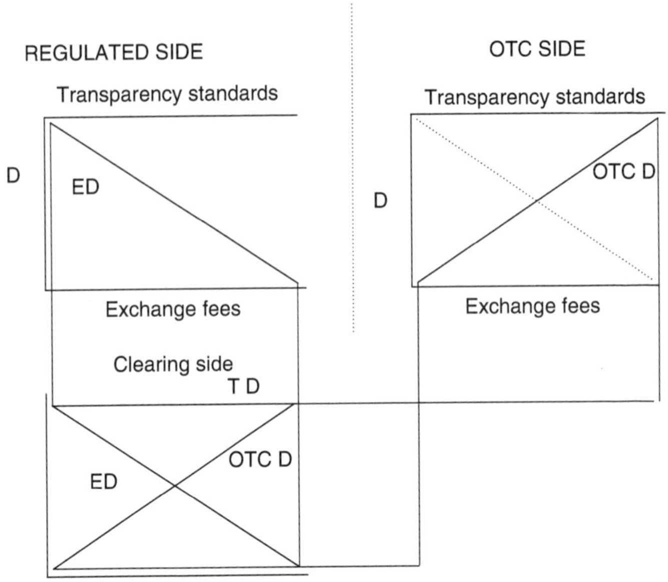

Figure 3.2 The economic impact of regulation

trading fees and transparency requirements. The second quadrant shows the demand (OTC D) flowing to the OTC side of the industry which, supposedly, rises as costs at exchanges rise and transparency standards become tighter. The regulated side of the exchange industry recovers the demand which has flown to OTC systems at a post-trading level, where regulated platforms now capture the entire demand for derivatives.

On an economic basis, it is clear that the choices pertaining to the array of products and services offered depend on the potential market the platform could reasonably expect to reach. Large platforms designed to clear transactions on a cross-border basis, and offering their services to a wide array of trading venues, obviously have the incentive to expand their offer. Currently, the post-trading industry is characterized by a few international CSDs, central counterparties and some regional operators. Should consolidation at the post-trading level go further, we may expect the industry to reorganize around a couple of dominant players acting on an oligopolistic basis and fighting energetically for large portions of the big OTC market. We note that something similar is happening in relation to the trading of derivatives.

The potential market for small operators is rather difficult to predict. While one may be tempted to argue that for regional post-trading operators the potential market is quite limited – notwithstanding the crowding-out effect by large international post-trading organizations – this is probably not an unavoidable outcome. The distribution of OTC transactions for post-trading processing between existing players is driven by the intermediaries designating the post-trading operators for the clearing of their transactions.

On an industry basis, an interesting point, which arguably has industry-wide governance implications (dealt with in Chapter 4), concerns the relations between platforms in different countries. The question is whether new regulation can be expected to impact on the industry's structure both vertically and horizontally, in the process promoting greater integration. Moreover, another relevant issue is whether new regulations may exacerbate the inherent conflicts of interest between platform operators and financial institutions, especially large investment banks.

The incentive to move forward with integration should be assessed bearing in mind the entire international regulatory architecture that has emerged from the various pieces of legislation adopted over the last decade: MiFID, EMIR and codes of conduct in Europe, Reg. NMS and the Dodd-Frank Act in the US. Should we expect further fragmentation or greater integration (horizontally both at the trading and post-trading level as well as vertically)?

As rivals threaten the competitive position of established exchanges at the trading level, a similar process leading to fragmentation may arise at the post-trading level. Certain ECNs are already developing a silo-like model by establishing their own post-trading entities, entering into competition with established clearing and settlement operators. Indeed, major investment banks trading very large volumes of OTC contracts might find it advantageous to introduce their post-trading business or to use those post-trading platforms created by major ECNs. Arguably, investment bank clearing and settlement entities would act as mutual-like organizations with the mandate to provide a low-cost environment for clearing a large portion of their trading business, that previously took place outside a regulated clearing environment, at low levels of transparency and cost.

Consortiums of investment banks setting up clearing entities broaden the opportunities for conflicting interests with platforms. The former normally have a stake in large trading and post-trading platforms. Acting as global custodians as part of their business, they divert large flows of transactions from platforms. The magnitude of this phenomena might become greater, should investment banks succeed in reinforcing their competitive position at the post-trading stage of the value chain.

Exchanges increasingly suffer from the competitive threats of new rivals. In derivatives, in particular, trading activity largely takes place in OTC trading venues. Mandated CCP clearing for certain types of derivatives provides exchanges that own their post-trading entities the opportunity to at least partially recover at the bottom of the value chain the order flow that they were not able to retain at the top. Provided that the economic benefits – lower revenue volatility and increasing margins – are sufficiently large, it is reasonable to expect trading platforms to be even more incentivized to retain some form of control over post-trading operators within the new framework, characterized by greater attention to financial stability.

At the same time, new business opportunities may provide the rationale for increasing horizontal integration at the post-trading level in order to gain the benefits of scale to extend clearing services to CCP products. Although it may appear to be an incentive for exchanges to move toward silo-like organizational solutions, the development path is still fluid and it is hard to predict where the balance will be reached.

One possible equilibrium would lead to greater polarization in the exchange industry with a few dominant, transnational exchanges owning clearing and settlement organizations. In such a case, a few super-vertical silos would manage almost all order flow, in almost every asset class along the value chain. In contrast, another possible equilibrium is one potentially leading to further fragmentation at all stages of the value chain. This is not restricted to traditional exchanges but is inherent in electronic communication networks as well, as shown by alternative platforms building up their post-trading business.

Yet despite this, there is a clear incentive for trading platforms to reinforce their control over post-trading operators. For this purpose, the forces driving towards vertical integration coexist with incentives to adopt open-access architectures. Indeed, there is evidence that cross-border exchanges are considering a cooperative solution, in other words the joint ownership of common post-trading platforms.

Both competitive policies and new pieces of regulation are currently leading to more interconnected market centres and post-trading entities. At first glance, it might be thought that the emerging network-like industry model is properly supported by all-encompassing regulations. But look more closely and the latent contradiction becomes evident: SRO responsibilities assigned to interconnected platform operators not only magnify potential conflicts of interest but also result in inefficient regulation as well. The SRO model was conceived in an era when capital markets were to a large extent segmented, international participation in trading and post-trading platforms quite subdued and inherent conflicts of interest between platforms and intermediaries manageable.

The situation has radically changed. With an increasingly integrated superstructure (industry level and primary regulation), segmentation in self-regulatory responsibilities is inefficient in terms of the duplication of regulatory costs, and contradictory. In fact, it leads to exchanges regulating their competitors. Hence, an argument can be made for taking a step forward in the regulation of securities, shifting certain regulatory responsibilities away from the exchanges as regards, in particular, the regulation of members.[24] Exchanges that voluntarily confer certain regulatory responsibilities on a common entity, apart from saving in duplicated regulatory costs, commit to better governance standards as they reduce their exposure to conflicts of interest. Although a greater integration in regulatory responsibilities has been advocated, in our view not all regulatory functions can, reasonably, be delegated. The monitoring of capital market integrity should remain within the inalienable functions of exchanges due to their proximity to the markets in which they operate. As for the definition of listing standards, whilst delegation to an independent authority might eliminate certain conflicts of interest, nonetheless it would dampen competition among market centres seeking to attract high-quality issuers. In our view, such competition is a vital part of the free movement of capital flows between countries.

6 Conclusions

Traditionally, regulators were concerned with the fair and efficient functioning of capital markets. The main objective in regulating the securities industry has ever been that of ensuring the quality of the overall price discovery process. As exchanges transform their status, and become private, for-profit entities, the firm view starts to pervade academic research. Regulation obviously impacts upon the management of exchanges as firms; nonetheless, such impacts have long been neglected. The most recent pieces of regulation attempt to both promote greater competition among trading and post-trading platforms and, subsequently to the crisis, foster financial stability. Pro-competitive policies are mainly targeted at the protection of *access rights*. The concept is multi-faceted and refers both to access to best quotations and fair access to platforms. Stability regulations cover the clearing and settlement on certain OTC derivatives trades on regulated platforms.

New regulatory reforms carry both economic and industrial implications, and bring new threats and new opportunities for platform operators in the meantime. In terms of economics, pro-competitive regulations might impact on the production technology and the optimal composition of capital and labour, or imply an increase in the costs of revenues. We discuss this point in Chapter 5. On industrial grounds, both competitive policies and new pieces of regulation are currently leading to more interconnected market centres and post-trading entities. Additionally, the regulation on OTC clearing has revealed new business opportunities to regulated platforms which should be able to recover, at a post-trading level, large flows of transactions that flowed to the opaque side of the exchange industry. In fact, it is the case that major central counterparties have already enlarged their range of services to take advantage of these new opportunities. Viewed in this perspective, it can be seen that such developments might stimulate further integration in the exchange industry on a vertical scale, with exchanges finding it worthwhile to leverage on growing post-trading businesses.

4
The Governance of Securities Exchanges. New Insights

1 Introduction

There is a bourgeoning strand of academic literature dealing with the subject of corporate governance in the exchange industry. A large part of that literature investigates the reasons why exchanges modify their legal status. In particular, it tries to find a viable economic explanation for the demutualization of exchanges and the subsequent listing of major exchanges. To accomplish that task academic literature has investigated the different incentives of various stakeholders. Broadly speaking, the corporatization of exchanges would seem to mirror the attempts that have been made to balance the vested interests of brokerage firms and outside shareholders, local and international intermediaries, listed firms and platform users.

The exchange industry has been rapidly evolving, especially during the last decade. Today the question of governance involves quite different concerns to those addressed when the demutualization process started to take place. The balancing of different vested interests is becoming even more challenging due to the institutionalization of the shareholder base in large exchanges, and the increasing convergence between exchanges on a cross-border scale as a result of mergers and acquisitions in the industry.

Alongside increasing consolidation, the exchange industry is following a specific development path towards a strengthening of links between platforms both at trading and post-trading level. Such a development is a by-product of the institutionalization of ownership, and it links platforms at an ownership level. What we are seeing is a limited number of large institutional investors holding considerable stakes in the same (major) exchanges, and hence exerting a joint control over the biggest players. This may be considered as a form of soft consolidation or clustering. It would, therefore, be interesting to delve deeper into the governance implications and challenges connected to the growth of exchange clusters.

This chapter is organized as follows. In section 2 we will provide a review of the prevailing literature on the governance of securities exchanges. In section 3 we will give an overview of the ownership structures of some of the major listed exchanges. Then, section 4, we will discuss the main features and criticalities of exchange governance in light of prevailing ownership structures. In section 5 we will consider the rationale of non-contractual governance; we point out that increasing relationships among exchanges result in a modification in the way exchange governance has been conceived. We argue that such relationships imply a changing paradigm in governance, from managing different vested interests within the exchange to governing networks. In section 6 the implications of networks will be discussed, with reference to control over flows of liquidity. Finally, section 7 concludes.

2 Literature review

Traditionally, securities exchanges were run as mutual organizations and owned by the intermediaries who were allowed to use the trading facilities on a membership basis. As members, their function was to mediate investors' transactions. Members' utility was, therefore, a decreasing function of trading costs (that is, the costs of using the exchange's facilities) and an increasing function of revenues from the brokerage business. The objective function of the exchanges when operated as not-for-profit entities was to provide a marketplace where members could trade securities at low costs.

However, the governance structure of exchanges has rapidly evolved. The evolutionary path started with the demutualization of many exchanges and the consequent separation between ownership and membership. In particular, the process sped up at the end of the 1990s and the beginning of the new century.

The financial literature has widely analysed the forces leading to this change. The analytical framework has focused on the competitive policies of stock exchanges and the degree of heterogeneity of vested interests. Competitive policies and conflicts of interests in the exchange industry constitute two dimensions which are strictly interconnected and they should be studied jointly in order to identify the incentives for changing governance paradigms.

The traditional governance literature focuses on the conflicting interests of various stakeholders which, in mutual exchanges, are the users of the exchange's services – listed companies and the brokerage firms that own the exchange. However, within mutual exchanges the degree of heterogeneity among brokerage firms is quite limited. As a result, potentially conflicting interests are those prevailing between the two main classes of customers, rather than those within the same class.

By contrast, within demutualized exchanges member–users constitute a heterogeneous class as they may comprise small local brokerage firms, large firms entitled with multiple memberships on a cross-border scale and intermediating huge capital flows, or big institutional investors trading on international exchanges. Members may be, therefore, entrusted with different vested interests.

It is accepted that mutual exchanges could survive as long as they were shielded from international competition and acted as natural monopolies within their national boundaries. In that era, membership was restricted de facto to local brokerage firms. Since the degree of heterogeneity among members was quite limited, conflicts occurred between listed companies and trading firms.

Reconciliation of the respective interests was attained in light of the consideration that exchanges needed both parties on board, according to the paradigms of the two-sided platform theory. Due to the isolation of exchanges from external competition, the members were able to block any reform that attempted to dis-intermediate trading on securities exchanges. Hence, the mutual structure was coherent with a natural-monopoly setting and designed to allow exchanges to extract monopoly rents (Pirrong, 2000) by limiting, for example, the number of members and enforcing member cartels.

By contrast, increasing financial centre competition, widening financing opportunities for issuers and greater investor access to foreign markets led to a substantial change in the incentive structure. Initially, the competition drivers were to be found in the massive technological developments that started to affect exchange trading. During the first stage of the evolutionary process improvements in IT facilitated remote access to exchange trading. These developments, coupled with a more pro-competitive regulatory framework (which did, however, only emerge a little later), were the most powerful incentives to exchange demutualization.

While one would be tempted to suggest that the increasing need for new capital was the main reason for demutualization, it has been pointed out that more strategic reasons were behind the process (Steil, 2002), namely the fact that exchanges were facing greater competition. Moreover, it has been pointed out that demutualization is a typical feature of those exchanges located in countries with higher levels of economic freedom and more competitive environments (Brito Ramos, 2006). The link between governance and efficiency was further investigated in Serifsoy and Tyrell (2006) who showed that whenever there is competition from a for-profit, outsider-owned platform, a mutual exchange is only able to survive by adopting a similar governance structure. However, although capital needs may not have been so compelling on the eve of exchange demutualization, we will show that in today's world access to equity financing is crucial in order to support the growth strategies of exchanges.

Nevertheless, in order to make the point clear, we should mention the potential conflicts of interest which were inherent in a mutual structure and, in particular, in the trading intermediation performed by members. Indeed, members sought to maximize their own utility to such an extent that the ability of the exchange to best serve its stakeholders, namely listed companies and investors, may have been impaired. Evidence (Domowitz and Steil, 2002; Steil, 2002) has shown that trading costs were higher in trading that occurred through broker members at a mutual organization than in the case of for-profit organizations.

The changing technological paradigm was at the heart of the transformations and marked a substantial shift in the way exchanges were managed and trading was conducted. The rapid substitution of traditional floors by electronic platforms also coincided with an evolutionary step in the nature of exchange itself. While previously the exchanges could have been seen just as a set of rules (or, otherwise, the entities setting them, adopting the *firm view*), today they are systems, that combine a set of rules and technological facilities, whose interaction plays an essential role in facilitating transactions. A striking feature of the strategic positioning of exchanges in the current trading environment is the massive investment in technology that has occurred.

These technological advances have reduced the costs of accessing exchange services and put pressure on the intermediation function of traditional members, a process that eventually caused the demise of monopolies (Domowitz and Steil, 1999). Moreover, as national boundaries have become less distinct, the restrictions for issuers to list abroad have become fewer (Macey and O'Hara, 1997). As a result, exchanges faced a more challenging competitive environment, which contributed to diminishing the role of financial intermediaries (Mishkin and Strahan, 1999; Allen, McAndrews and Strahan, 2002).

It is not surprising that the early stages of governance reform witnessed the engagement of northern European exchanges, since they served the needs of small and open economies and were particularly exposed to competition from the London Stock Exchange (LSE). By contrast, in other jurisdictions change came later. For example, the trading specialists that dominated in the largest American exchanges (namely, NYSE and NASDAQ) succeeded in blocking any attempt at governance reform for some years. More recently, the diffusion of the so-called ECNs has taken the evolution of the exchange industry a step further. These systems have magnified the impact of technology; since they succeeded in capturing large flows of orders, they strongly incentivized large exchanges to demutualize. Hence, demutualization was conceived as a means to endow exchanges with the flexibility required to facilitate innovation. The biggest international intermediaries were the main actors striving for the change: banks operating across borders were members of a variety of exchanges, and such banks had less interest in defending the traditional governance structure than local banks.

Demutualization of exchanges has significant implications. On the one hand, it implies an important change in the incentives they face; on the other hand, it has a huge impact on their efficiency compared with traditional mutual organizations. Incentives are strictly related to the self-regulatory role of exchanges, and to their attitude towards risk. A major concern regarding demutualization was a presumed inconsistency with self-regulatory responsibilities. In particular it was questioned whether a for-profit organization would have the right incentives to correctly regulate listing, trading and settlement, and exert an efficient surveillance of market participants. However, there is widespread consensus that demutualization and listing are no less consistent with regulatory duties than a mutual status (Steil, 2002). Another concern was the presumed incentive for a for-profit exchange to engage in high-risk activities that might threaten the viability of business on an ongoing basis, thus damaging members and the economy as a whole.

It has been argued (Oesterle et al., 1992) that the even more compelling need to innovate constitutes the prime rationale for exchanges to move from a not-for-profit to a for-profit status. A for-profit exchange generally widens the catalogue of potentially conflicting interests, and thus requires an in-depth comprehension of corporate governance arrangements and controlling mechanisms. Moreover, striving for profit maximization, which admittedly might prompt the management to engage in riskier activities, increases the need to adopt a well-designed risk management framework.

Academic literature has compared the relative efficiency conditions of cooperatives and demutualized exchanges. One of the prevailing features in this field has been the support of a contraposition between outside ownership and member ownership, in so much that outside owners do not use the exchange facilities and services (which means that their utility function is arguably focused on value maximization), whereas member ownership is identified with owners that act as customers as well. It has been pointed out (Hart and Moore, 1996) that as the exchanges are facing greater competition, and the vested interests of members are becoming more skewed, outside ownership is proving even more efficient than a mutual organization. Although proponents of this view argue that both the mutual model and the outside-ownership model are inefficient, the more intense the competition and the greater the degree of member inconsistency, the more efficient outside ownership appears to be.

The Hart and Moore model focuses purely on voting rules and ignores the specific governance arrangements designed to support bargains between members. In fact, how bargains within the organization are governed is of central importance if we are to understand the economics of exchange decision making and reveal significant features of the exchange industry structure.

We would contend that what differentiates a demutualized governance structure is a different allocation of the residual rights of control compared to a mutual organization, and the distribution of surplus. While a corporate for-profit exchange seeks to maximize profits that are then distributed to owners, a not-for-profit exchange does not distribute profits. Rather, it may be tempted to facilitate profit maximization by reducing competition between members.

However, it should be emphasized that the changes in statutory arrangements did not lead to a substantial and immediate transformation of the ownership base. Some exchanges, de facto, continued to be largely controlled by intermediaries – members even after demutualization – and thus resembled the governing mechanisms of the old paradigm. It took a while for outside ownership to take root in securities exchanges.

With the *listing* of securities exchanges outside ownership widened to a considerable extent and radically changed incentives. In particular, new forms of conflicting interest emerged between different stakeholders. Within this conceptual framework the listing of exchanges actually represents a successive stage of governance reform which is logically related to demutualization. The reasons behind the self-listing of exchanges were almost the same as those that forced the mutual structure to be abandoned. There is general consensus that self-listing was a response to the need to endow stock exchanges with the most suitable instruments (the public company model) to deal with growing international competition (Fleckner, 2006). In fact, the changing competitive landscape forced almost all of the major exchanges across the world to seek alliances or, more frequently, to negotiate mergers for which public ownership was particularly suitable. Indeed, almost all the deals completed so far have involved, to a greater or lesser extent, exchanges of shares. Therefore, listing facilitates value measurement in mergers and acquisitions (M&As) and further capital raising to support expansion plans. Incidentally, listing and consolidation determines the adoption of a shareholder value perspective when investigating the pros and cons of demutualization and stock exchange IPOs. Mendiola and O'Hara (2004) were among the first to embrace such a perspective, and they argued that the benefits overweighed potential costs. How value is distributed is another challenging issue that is dependent on the structure of the exchange industry, the competitive environment and the behaviour of the entities involved: in short, it may be summarized as cooperative strategies versus non-cooperative strategies. We will explore the topic of value creation in more detail in the following chapters.

At the beginning of the 2000s the debate on the future of the securities industry spurred predictions that there would be a trading environment dominated by a few large exchanges. It was asserted that the need for integration would be triggered by increasing competition and the new status of exchanges as profit-maximizing entities. Subsequent events have seemingly confirmed these predictions: an intense consolidation process that started during the 1990s has sped up in recent years. Theoretically, competition may lead to consolidation through mergers, joint ventures, reciprocal ownership and other forms of alliances. For example, exchanges may negotiate alliances by signing cooperation and technology agreements, while remaining independent legal entities (Di Noia, 1998).

In recent years M&As have emerged as the predominant integration model, leading to the formation of large conglomerates. However, alongside polarization, a networking model is emerging among the major groups in which conglomerates have common significant shareholders. Such developments may have interesting consequences for the operation of network economies, as well as raising several concerns. The application of network theory to the stock exchange industry (Economides, 1993) shows that network economies lead to increases in liquidity and the quality of price discovery. It should be noted that the unfolding of network externalities is dependent on compatibility and coordination among the constituent parts. Competition should be promoted so that users have the right to access all exchange trading services and choose the provider offering the best conditions. Coordination is ensured as long as exchanges adhere to common standards (compatibility) that grant equal access to users (Economides and Flyer, 1997). The equilibrium between competition and coordination in the new industry setting constitutes the most prominent feature of modern exchange governance. It is expected to change the way in which governance is conceived, conferring even more importance on external governance arrangements.

3 Securities exchanges and ownership structures

Nowadays, the majority of publicly listed exchanges operate in high-income economies,although a few are located in low–middle-income economies. Table 4.1 records the evolution of governance structure for exchanges that are members of the WFE.

According to WFE data, mutual exchanges or associations constitute a marginal class in the international landscape. As we can observe, the majority of securities exchanges are corporations (publicly listed companies, demutualized exchanges and private limited companies), although there are, arguably, substantial differences among them. Some 44 per cent of WFE members are listed exchanges and comprise the largest players in the world in terms of turnover, IPOs and capital raised: more specifically, the NYSE Euronext, NASDAQ OMX, the LSEG, Deutsche Börse and the largest derivatives centres such as the CME, the CBOE and Intercontinental Exchange (ICE).[1] The emerging landscape is quite different if compared with the morphology of the industry prevailing

Table 4.1 Changing governance

Legal status	2007	2008	2009	2010	2011
Publicly listed companies	21	19	19	22	23
Demutualized exchanges with transferable ownership	11	8	9	9	8
Private limited companies mainly owned by members	7	7	8	7	8
Associations or mutual exchanges	4	4	4	3	4
Other legal status	8	7	8	9	9

Source: WFE, Cost &Revenue Survey (various years).

around 2000. Excluding the long-standing listed exchanges – LSE, Deutsche Börse and the Stockholm Exchange – at that point just a few exchanges were listed. Many others operated as demutualized exchanges, albeit unlisted. Most of the listed exchanges went public in the years immediately before the financial crisis, while others followed later.[2] Today, listed exchanges are largely predominant in terms of assets, profits and volumes traded.

While such exchanges have substantially different vested interests when compared with traditional mutual organizations, the same cannot be said for incorporated exchanges, which are still dominated by traders. Although formally vesting a different legal status, the latter arguably have the same structure of incentives as cooperatives.

However, the classification adopted by the WFE suffers from a lack of clarity. De facto, it may be difficult to distinguish between demutualized exchanges and private limited companies. In fact, excluding listed exchanges, other incorporated exchanges have quite similar ownership structures, characterized by low levels of dispersion in the shareholder base. Moreover, listed exchanges themselves do not necessarily have a dispersed ownership structure.

From a corporate governance perspective, the listing of securities exchanges poses a wide array of questions with regard to managerial incentives and minority shareholder protection, as well as exchange governance issues (that is, the relationships among user-owners, non-owner members and other outside shareholders, and the potential conflicts between local and international members).

Currently, the ownership structure of listed exchanges is somewhat fragmented and displays the typical features of public companies. In almost all listed exchanges there is a large proportion of institutional ownership (Table 4.2), whose distribution is widespread (Table 4.3). Apart from the Spanish Exchange, there is extensive institutional ownership especially as regards American exchanges such as the NASDAQ OMX Group and the Intercontinental Exchange, which are almost totally owned by institutions. Moreover, the distribution of ownership for the top ten investor holdings is also distinctly widespread.

The massive presence of institutional investors in the capital base of securities exchanges marks a new step in the evolutionary process of exchange governance. The process appears of particular interest for at least two reasons. First of all, it reflects an acceleration in the process of separation between ownership and control. Then, more importantly, it depicts a substantially different picture to the traditional member–owner paradigm. This separation between membership and ownership

Table 4.2 Institutional ownership across listed exchanges

	Institutional ownership			Top ten institutional owners	Mutual funds
		North American	Non-North American		
NASDAQ OMX Group	95.89%	*58.06%*	*37.83%*	54.61%	31.14%
NYSE Euronext	73.11%	*66.64%*	*6.46%*	34.27%	32.79%
CME Group	73.66%	*64.55%*	*9.11%*	28.41%	29.34%
CBOE	54.04%	*52.30%*	*1.74%*	31.99%	28.73%
ICE	93.98%	*84.81%*	*9.17%*	44.12%	46.51%
TMX	31.33%	*28%*	*3.34%*	16.91%	30.64%
LSEG	74.88%	*8.42%*	*66.47%*	43.94%	21.87%
Deutsche Börse Group	43.03%	*17.81%*	*25.23%*	21.94%	36.49%
Bolsas y Mercados Españoles	17.90%	*2.64%*	*15.26%*	8.36%	17.07%

Source: SNL Financial.

may entail a refocusing of the entire structure of incentives. However, in order to define the exact nature of securities exchange incentives a more comprehensive knowledge of the ownership base is required. Building on the SNL Financial dataset we focus on two dimensions: the presence of one or more controlling shareholders and the existence of cross-ownerships.

In the cases of NASDAQ OMX and the LSEG the distribution appears to have a long right tail, probably owing to the specific stakes that a single shareholder holds in each group. Analysis of the ownership structure of the main securities exchanges reveals several implications for their governance and management, which are summarized below.

The predominant listed exchanges have a widespread shareholder base (see the mean and median ownership share in Table 4.3). As public companies such exchanges exemplify the classical problem of the separation of ownership and control.

However, looking at ownership structure in more detail we can identify a core of shareholders holding significant stakes. This is shown by the means above the median values and the stakes held by the outliers. In some exchanges the outlier shareholders control around a 50 per cent stake or more. Narrowing the analysis to American exchanges, a few shareholders control nearly 20 per cent of stakes.

Nevertheless, not all of the listed exchanges have a widespread ownership base. For example, the Warsaw Stock Exchange is controlled by the Polish government, a fact which questions the similarities with other listed exchanges in terms of vested interests.[3]

Therefore, in the case of relations between shareholders, very low median shareholdings combined with the presence of a large controlling shareholder implies that there may be agency problems involving major and minority shareholders.

Table 4.3 Institutional ownership distribution across listed exchanges

	NASDAQ	NYSE Euronext	LSEG	BME	DB	TMX	CME	CBOE	ICE
Mean	0.37%	0.28%	0.33%	0.08%	0.17%	0.18%	0.28%	0.21%	0.37%
Median	0.09%	0.07%	0.04%	0.02%	0.03%	0.02%	0.08%	0.03%	0.08%
5% perc.	0.02%	0.02%	0.01%	0.00	0.01%	0	0.03%	0	0.02%
95% perc.	1.16%	1.10%	1.09%	0.4%	0.82%	1.27%	1.05%	0.93%	1.51%
outlier	13	13	13	10	12	9	13	13	13
% outlier	58.5%	37.8%	51.2%	8.3%	23.8%	15.6%	32.1%	35.3%	49.6%

Source: Calculations based on SNL Financial data.

Cross-ownership is an important feature in today's exchange industry. Examining the ownership structures we can find tight links across major listed exchanges, in particular the North American ones. In fact, the figures show that such exchanges are controlled by a common nucleus of institutional shareholders. In particular, the CBOE, the CME, the Intercontinental Exchange and the NYSE Euronext Group have four common shareholders with stakes ranging from 15 per cent to more than 19 per cent (see Table 4.4).

The figures above are quite interesting because they suggest that there may be some form of coordination between major exchanges, in spite of the fact that they are formally distinct juridical entities. Indeed, the results are even more significant in light of the consolidation process, which is reshaping the morphology of the industry. It could be argued that the resulting ownership structure would resemble a sort of implicit merger between exchanges accounting for the great majority of capitalization and turnover value throughout the world. In turn, this may imply that a few institutional investors would be able to control flows of listings and investments that are channelled through the capital markets.

Ownership of securities exchanges is, however, evolving along a new path that involves links between Western and Arab exchanges. Western exchanges include the LSEG and NASDAQ OMX, whereas on the Arab side coordinating power is in the hands of the Borse Dubai, a holding company controlled by the Investment Corporation of Dubai (ICD). The ICD is the sovereign fund of Dubai and holds large stakes in both the LSE group (21 per cent) and NASDAQ OMX (16 per cent). The Borse Dubai has about an 80 per cent stake in the Dubai Financial Market (DFM), one of the main exchanges in the UAE, in which NASDAQ OMX itself is a shareholder. The DIFIX Exchange (today NASDAQ Dubai) was the result of a partnership agreement between Borse Dubai and

Table 4.4 Common ownership across exchanges

	CBOE	CME Group	ICE	NYSE Euronext
Vanguard Group Inc.	4.32%	3.90%	5.57%	5.61%
State Street Global Advisors Inc.	1.98%	3.78%	3.81%	4.06%
T. Rowe Price Associates Inc.	7.41%	3.71%	5.94%	3.25%
BlackRock Fund Advisors	4.24%	3.67%	4.03%	4.67%

Source: SNL Financial.

NASDAQ OMX that aimed to establish a marketplace for international securities. Recently, the DFM acquired a two-thirds stake in NASDAQ Dubai, leaving the remainder in the hands of Borse Dubai.

The above-mentioned relationships between DFM, NASDAQ OMX and the LSEG derived from the battle for control of the London market place. Incidentally, the struggle for control of the LSEG resulted in the Qatar Investment Authority's entry into the shareholder base with a 15 per cent stake. From a corporate governance perspective it is quite interesting to note that the same Arab group holds significant stakes in both NASDAQ OMX and the LSEG. Increasing convergence between Western and Arab capital markets has significant macroeconomic implications, as such integration has a strong impact on the development of capital markets in an area which is intermediating high capital flows.

In general terms, such developments raise concerns regarding the future of the exchange industry. In light of the weakening influence of brokerage firms on securities exchanges, it is difficult to identify who, ultimately, controls and exercises power over trading platforms. There is no doubt that growing links between exchanges and other platforms, as well as the affirmation of corporate chains, result in the substantial reallocation (and spreading) of control rights over exchange franchisees.

As an incidental aside, we might also note that increasing linkages among platforms will certainly have consequences for the exercise of supervisory and regulatory powers, alongside the impact on value creation. Indeed, it may become difficult to ascertain who actually decides the strategic policies of exchanges. Moreover, increasing complexity in ownership architectures interferes substantially with the role of exchanges as SROs are entrusted with the regulation (and supervision) of the markets they manage. As a result, the overall reputational capital of platform operators may be affected.

Turning to objective functions we would expect listed institutionally owned exchanges to have a strong focus on profit maximization compared with other legal statuses. In particular, this should be true of cooperatives and private member-owned exchanges. The fact that value creation is an important objective for listed exchanges has emerged following recent events occurring within the exchanges industry. In particular, merger proposals between exchanges place strong emphasis on value and its distribution among shareholders.[4] Theoretically, market discipline may be expected to act as a powerful incentive for managers to pursue value creating strategies in order to dampen the risk of a takeover. The matter has recently been investigated by Otchere (2006) with reference to securities exchanges. By analysing the determinants of listing decisions, he found that the more profitable exchanges or, alternatively, those that are highly active in the market (despite their subdued profitability ratios) have the strongest incentive to list. Consequently, listing would be a means of unlocking growth opportunities and creating value for shareholders through better monitoring of managerial behaviour and by lowering those agency problems which typically characterize a cooperative exchange. Hence, the market for corporate control operates as a powerful disciplining mechanism. However, the actual functioning of such forces is dependent on the specific ownership structure.

4 Governance arrangements, objective function and conflicts of interest

The large diversity in the ownership structure of stock exchanges around the world requires a discussion of the main implications this has for corporate governance, corporate strategies and the incentives driving management. As a first stage we have to address the issue of whether or not differences in the shareholder base affect the objective function of exchanges. Here, we put on the table some basic considerations about the exchange's objective function; we develop our points in more detail throughout the book.

Given the objectives of the present work consideration of this issue elicits some important points. The central idea is that the strategic dimension of exchange management is of paramount importance in a highly competitive environment, marking a substantial discontinuity with the era when exchanges operated as local monopolies. On one hand these developments have an impact on the incentives of exchange management; on the other hand, they introduce new sources of conflict.

While issues of governance entailed by mutual organizations and demutualized but unlisted exchanges (at least those with a homogeneous shareholder base) are widely recognized in the literature, particular concerns emerge with reference to listed exchanges.

The governance of listed exchanges is sharply different in comparison with other exchanges as they are more exposed to external influences. It is also different from that of other public companies. What actually distinguishes a listed exchange compared with other public companies is its double role in corporate governance which requires it to set, oversee and comply with:

a) Corporate governance rules and arrangements as a listed company.
b) Corporate governance rules and arrangements as an SRO.

This double role mirrors the particular nature of a stock exchange as a firm operating in a strictly regulated environment. As a regulator and listed company, the listed exchange has responsibilities towards a variety of stakeholders, including shareholders, the financial authorities and supervisors, and the market, which, within this context, comprises all those entities (issuers, traders and brokerage firms) interested in the integrity of the marketplace.

As a listed company the exchange owes a duty of transparency and disclosure on relevant corporate matters to shareholders. Sound and effective corporate governance rests on the independence of the board of directors and the resolution of potential conflicting interests, entrusted to specific committees constituted under the exchange's governance framework. Like other listed companies, the governance arrangements of listed exchanges sets up various committees entrusted with specific functions, such as remuneration and corporate strategies.

As an SRO the exchange is mainly accountable to regulators and supervisors as regards compliance with high-level rules and regulations. While obviously of concern to supervisors, compliance with rules is of great interest to shareholders as well. In fact, compliance has much to do with the reputational capital of the exchange and, ultimately, with the viability of the business and the attitude of the exchange to the creation of value.

Traditionally, the governance arrangements of an exchange were designed as a system of accountability to customers and supervisors, the latter being entrusted with a public interest in preserving an orderly and fair market and, therefore, acting as guarantors of fair and non-discriminating behaviour of exchanges in their relations with the market.

With the listing of securities exchanges, the advent of minority shareholders has led to the affirmation of new vested interests. And, in turn, the affirmation of a new category of stakeholders has resulted in an enlargement of the catalogue of potential conflicting interests. Nowadays, the contraposition of issuers and brokerage firms, locals and internationally active brokers, inside and outside shareholders, is not an exhaustive list of the overall vested interests.

Broadly speaking, minority shareholders should pose the same governance problems that public companies normally face. Arguably, the listing of exchanges may turn out to substantially transform the nature of agency problems related to the ownership structure. Provided that the listing gives rise to a dispersed and diversified ownership, a trade-off between user–owners and outside owners would become less compelling.

At the same time, we might argue that the outside owners of publicly traded and widely held exchanges do not have the incentive to expropriate the members. By contrast, listed exchanges would face the well known agency problems that characterize listed companies. Within this framework the potentially conflicting interests of managers and shareholders are of particular relevance (Berle and Means, 1932). Were a few large shareholders to emerge, the agency problems opposing controlling shareholders to minority shareholders (and other stakeholders) would be a particular concern as well (Shleifer and Vishny, 1997).[5]

The core of relevant and relatively stable shareholders (institutional investors) has, arguably, a multifaceted utility function where value creation may come to combine or conflict with other objectives. These shareholders might act as strategic investors with the aim of leading change in the exchange industry or pursuing specific interests in contiguous businesses. Their position may also drive a wedge between their interests and the interests of minority shareholders who, arguably, strive for value maximization.

The process of governing listed exchanges with a great variety of stakeholders – arguably all having different objectives and utility functions – is undoubtedly complex and challenging since it expands the risks of poor management practices. According to the governance literature, separation between ownership and control creates an area of contraposition between managers and shareholders. At the same time, there is a potential source of conflicting interests between managers and customers.

In today's exchange industry these issues come to the forefront with reference to the expansion policies that exchanges are pursuing. At least for those listed exchanges where a few large institutional investors hold relevant stakes, we might expect that effective monitoring is achievable; nevertheless, there remains the risk that certain strategic options are conceived by the management simply as a means of consuming perquisites.

These concerns should be assessed with reference to shareholders' value maximization and the availability of exchanges' services to customers (with regard to both costs and access rights). While large controlling shareholders might be expected to strive for value maximization, their strategic vision might nevertheless be inspired by other interests (these may encompass prestige and the ambition to expand control over global capital flows). The phenomena of common shareholdings, which we accounted for in section 3, poses the problem of operations with (or between) *related parties*, which is one of the most interesting governance issues in the modern exchange industry. Obviously, such operations might be beneficial to both exchanges and customers in several respects (we may cite the favouring of technology transfers, the adoption of common standards by a variety of platforms or facilitating trading to their respective members), notwithstanding that they require adequate transparency and oversight in order to ensure that such relations are conceived as a means to effectively address the interests of minority shareholders and customers rather than just responding to the needs of controlling shareholders.

Whether increasing relations between exchanges encourages the free access of customers to services across the exchange industry or whether this will, rather, turn out to erect competitive barriers is a contentious issue which we discuss in section 5. In Figure 4.1 we contextualize the matter of corporate governance within the system of value, intended as both shareholder value and value for the market.

Creating value for shareholders and the community means managing three competitive levers which are sharply influenced by pressures coming from the external environment and pertain to sustainable growth, sustainable value and prime capabilities and skills. The aim of achieving sustainable value influences decisions taken to obtain sustained (and sustainable) commercial growth and to endow the firm with the best human and physical capital. Within this framework, strategic engagement requires the management of three focus areas pertaining to product and service development (on which depends the sustainable growth), investments in IT systems and human skills (achieving prime capabilities) and corporate governance. More generally, it requires an engaging approach to exchange's management which is inclusive of all relevant stakeholders (owners, customers and the market or the community as a whole).

At the heart of the overall system of corporate governance stands the sustainability of the business. This objective is of paramount importance

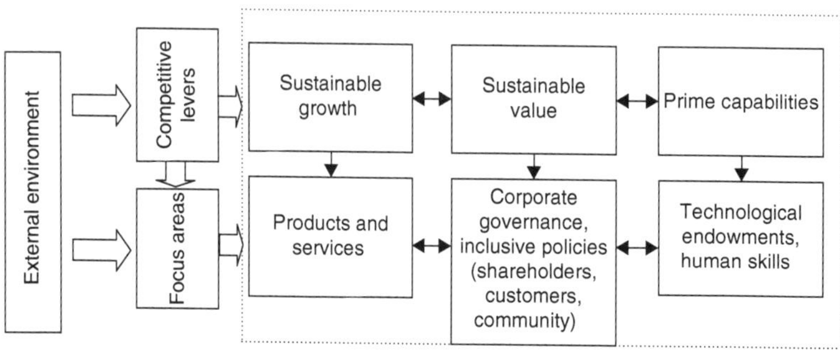

Figure 4.1 The value system

for regulators, supervisors and the market. The sustainability of an exchange's business (and of platform operators), in fact ensures an effective and efficient channelling of savings to investment opportunities and prevents disruptions in the financial system. Conceived of in this way, sustainability reconciles the interests of listed exchanges as for-profit organizations with the public interest in a fair and well-functioning capital market.

Figure 4.2 describes the governance arrangements for listed exchanges and the relations with stakeholders.

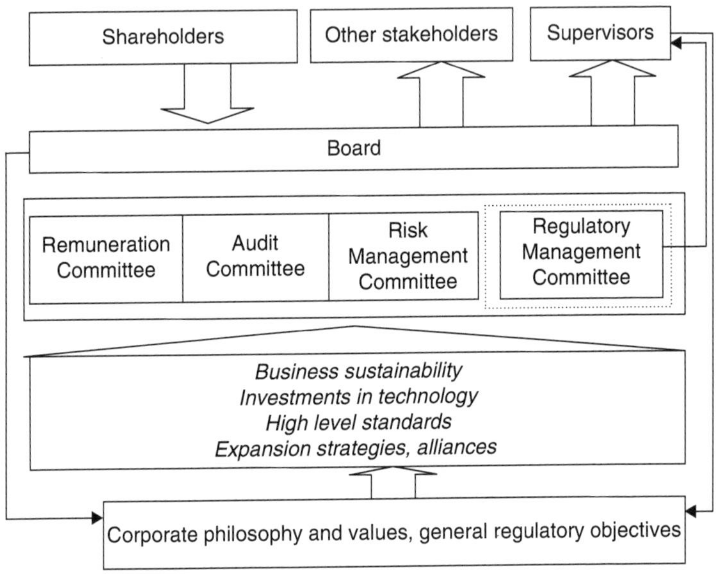

Figure 4.2 The system of corporate governance

The joint influence of both the corporate philosophy and values (which are expressions of the competencies and sensibilities of the board) and the general objectives of regulators and supervisory authorities sharply influences business sustainability.

Corporate philosophy is a multidimensional concept; it pertains to the model of growth, the striving of the management to promote fair and well-functioning markets and, more generally, attitudes toward risk. In that sense, corporate philosophy is a function of the specific strategic choices of the exchange in terms of capital investments (mainly devoted to improve platforms), mergers and other alliances with other platform operators, self-regulatory and monitoring standards.

Corporate value refers to the attitude of the exchange in its relations with all the relevant stakeholders (shareholders, issuers, market operators) and goes far beyond the compliance duties owed to the supervisors and the market according to rules and regulations. Rather, it comprises commitment to a market-friendly mode of conducting business in terms of high-level monitoring and admission standards and the proper communication of such a philosophy to the market.

Within this framework, it is the responsibility of the board to spread the particular corporate philosophy and values across each level of the firm. In turn, the overall aim of running a sustainable business should drive the decision-making process of each corporate committee. By integrating the general objective of sustainability into each committee, the system of corporate governance realizes the coordination of their specific functions and their joint commitment to value-oriented, rule-compliant corporate policies. Within this framework, the most important relations are the following:

a) The relation between the sustainability objective and remuneration policies. A good principle of corporate governance would require that stock option plans and other bonuses cohere with the long-term viability of the business. There should be a good principle of governance to link remuneration policies to certain measures of performance adjusted for risks.
b) The relation between the sustainability objective and overall corporate strategies. This is a particularly important relationship when it comes to growth strategies by means of mergers and acquisitions and other alliances which, while responding to efficiency reasons, still entail risks for sound management and overall corporate stability. As noted in previous chapters, strategic management involves a strictly correct relationship between exchange and regulators; the latter should, for example, be informed about mergers and alliances.
c) The relation between the sustainability objective and risk management. Controlling and managing risk should receive particular attention within the system of corporate governance. Demutualized and, in particular, listed exchanges have, supposedly, the incentive to expand risks, although there is no clear evidence on that point. Notwithstanding, increasing competitive pressures boost exchanges to pursue expansion policies either investing in new business lines or through M&As. In either case, they need sound risk management policies.

In particular, risk control and management claims to set clear risk objectives for each business unit and continuous reporting to the board. A central role in the entire system of governance is played by *regulatory management*. A sound principle of governance would require such a function to be accountable to the board and regulators and be, more importantly, independent of other functions and committees. As such a function should be entrusted with the responsibility of regulating and monitoring markets and managing overall conflicts of interest, it should not be influenced by the strategic and commercial functions of the exchange. Within conglomerate exchanges it is, in particular, important that the directors responsible for each division (cash markets, derivatives markets, post-trading and so on) are not in touch with regulatory management.[6]

5 Controlling chains. Which kind of governance?

In this section we analyse in greater detail the relationship between ownership and governance arrangements. The transformation of the exchange industry over the last few years gave rise to a particular structure where national or regional exchanges, with a relatively closed ownership structure, coexist with large groups with cross-border extension. Within regional exchanges the managing company overlaps the local market. By contrast, within conglomerate groups this proximity vanishes. In the latter case, controlling shareholders have far reaching power over a wide array of business activities that span different geographical areas. In fact, the consolidation process in the industry gave rise to the *'holding model'* for the control of exchanges, linking together platforms at all stages in the value chain.

Such a model proves, due to its flexibility, to be particularly efficient in managing mergers on both horizontal and vertical scales. It is particularly suitable for combining different corporate cultures and integrating complementary businesses along the value chain. Looking at major groups across the world a paradigmatic example of vertical silo is that of Deutsche Börse Group, which internalizes under the same controlling holding both the security exchange and post-trading activities. The federative model is, in contrast, that of NYSE Euronext, which brings under a common coordinating entity different exchanges across America and Europe. At the post-trading stage of the value chain NYSE Euronext does not control an own operator; nevertheless it holds relevant stakes in major CSDs and clearing houses (the DTCC in the US and Euroclear in Europe) in conjunction with other user–shareholders.

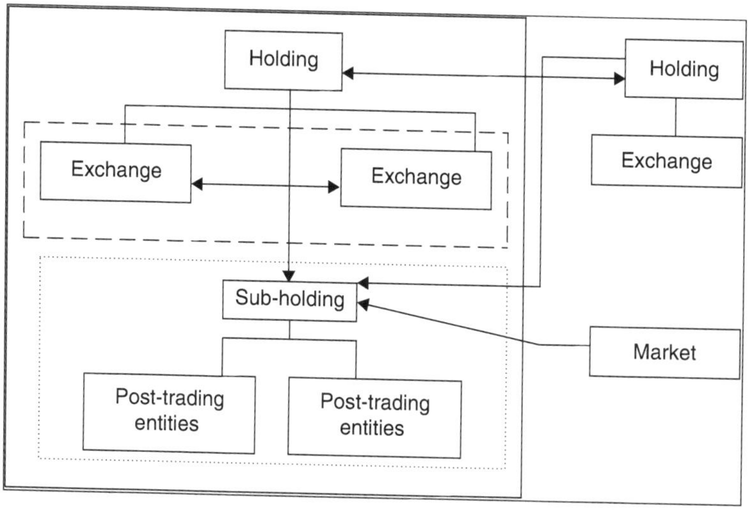

Figure 4.3 The holding model

In a practical sense, the holding model answers the question of whether the advantages of flexibly managing the consolidation process (through formal mergers or mere alliances among trading platforms) outweighs the potential drawbacks in terms of poor corporate governance or inefficient supervision. The topic should be considered in light of both *contractual governance* and *non-contractual governance* arrangements.

Contractual governance refers to all of those mechanisms formally established to govern relations between different stakeholders, promote a managerial style that is in line with best practices, improve efficient internal control systems and design a coherent system of incentives. Securities exchanges around the world (in particular listed ones) have come up with complex systems of corporate governance. Internal controls and risk management procedures have been particularly developed, and are entrusted to specific committees reporting to top management. While constituting an important piece of the entire corporate governance architecture, contractual governance is too narrow to define the vast system of relations that is at the heart of exchange management. Actually, it misses taking into account the complex flux of influences coming from the external environment. And in fact when pursuing expansion strategies, and furthering the integration process within international capital markets, the exchange becomes increasingly exposed to many more external influences.

Non-contractual governance becomes, therefore, of paramount importance in orienting the management of securities exchanges. While it is certain that almost all firms are subject to external influences, conglomerate exchanges are particularly affected by the external environment for technological reasons (remote trading) and as a result of the increasing links at ownership level among multiple platforms. To define the concept, non-contractual governance refers to the effects deployed by the so-called *network embeddedness*[7] which is related to the ability of platform users to resort to other providers (exchanges or post-trading entities) that provide a better service (which may take the form of better prices, lower costs, high-quality monitoring or higher transparency standards). Provided that an *exit network* such as this functions well, it would act as a powerful mechanism for regulating industrial relationships. It would, therefore, promote fair competitive practices and ensure a non-discriminatory treatment for platform users.

It can be seen, therefore, that the main features of corporate governance in the modern exchange industry seek to regulate networks and relations between exchanges rather than just simply resolving conflicting interests within the single exchange. It follows that the concept of the stakeholder is much wider than the body of exchange members, embracing as it now does the market as a whole.

From a theoretical point of view, the proper functioning of an exit network mechanism would set questions about how to conceive corporate governance within the exchange industry. In particular, the value of reputational capital and the threats coming from the exit network would themselves act in a way to prevent opportunistic behaviour by the exchange. In this regard, Lee (1996) argues for the irrelevance of governance arrangements whenever the exchange is deemed to face massive competition. Obviously, the issue is strictly related to the regulation of the exchange industry and the influence that regulation has on competition and behaviour. In the literature it has been argued (Fischel and Grossman, 1984) that there is a strict relationship between the quality of regulation and the trading volumes that the exchange is able to attract. It would, therefore, follow that the functioning of the exit network is something that is exogenous to the exchange and attributable to the incentives emanating from regulators. Nevertheless, the exchange industry is distinguished by the extensive powers of self-regulation that lie in the hands of exchanges. Therefore, the proper functioning of competition and the effectiveness of market discipline is, to a large extent, endogenous and dependent on the strategic behaviour of the exchange's management; it is at this level that non-contractual governance merges with contractual governance.

Within platform industries the conditions for the exit network to properly work suggest complementarities which may be conceived in two forms:

a) Technical complementarities, implying the adoption of common platforms, or otherwise the full interoperability of different platforms alongside the homogenization of standards and protocols.
b) Economic complementarities, implying a strategic coordination between different platform operators favouring cross-memberships, cross-listings and smooth post-trading procedures.

It could be questioned if the affirmation of a federative model among platforms would harm the fair access to trading and post-trading services. We may address the issue in light of the following considerations. At trading level, aggregations between exchanges generally lead to the adoption of a common platform in order to fully exploit potential synergies, ensure interoperability and facilitate the trading of securities listed in the markets involved in the merger. Relevant advantages may be related to the reduction in trading costs and easier cross-listing opportunities.

It is, however, at a post-trading level that the issues of most concern arise. Different situations may emerge: we may find two or more post-trading platforms owned by the same holding company; post-trading platforms may be subject to joint shareholdings by a variety of platform users (at most, securities exchanges); we may, then, find a post-trading platform with two or more exchanges as the relevant shareholders; and, finally, a vertical silo may emerge.

As a matter of fact the effective functioning of non-contractual governance arrangements might be undermined as large exchanges that integrate all the stages of the security industries' value chain emerge. This may happen whenever full integration hinders transparency on prices and other relevant attributes of trading and post-trading services. In fact, vertical integration entails significant risks associated with the bundling of complementary services. First of all, it might become difficult to recognize the price of each single service in the bundle; moreover, bundling of services might boost cross-subsidization policies.

Turning now to the competitive implications, the integration of capital markets around the world is not necessarily incompatible with a competitive setting of the market for securities trading. While antitrust authorities block mergers which would arguably result in harming competition, nevertheless the holding model may actually promote a *levelling of the playing field*. When acting as vehicles with both controlling or non-controlling interests in trading or post-trading entities, holding companies might stimulate *inter-group* and *intra-group competition*. Inter-group competition develops across legally autonomous entities subject to a common coordination, as a result of the adoption of common infrastructures and the offering of products and services which may be deemed as substitutes. In that case, platforms belonging to the same group constitute different access points to the same pool of liquidity.

The main concerns arise with reference to the links between trading platforms and post-trading entities. Several stock exchanges pursue vertical integration strategies with post-trading companies by taking advantage of: a) complementary operations between the two stages of the value chain; b) the recurrence of the relationship between stock exchange and post-trading companies; c) specific investment in the relationship; and d) the divergence of interest among the parties, which can lead to opportunistic behaviour. The literature of industrial organization identifies as incentives to integration specific investment in the relationship (Williamson, 1985) and difficulty in drawing up contracts that will be able to meet all future contingencies (Grossman and Hart, 1986). Should the vertical silo imprison the customer in a tight relationship through bundling of services and poor transparency, it would undermine the full operation of the exit network and prevent efficient governance of networks.

6 Global exchange governance. Who controls platforms?

The traditional securities exchange governance literature has a quite limited focus. As noted previously, it tends to concentrate on the incentives of securities exchanges to change their legal status, in particular their shift towards a demutualized ownership structure and, eventually, the move to going public. Other contributors within the stream of literature address the issue of compromise among different vested interests, namely those of outside shareholders, platform users, listed companies and others.

Despite providing an excellent insight into the mechanics of exchange governance, the established literature is deficient in providing a satisfactory overview of the implications for governance in view of recent developments in the exchange industry. Demutualization and the listing of major exchanges has changed their objective function.

The aim of seeking profitable markets and activities stimulated expansion strategies. Therefore, the exchange industry is moving toward a pattern of development where small and medium regional exchanges coexist with a few big players whose ownership links constitute a network characterized by economically and strategically interconnected platforms. When a few common shareholders have an effective controlling power over them, the interconnected exchanges come to form a cluster whose scale may deeply influence the overall competitive dynamics within the industry.

The most relevant implications of these changes concern the objective function. While assuming profit maximization as the relevant objective at cluster-wide level, some form of cross-subsidization across exchanges within the cluster might be expected to occur, and hence the distribution of value among exchanges becomes a relevant issue. A related question involves the changing nature of the conflicting interests that a network might imply.

On the one hand, while clustering might stimulate interoperability it brings conflicts of interest outside the perimeters of the firm. This means that the perspective should be widened to comprise all relevant stakeholders at cluster-wide level. In such a setting, the governance paradigms should be deemed to change their essence. This is precisely why a mere microeconomic approach (managing conflicts within the firm) to exchange governance might be misleading. Rather, it should proceed side by side with an industry-wide perspective. Analysis of the microeconomic level causes concern about the creation and distribution of value between relevant shareholders, minority shareholders and other stakeholders, by which we primarily mean listed companies and brokers.

From an industrial perspective corporate governance implies the reconciliation of conflicting interests between multiple trading and post-trading platforms. Within this framework, shareholders should be concerned with redistribution of value to other exchanges within the cluster. The relevant conflicting interests, at this level, are those opposing the controlling shareholders with minorities at each exchange.

On the other hand, users (issuers and traders) at a specific node of the cluster might be worse off in the event that the exchange charges heavier fees in order to subsidize tariff cuts on the other platforms. The issue here is related to potential distortions in access rights at each node of the cluster.

To the extent that networks among exchanges are deepening, it becomes obvious that the relevant perspective of corporate governance encompasses the industry as a whole and is connected with the conditions governing access to all trading-related services offered by different platforms. However, industry-wide networks of relations among trading platforms carry relevant implications at a macroeconomic level as well. By bringing trading platform operations in different macro-areas under a common control, ownership structures might heavily impact on international capital flows. Provided that the common shareholders have effective powers of strategic coordination, this may sharply affect the cost of rising capital for issuers and the overall trading costs for brokers, dealers and final investors. At a macroeconomic level, moreover, there are implications for the distribution (and management) of risks across the entire financial system.

Clustering is the most recent phenomenon to cause concern with respect to both industrial and macroeconomic perspectives. It responds, arguably, to the needs of large institutional shareholders – directly interested in the functioning of the exchange industry – to reinforce control:

a) Over global liquidity pools, arguably in light of recent tendencies in exchange regulation.
b) Over the competitive dynamics within the exchange industry, eventually influencing the course of competitive forces.

With reference to the first point, we may recall, in light of the network theory, that liquidity is the key value driver for exchanges. Clusters may result in a way that counteracts centripetal tendencies due to increasing competition among platforms. We think that it is interesting to interpret the tendency toward clusters in light of regulatory reforms. For example, the US interlinking system established and promoted by Reg. NMS potentially implies a great mobility of flows among exchanges. By controlling major exchanges shareholders may be better able to retain control of liquidity flows in their moves.

We remarked earlier how the competitive positioning of an exchange may be captured by highlighting the relevance of a stock exchange in intermediating capital flows measured in relation to GDP. As a step forward from this basic assertion, we may derive a similar measure for the intensity of market activity by reference to a cluster of exchanges subject to joint coordination by a dominant shareholder (or group of shareholders) that exerts power over the capital flows controlled by the cluster.

Let us suppose that the *i-th* exchange is incorporated in the *j-th* country. We may measure its involvement in capital flows as a function of three ratios, the first being the *market capitalization on GDP* (Mcap_GDP), and the other two capturing exchanges' liquidity on primary and secondary markets respectively. Liquidity on primary markets may be measured by the ratio of *new capital raised* (by means of new IPOs or secondary offerings) *on GDP*. Formally: $Ncr_{GDP_i} = \frac{New\ capital\ raised_i}{GDP_j}$.

Secondary market liquidity may be measured in terms of *value of equity trading on GDP*. Formally: $Vse_{GDP_i} = \frac{Value\ of\ equity\ trading_i}{GDP_j}$. To this end, we use the *GDP* measure of the country where the exchange is incorporated, although it could enjoy a widespread international extension by incorporating other foreign exchanges or simply attracting many foreign issuers and traders. For listed exchanges it would be possible to adopt the *GDP* of the country where the exchange is listed which, de facto, corresponds to the country of incorporation. Both of the two aforementioned ratios express the engagement of the exchange in linking savings and investments, either within the domestic economic space or a wider international arena.

Building on these ratios, we define the overall liquidity of the *i-th* exchange as the sum of the contributions of primary markets and secondary markets. The contribution of primary markets (PML_i) may be defined as follows:

$$PML_i = \frac{\frac{Ncr_i}{GDP_j} \cdot \frac{Vet_i}{GDP_j}}{\frac{Mcap_i}{GDP_j}} = \frac{Ncr_i}{GDP_j} \cdot \frac{Vet_i}{Mcap_i} \qquad [1]$$

This represents the value of equity attributable to new capital raised. The idea we want to capture is that the flow of new capital raised (Ncr_GDP_i) on primary markets transforms in value of equity trading according to the ratio Vet_GDP_i. We divide by $Mcap\_GDP$ in order to represent the magnitude on which the stock (market capitalization) transforms into streams of liquidity. We may define $\frac{Vet_i}{Mcap_i}$ as the turnover velocity of the *i-th* exchange.

On the same basis we can express the contribution of secondary market liquidity (SML_i) as follows:

$$SML_i = \frac{\frac{Vet_i}{GDP_j}}{\frac{Mcap_i}{GDP_j}} = \frac{Vet_i}{Mcap_i} \qquad [2]$$

The index of liquidity of the *i-th* exchange therefore becomes:

$$I_i = PML_i + SML_i = \frac{Vet_i}{Mcap_i}\left(1 + \frac{Ncr_i}{GDP_j}\right) \quad [3]$$

We may express the liquidity index of the cluster as the sum of single indexes: $\sum_{i=1}^{n} I_i$. The effective control over liquidity depends on the behaviour of single relevant shareholders on the board of each exchange. Provided that they adopt cooperative behaviour (for example, in exercising voting rights) their control over the cluster's overall liquidity is $\sum_{i=1}^{n} a_i \cdot I_i$, where a_i expresses the controlling interest of the coalition on exchange *i*.

Turning to point b) above, coalitions of shareholders in multiple exchanges may influence how competition and coordination combine. Theoretically, with interlinks expanding and becoming even stronger, the exchange and industry level may come to overlap. Arguably, the aforementioned developments will act in a way that would result in substantial changes in the nature of competition. More precisely, competition is expected to develop between large conglomerates (or clusters), while within each conglomerate a model of cooperation would prevail.

At a managerial level, the cluster model poses interesting challenges for the strategic behaviour within the group and its interrelations with the behaviour of stakeholders (mainly traders and issuers). Value creation becomes even more challenging when it depends on the new equilibrium that is entailed by strategic coordination at an industry-wide level. The distribution of value, on the other hand, may cause concern as well; eventually, it may be affected by the contraposition of the interests of a very few shareholders and those of the international capital market. Should such links come to lock control of the cluster, the utility function of the main shareholders would entail the joint-maximization of profits of all the constituents of the group, thus realizing a kind of implicit merger. Profit maximization becomes relevant at conglomerate or cluster level, with implications for the pricing policies and the manifestation of cross-network effects.

Whether the controlling shareholder is able to seize value or not depends on the level of competition at each node of the cluster. The joint profit-maximization at cluster level leads to coordination in setting fees (both for listing and trading business) across the platforms involved. More precisely, the cluster is able to internalize cross-network effects. Each exchange becomes a node of the cluster and sets its listing and trading fees as a result of the decisions of other exchanges in the node. We may assume, therefore, that the conjectural variations in prices equals zero. In such a setting conjectural variations become relevant for those nodes that, eventually, are exposed to external competition. These nodes might be forced to adopt aggressive pricing policies, while the nodes not suffering from fierce external competition might behave as if they have some form of market power. We will deal in more detail with this topic in Chapter 5.

For traders and listed companies there emerges a multiple-choice problem. They can alternatively choose not to move from the elective exchange, to move to another exchange of the cluster or to move away from the cluster. The emerging equilibrium depends on the strength of external competitive forces, that is, the competitive threats that platforms outside the cluster are able to exert. Arguably, the interactions between global platforms and users may develop as follows:

a) When common shareholdings give rise to a cluster covering a wide macro-area (for instance, the US or the European Union), it would, eventually, gain a monopolistic power over capital flows within that area and over incoming flows (the listings coming from another economic space and the order flow coming from international traders).
b) Otherwise, the links at ownership level may involve exchanges or other trading platforms located in different jurisdictions or economic areas despite not gaining a monopolistic power over capital flows on each area.

Looking at the current morphology of the exchange industry, we may identify both models of clustering. As noted in section 3 of this chapter, the American macro-area has tended to develop around a cluster of exchanges (namely, NYSE Euronext, NASDAQ OMX and the three large derivatives markets) which occupy the same economic space. The convergence between platforms located in different economic areas, on the other hand, is only now emerging with reference to the links between Western exchanges and Arab markets. These links are a by-product of the battle for the control of the LSEG and involve the LSEG itself, the NASDAQ OMX Group and the Dubai marketplace.

The above-mentioned cases are, arguably, a challenge to regulators and supervisors in relation to the reputational standards which the exchanges commit to and the effective functioning of competition. Although operating as separate legal entities, exchanges or other platforms with relevant common shareholders may act in a way that undermines fair competition within the industry. Were common shareholders able to exploit their innate coordinating power they would realize a sort of implicit merger. Yet so far, regulators and antitrust authorities have been widely concerned only with explicit mergers among securities exchanges, and certain deals (the planned merger between Deutsche Börse and NYSE Euronext is a noteworthy example) have indeed been blocked for antitrust reasons.

Theoretically, the cluster model might stifle either price competition or product innovations which may benefit customers. Arguably, major concerns would arise from clustering in the same macro-area. In such a case both issuers and trading firms might not be able to improve their circumstances by listing or trading on another trading platform. By contrast, clustering across macro-areas would result in bridging different capital markets which may help to promote links among contiguous economies while preserving competition within each area.

Yet the cluster model might not always hamper the formation of a free capital market. Collusion on tariffs can be detected and sanctioned by applying the normal antitrust tools. Moreover, to the extent that international competition works efficiently, the threats coming from outside the cluster would sustain market discipline. In the recent past, improvements in IT caused barriers on the trading side to fall helping to create the exchange landscape we see today.[8] As for issuers, the evidence points to an effective functioning of competition in international listings. This is particularly true for large stocks or companies seeking a dual listing outside their national jurisdiction. The evidence is based on trends in IPOs in both the US and the London-based capital market. Following the adoption of the Sarbanes–Oxley Act in the US, statistical books registered a fall of listings on American exchanges and an increase of IPOs on the LSEG.

Within this framework, however, the focus of corporate governance is expected to leverage to a greater extent on the compliance function. It is anticipated that this will become the function that realizes the coordination between the microeconomic and macroeconomic levels of governance through the workings of market discipline. In that way, the effective functioning of market discipline (as a result of the competitive struggle among major international capital markets) would provide an incentive for strict compliance with regulations and, more generally, for establishing and maintaining prime monitoring standards. The incentives for product innovation are then, an interesting matter to analyse. Given that large exchanges operate as conglomerate organizations, effective coordination driven by common shareholders may lead to leverage on respective excellence in certain product lines and produce joint commercial offerings. Should competition be strong enough throughout the cluster, there would be an alignment of interests between issuers and trader on the one side and the controlling shareholder on the other, with the latter being constrained in seizing value.

7 Conclusions

Governance arrangements have been rapidly changing during the last few years as a result of the listing of major exchanges. In this chapter we have accounted for how the pattern of development in the exchange industry is pointing toward a cluster model where interrelations among exchanges at ownership level has certain ramifications for corporate governance.

The main point, in our view, is that the microeconomic approach is too narrow to properly describe exchange governance. Rather, the most relevant issue is related to non-contractual governance arrangements regulating incentives and relations among exchanges at industry level. Governance of networks is important for value creation since it can alter the entire structure of incentives and the competitive jostle among the cluster. Clustering may eventually dampen competition when external competitive threats are low. An interesting topic for further research is related to the macroeconomic impact of evolving ownership structures, but here we merely refer to the control of capital flows and the powers that a few large shareholders may exert on large pools of liquidity as a result of aggregations (both explicit and implicit) within the industry.

5
The Economics of Exchanges

1 Introduction

The consolidation process which has occurred during the last few years has changed the morphology of the exchange industry in a substantial way, and also effected a widespread transformation of the business model of major exchanges. We noted in Chapter 2 that business diversification is a strategic choice in an industry landscape where exchanges' revenues are under pressure. To this end, exchanges have attempted to counteract the adverse effects of both competition and economic downturns on trading revenues. The most striking example of this is the combination of cash market and derivatives market activities – something which constitutes the case for almost all of the exchanges involved in mergers, given the countercyclical nature of derivatives trading.

Business diversification has important ramifications, together with two dimensions which are related to the revenue function and value creation for securities exchanges. On the one hand, a diversified business model would reduce overall exposure of exchanges to business risk by reducing revenue (and earnings) volatility. The contribution to reducing *earnings at risk* and the cost of capital, in turn, would positively affect value creation for shareholders. Moreover, business diversification would improve synergies across business lines, primarily by exploiting cross-selling opportunities. In conjunction with cost savings, revenue synergies are powerful drivers of mergers across securities exchanges. Assuming a managerial perspective, multi-business exchanges entail a quite complex maximization problem in which projected synergies should explicitly be modelled.

We will examine value creation and measurement in the exchange industry in Chapter 6, but in this chapter we discuss sources of value for securities exchanges focusing, in particular, on industry-specific examples. The aim is to provide a general framework for contextualizing value creation in the exchange industry and bridging the economics of exchanges throughout the macroeconomic environment. This framework will be the base for defining the demand and supply side of exchanges and sketching out their maximization problem.

Finally, an important feature of the industry's structure is represented by the links between major exchanges at an ownership level. While such links may mirror the attempt of a few large institutional investors to gain control over capital flows they may alter the structure of incentives driving exchanges' behaviour. To the extent that the evolution in ownership structure may induce some form of coordination among exchanges, their maximization functions would be affected with each setting its own prices while taking into account the others' decisions.

This chapter is organized as follows. Section 2 provides a discussion of the relevant literature on the economics of exchanges. Section 3 moves in greater detail into the economics of exchanges by describing their objective function. Sections 4 and 5 discuss the revenue and cost functions, respectively, of exchanges. Section 6 discusses the maximization problem for platform operators under different assumptions regarding the industry structure and ownership models. Section 7 provides some concluding remarks.

2 Literature review

The bourgeoning strand of academic research in this field of the exchange industry has for a long time dealt with the economics of securities exchanges, although not in a systematic way. The corporatization (and subsequent listing) of major exchanges stimulated interest in various types of research on such topics as efficiency and economic performance. In this section we aim to provide a broad overview of the literature as it has been evolving.

The approaches that have been followed by commentators are quite different. In most cases efficiency or value creation are examined in relation to issues such as the comparative advantages of certain governance arrangements or the economic implications of mergers between exchanges. Other works build on the microeconomic approach, and describe the profit function and the maximization problem for exchanges. All these models, however, provide a stylized representation of the business of securities exchanges focusing on a narrow definition of the profit function.

Some theoretical works also present stylized models of exchanges' behaviour. Andersen (2005) provides a theoretical framework which jointly analyses the industry structure and exchange behaviour. In his stylized model the author assumes a monopolistic setting in which the exchange maximizes its profits. The outcomes depend on the network externalities at investor level (which are explicitly considered in the model) and the interaction among brokers and of the latter with the exchange. Andersen's study has several interesting implications for exchange management. First of all, it gauges implications for pricing. Moreover, by explicitly making endogenous the role of users (brokers) in driving pricing decisions Andersen elicits some considerations in regard to governance mechanisms, despite the governance argument not being properly addressed in the work. In its simplicity, however, the model does not take into account the double role that brokers (and other users) often play as platform users and owners, nor is the impact that this double role may have for the objective function of exchanges considered. In regard to an exchange's pricing policies, and notwithstanding the fact that it explicitly addresses the role of externalities, the model focuses on trading services only.

Another strand of the literature focuses on value creation following mergers and alliances and investigates how changing ownership impacts on value. The main contributions in the strategic literature comprise those of Arnold et al. (1999), Anand and Khanna (2000), Hasan and Malkamäki (2001), Dessein (2005), Gomes-Casseres et al. (2006) and Hasan et al. (2010).

Hasan and Malkamäki's study is relevant in that it represents one of the first attempts to gain an insight into both cost and revenues of stock exchanges. However, their study does not provide a formal representation of cost and revenue functions; rather, it empirically investigates the productivity of stock exchanges over time. The study models a relationship between inputs and outputs of stock exchanges with the specific purpose of investigating revenue and cost efficiency. Their findings suggest that investments in technology and competition both positively affect cost and revenue efficiency. In contrast, market size and quality seem to have a positive impact only on revenue efficiency.

Another body of research focuses on the distribution of value amongst stakeholders; the contributions in this field place to one side governance matters. The value and governance literature constitutes a stream of research in studies dealing with the exchange industry. The contributions within this field are, it must be said, quite heterogeneous, at least in relation to the notion of value, on which they all rely. However, they share the same goal, which is to investigate whether shifting governance from mutual structures to corporate structures is value enhancing[1] and determine how governance affects corporate strategies.

Some of the literature focuses on share performances while other aspects build on operative performances and, in particular, on accounting measures (ROE, return on assets (ROA) operating margins). The major contributions in this field (Aggarwal, 2002; Mendiola and O'Hara, 2004; Otchere, 2006) are mainly empirical, comparing the pre- and post-privatization operating performances of listed exchanges. These studies provide support to the intuitive view that self-listing leads to increases in profitability and efficiency.

Mendiola and O'Hara find that exchange privatization provides a value enhancing contribution. The authors analyse how corporate exchanges have performed, taking into account both accounting data and return performances. Provided that listed exchanges qualify as self-listed companies, the most obvious benchmark is the return of the exchange's underlying index. The authors then perform a comparison between the performances of newly listed exchanges and those of the IPOs on their own markets. Finally, they analyse the impact of economic factors on performance. According to their results, the equitization of securities exchanges is indeed value enhancing. Not only have the exchanges involved increased their performances after changing the governance structure they also tend to outperform the stocks listed on their index and the other IPOs in their home markets as well.

Aggarwal and Dahiya (2006) come to the same conclusion, accounting for the superiority of listed exchanges in terms of both operating and stock market performance compared with demutualized exchanges. Moreover, they expect the transformations that are reshaping the exchange industry to lead to the formation of one or two large exchanges dominating trading.

All of the above mentioned contributions agree on the positive impact of privatization on exchange performances, but notwithstanding this firm conclusion there remains an open question. Although improvements in performances may theoretically result from the adoption of a profit-oriented objective function, the effects of market discipline might play a role here as well. The issue has been recently investigated by Otchere and Oldford (2011). Their study examines changes in operating performances at each stage of the exchange governance continuum, focusing on ROE, ROA, net income margin and share performances. The sample consists of 12 mutually-owned exchanges, 12 demutualized, privately-owned exchanges and 21 listed exchanges, with the evidence showing that while publicly traded exchanges fare better than customer-owned exchanges, the comparison between *pre-* and *post-listing* operating performances does not show improvements in profitability. According to the authors these findings would imply that demutualization itself is sufficient for the owners to extract rents from the new, for-profit mandate.

Other research considers various measures of liquidity generally related to the value of trading. The focus here is on the links between ownership structures, developments in market activity and exchange value. The liquidity-based literature focuses, more precisely, on the relationships between trading values and revenues.

The most recent output in this field explores the rationale of consolidation in the industry in light of the improving effects on liquidity and revenues. The specific sources of value are identified in the liquidity pools managed by platform operators. Pownall et al. (2012) investigate the liquidity effects with reference to the formation of Euronext. After recognizing the benefits of stock exchange mergers in terms of deeper pools of liquidity and, consequently, increased listing and trading revenues, the authors focus on the structural changes of newly consolidated exchanges. We might mention in passing that they make an interesting contribution to the debate around market microstructure, studying the impact of market segmentation on liquidity. More precisely, they put under scrutiny the Euronext strategy of creating two market segments characterized by improved transparency and accounting standards. Their findings show that such segments succeed in attracting deeper liquidity and that these increases are to be ascribed to the pre-commitment of listed firms to comply with prime listing standards. As for exchanges' policies these results are highly relevant. The most interesting fact is that cross-border consolidation would not be per se sufficient to improve liquidity, without a single national regulator entitled to carry out effective monitoring and armed with enforcement powers. In this scenario, the improvement in liquidity would occur only in the presence of a mechanism credibly signalling stricter financial reporting and disclosure.

The literature focusing on share performances is less developed. Worthington and Higgs (2005) examine the distribution of share performances with reference to a limited sample of listed exchanges (Deutsche Börse, LSE, the Australian Exchange and the Singapore Exchange) as a basis for determining the market risk (the exchanges' beta). In doing so, they relate exchanges' share performances with those of the market index, and find that all the returns of the exchanges are positively skewed.

The existing literature, however, lacks a comprehensive framework that describes value drivers, addresses exchange behaviour and deals with performance measurement. What is lacking, in particular we feel, is an organic approach that examines the objective function of exchanges and other platforms and considers its influences on their behaviour. There remains, therefore, room to further expand the analysis in several directions. One potentially fruitful area of research pertains to a formal representation of the revenue function for exchanges and other trading systems, so as to capture the contribution of different value generating activities to the total revenues; this could also take into account the impact of cross-selling opportunities as well. A subsequent step forward from this would be to explicitly take into account the interactions of various business units in pricing exchange services. Here, the application of two-sided platform theory to the exchange industry is needed. The characterization of the maximization problem for platforms, therefore, requires formal representation of the cost function. One of the main limits of the prevailing models in the literature is that they provide only a stylized framework which does not specifically investigate either the form of the cost functions across exchanges or the impact of competitive policies on cost structures. Certain academic research does address the cost effectiveness issue as related to the consolidation process among exchanges, but the most relevant contributions in this field are mainly empirical and are devoted to testing whether or not expansions in the exchange industry are potentially able to spur scale and scope economies. We maintain that an in-depth understanding of the objective function of trading platforms and the formal representation of their behaviour requires a microeconomic approach with the aim of theoretically representing economies of scale and scope and their impact on the platform's profitability. We will endeavour to bridge the gap we have identified by describing in formal terms in this Chapter the objective function of exchanges and their maximizing behaviour alongside a model for measuring performances (Chapter 6).

3 What is the objective function of exchanges and other platforms?

Unlike the prevailing literature on the exchange industry, we aim in this section to represent the objective function of platforms, adopting a formal microeconomic model which focuses on the mutual interrelations between governance arrangements and corporate objectives.

In light of the particular morphology of the exchange industry (which we addressed in Chapter 2) and the prominent contributions prevailing in the literature, we aim to discuss the actual objective function of exchanges and other platform operators. It will be seen that we broadly refer to 'platform operators': in order to properly capture the features of the industry and the economic and financial implications of running markets we need to widen the focus outside the sphere of traditional securities exchanges and include all of the main actors playing the competitive game. This means that we cannot neglect those trading venues that although not having the status of regulated markets, nevertheless perform the same functions. As for their corporate structure, however, they do have some peculiarities which may distinguish them in terms of their objective functions and managerial incentives.

Corporate strategies partially differ across trading platforms, although their respective competitive space now tends to overlap due to increasing competition; competitive policies share some common features, in particular cross-border expansion and massive investments in IT. What really contributes to differentiate market operators is a certain heterogeneity of vested interests that are hindered by different ownership structures. In an era when exchanges were mutual organizations owned by their members, the objective function was quite simple to define, as it was designed to maximize their utility derived from using the trading system. With the opening of the capital base to outsiders the exchanges are supposed, theoretically, to endorse a variety of vested interests. The manner in which the objective function is actually changing is, however, not easy to understand.

It could be questioned as to whether changing ownership should be deemed to impact on exchanges' management and objective functions. After all, theoretically value creation should not be affected by a specific firm's governance arrangements. On the one hand, the viability of exchanges depends closely on the ability to provide value added services to their customers in terms of integrity of the market and fast and reliable trading platforms. On the other hand, management is expected to maximize value for shareholders. Albeit the aforementioned interests may appear to be conflicting, nevertheless there may be good reasons to expect a substantial convergence between them. In today's competitive environment the more the exchange (and, more generally, trading platforms) succeeds in efficiently meeting the demand of customers the greater would be its competitive advantage over peers. Although one may be sceptical about the proper functioning of market discipline, the peculiar ownership structures that currently prevail may give some support to this view. In the first instance, the firm decides upon value-maximizing strategies whilst corporate governance and ownership structure matters for distribution of value. Notwithstanding this, changing governance arrangements may well interfere with the incentives of the firm's management.

The problem with incentives in the exchange industry is subsequently related to risk taking and risk management. Risk management is directly related to the corporate structure, and refers to the monitoring of a variety of risks pertaining to securities exchanges; these range from risk of failure in market integrity to platform breakouts and systemic risks entailed by post-trading activities. It could be argued that the risk profile of platforms has increased significantly during the past few years, partly due to the changing governance of exchanges and partly because of increasing competition. Where members no longer hold the majority of stakes in exchanges they would not have an incentive to bear the responsibility and costs of ensuring market integrity. Advocates of market discipline may respond that increasing competition itself might guarantee a convergence of incentives. Moreover, to the extent that institutional ownership may not have the incentive to expropriate other stakeholders, we can expect that it could have incentives to monitor the integrity of capital markets.

Institutional investors, such as mutual funds and hedge funds, holding relevant stakes in securities exchanges are directly interested in the proper functioning of capital markets. Alternative platforms are backed by the major investment banks which also have a clear interest in enjoying efficient trading facilities.[2]

The nature of incentives in the exchange industry is complex as shareholders, in most cases, are directly involved in trading activity. Balancing the interest in an efficient, low-cost trading platform with the incentive for value creation is a peculiar feature of running securities markets.

In posing the problem of the objective function of platform operators we should recall the variety of governance arrangements now prevailing in the exchange industry, even though there is not always an obvious and intuitive correspondence between *formal* governance structure and objective function. Although the main exchanges are publicly owned listed companies, there are a few surviving entities that still preserve the legal status of non-profit mutual organizations. As clubs of intermediaries they are expected to pursue the maximization of value for their customers – which means lowering the costs of trading – rather than profit maximization. Demutualized exchanges, despite being incorporated as for-profit entities, continue to be mainly owned by intermediaries–customers. Here the objective function of the exchange is shaped by the equilibrium that is obtained by adjusting the interest of intermediaries–owners to a share of the exchange's profit with their interest in rising trading values and deepening liquidity. It is reasonable to assume the objective function of a demutualized exchange as being constrained by the need to keep trading costs as low as possible.

We should also assume that alternative platforms, at least those established and owned by large intermediaries, have an objective function which resembles that of demutualized exchanges. As pointed out in Chapter 2 the genesis of such platforms is often diverse, where intermediaries-owned platforms coexist with alternative platforms operated and managed by exchanges. There are no reasons to assume the former as having a different objective function to securities exchanges. Apart from having a different qualification for regulatory purposes (multilateral trading facilities rather than regulated markets, according to the language of European legislation) they have the same incentive structure as demutualized exchanges. The latter, by contrast, are part of the business model of the exchange operator and are, therefore, absorbed within its overall objective function.

The crucial point when examining the objective function of platform operators is with publicly owned listed exchanges. The fact that they pursue strategies targeted at value creation is coherent with the presence of outside owners. In the literature they are generally regarded as value maximizing entities. We do not think that there are any reasons to believe listed exchanges have an objective function other than that of profit maximization. However, the peculiar nature of outside shareholders requires us to delve in more detail into their objective function.

Institutional owners holding large stakes in listed exchanges are not merely shareholders: large mutual funds, private equities and other institutional investors have a clear interest in the proper functioning of the capital markets. Since they have the ability to directly access the trading system without the intermediation of brokers they should be expected to place a great deal of importance on matters such as the conditions and costs of access and the efficiency of the trading system.

The joint control of a few large institutional investors over a few trading platforms, which may resemble an informal coalition, can be seen as an attempt to exert some form of coordination among the controlled entities. Viewed from this perspective, institutional ownership arguably has the potential to constrain exchanges' profit maximization. A constrained profit maximization requires to treat the utility function of controlling institutional owners as endogenous into the profit function of the exchange. For example, institutional owners might promote the use of the pricing lever (the fee schedule and the rebate schemes) to retain or improve the liquidity pool of the exchange. They might also promote a strategic coordination of the pricing policies among the exchanges comprised in the cluster.

Differences in ownership structures, governance arrangements and industrial settings all have an affect on the utility function of exchanges, and introduce complexity into our analytical framework. We formalize our model by assuming an exchange competing on listing and cash trading. The technology is described by the isoquants combining the inputs employed by the trading venue, namely labour costs and the trading system (that we may express in terms of capital investments). In so doing, we characterize the inputs of the exchange's production as Hasan and Malkamäki (2001).[3]

For those platforms (that is, alternative trading systems) that do not perform a listing function, utility depends on the number of companies whose shares are admitted to trading. In light of the discussion in previous chapters we assume the inputs as being complements, provided that each side of the market takes an advantage from the exchange bringing the other side on board. These inputs are mutually essential in gaining the output. This implies that the isoquants may be described by a *Cobb–Douglas* function. Employing the notations we have just used we gain the following:

$$Tv = L^{\frac{L}{K}} \cdot K^{1-\frac{L}{K}}; U' > 0 \qquad [1]$$

where *Tv* is the output of the exchanges expressed as a trading value, *L* and *K* are the inputs (labour costs and capital expenses respectively) and *L/K* is the labour capital ratio.[4] The arguments of the function need an explanation. In our setting the platform operator works with technology employing labour and capital. Labour is mainly used in listing services whereas capital is needed in order to develop the trading platform. In the economics of platform operators *K* represents the capital investments for developing trading platforms. Investments in platforms are crucial to the competitiveness of trading venues. We may express volumes traded as a function of K: $TV = f(K)$ More precisely, we define the function as follows:

$$\frac{Tv}{K} = \beta^{e} \qquad [2]$$

where *Tv/K* is the average productivity of capital employed; we think of it as a measure of the efficiency of trading platforms. By differentiating the function above we have $f'(K)>0$ and $f''(K)<0$. Therefore, trading volumes increase with capital investments, but at a decreasing rate. This means that the marginal productivity of capital is decreasing. This standard assumption in microeconomic analysis may help us to give a solid theoretical grounding to the consolidation strategies in the exchange industry. We will develop these concepts in more detail throughout this chapter.

Accordingly, we define the *labour/capital* ratio as the proportion in which personnel costs enter the production function. The complement, therefore, expresses the weight of capital in the technology function, and we may think of it as the proxy of the rate at which the number of trading companies gives rise to trading volumes.

Given the production technology, the platform operator may increase its output (trading values) by increasing, in some proportion, both the labour employed and capital expenditures with the aim of improving the efficiency of the trading platform; an alternative would be to simply spend more on technology leaving labour unchanged.

At a managerial level the problem of platform operators is to decide upon the mix of capital endowment and labour and, ultimately, upon the optimal labour/capital ratio. The combination of the two inputs depends on the specific business model. A two-sided platform engaged both in listing and trading business would be expected to operate at a higher level of that ratio than that of a mono-business platform. When engaged only on the trading side of the exchange business the technology would mainly consist of capital investments, allowing operation at a lower level of the ratio.

Taking an evolutionary perspective on this, it is reasonable to assume trading platforms moving toward the lower levels of the labour/capital ratio. Increasing competition, driven by new venues and cross-border integration, leads to consistent investments in order to improve the platform's speed and efficiency and attract more traders. Labour costs, by contrast, are generally assumed to be fixed. Expansion in trading values may entail, to some extent, increases in labour where the exchange tries to target an increase in values traded by increasing the number of companies listed; this would, quite reasonably, imply the need to strengthen screening and monitoring functions. Taking such considerations in mind, we may identify two models of growth, the first relying on the exploitation of the growth potentials in primary markets, and the second occurring at the technological frontier when the platform has already caught the long-term growth rate in listings.

The first model identifies a demand-driven growth path, fuelled by a strong demand for equity financing coming from issuers. Actually, in such an environment there may be room to expand trading activity, as also in a situation in which the trading venue operates at low levels of investments in trading platforms and, arguably, poor efficiency.[5] The latter case reflects a scenario in which further increases in trading values, after exploiting demand opportunities, requires a move to a higher combination of trading values and capital expenditures. Figure 5.1 describes the growth opportunities in trading markets through primary market expansion and along the technological frontier.

We define the potential growth rate in primary markets as a function of economic growth, in accordance with the analysis in Chapter 2. As we noted, the penetration of capital markets in finance intermediation may be measured (on primary markets) by the incidence of new capital raised on GDP. An exchange has fast-growth opportunities up to the point where it reaches a normal *Ncr/GDP* ratio.[6] Figure 5.1 represents a three-dimensional space with a coordinate system described by the axis representing the *Ncr/GDP* ratio, the *trading values* (*Tv*) and the *capital endowment* (*K*).

The *OB* curve represents the *technological frontier*, which itself represents the trading opportunities for various levels of capital expenditures. We assume that the there is a long-term normal growth rate in trading volumes (*N* in Figure 5.1). At a first stage of development, (where we could assume a fast expansion in the demand of capital through capital markets) arguably characterized by low levels of capital investments,

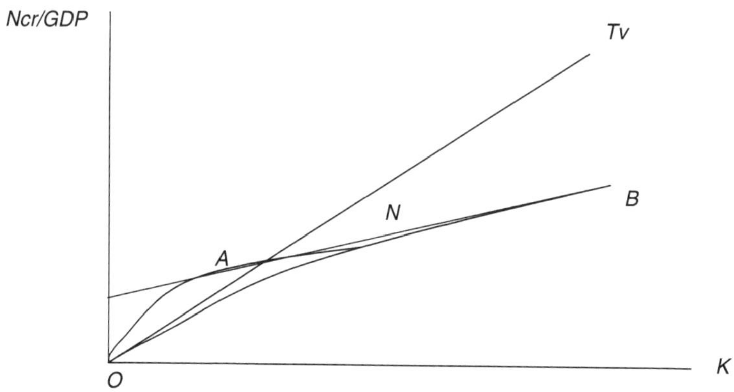

Figure 5.1 Growth opportunities in trading value

taking advantage of this long-term trend requires exchanges or other platforms to exploit their ability to catch the demand of issuers on both primary and secondary listings. The OA segment represents the growing opportunities reflected by increases in the *Ncr/GDP* ratio. At this stage, we expect investments in organizational arrangements (and, mainly, labour costs) to increase. Here the firm exploits latent growth opportunities by bridging the gap between the growth potentials embedded in one's country economic structure and the current penetration of the securities industry in the intermediation of funds. This model of growth could be deemed to characterize fast-growing economies, and also those countries whose financial system is undergoing structural changes with a growing importance of capital markets in providing equity financing. This demand-driven model of development may result in fast growth rates in trading values at an early stage, far beyond the natural expansion rate implied by the capital endowment.

Once these growth potentials are absorbed, the growth in trading values tends to approach a long-term growth rate. In order to sustain this rate of growth platform operators need to improve the efficiency of their trading platforms. The *AB* segment represents growth opportunities which are achievable only by moving along the technological frontier. Investments in capital endowments depend on the return that the operator expects to extract upon them. The productivity of capital is a function of the labour/capital ratio and may be expressed in terms of the output (the trading value). In particular, the average productivity of capital is defined as the ratio of the value traded on the capital endowment (*K*), whereas the inverse (the *K/Tv* ratio) defines the capital intensity. We may think of the capital intensity as the demand of capital, which is a function of the expected return of capital:

$$\frac{K}{Tv} = W(r) \qquad [3]$$

We define such a return as the expected return to shareholders. It corresponds then, to the cost of capital for the exchange. The inverse of the function above, $r = W^{-1}\left(\frac{K}{Tv}\right)$ expresses the expected return as a function of the demand of capital. Such a return increases with the demand for capital.

We then need to define the isocosts for platform operators and combine them with the isoquant map in order to derive the combination of inputs that would permit output to be obtained at lower costs. The proportion of capital and labour depends on the price of the two inputs. The optimal combination of inputs is located at the tangency between the isoquant curve and the lowest isocost.

In the short run, we may assume the endowment of capital to be fixed. By contrast, in the long run cost function may be characterized assuming both factors to be flexible. Therefore, for each level of output there is more than one efficient combination of the two factors.

Figure 5.2 describes the equilibrium. The first quadrant depicts the average productivity of capital (the 1/v curve) for each level of the *labour/capital* ratio. The *l* curve in the first quadrant represents the natural growth rate in the labour force.[7] Equilibrium is achieved at the point where the *l* curve is crossed by the *r* curve which, in our model, describes the expected return on capital employed.

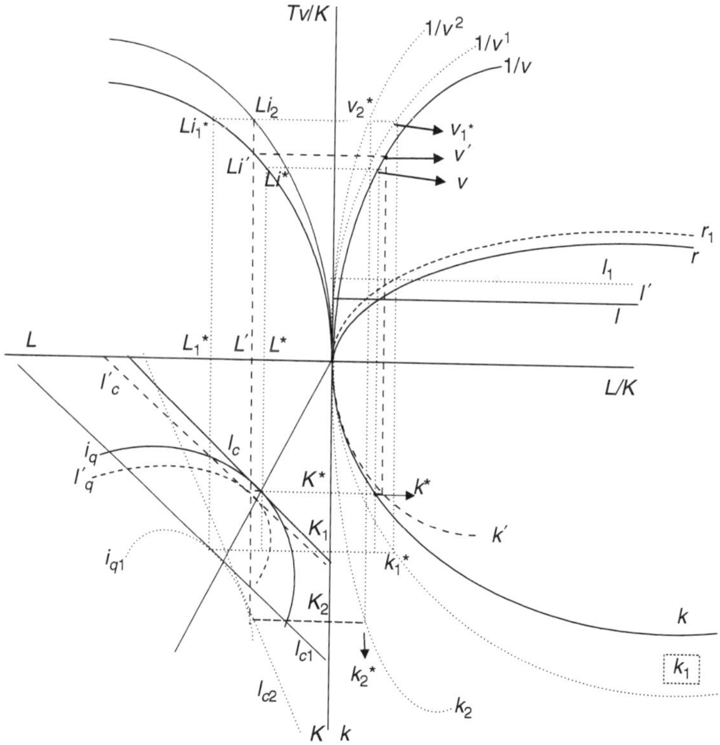

Figure 5.2 The technology function

The translation of the $1/v$ *curve* into the fourth quadrant describes the relationship between the average productivity of capital and labour costs. It could be seen as a proxy of labour productivity. The third quadrant represents the isocost and the isoquant curves, and describes the optimal choice of L and T. In our framework, therefore, each combination of the inputs on the isocost curve corresponds to a specified capital intensity. The second quadrant represents the marginal productivity of capital.

In the first instance, it is useful to represent a situation in which platform operators run a fixed-costs business. Costs do not change either with the output or with the combination of inputs; the isocost curve is, therefore, unique.

We assume the ownership structure as influencing the optimal choice for the combination of inputs. For those entities dominated by trading firms (usually mutual entities, but it could include demutualized exchanges as well, in the sense that there is no participation of outside shareholders) the utility of owners is a function of the trading costs. Their objective is the minimization of costs per unit of value traded defined by $\frac{C}{Tv}$. Building on Equation [1] we derive the minimization problem as follows:

$$\underset{Tv}{\min} \frac{C}{L^{\frac{L}{K}} \cdot K^{1-\frac{L}{K}}} \qquad [4]$$

Differentiating the value traded we obtain the target level ($\overline{Tv}$) of Tv which is coherent with the minimization of unit costs. Given the labour/capital ratio, Equation [1] returns the correspondent combination of L and K. The operator chooses, therefore, the combination (L^*,K^*) at the tangency of i_q to i_c for which the growth rate in labour costs equals the return on the capital endowment. Such a combination corresponds to the marginal productivity of capital labelled k^* on the k curve in the second quadrant and to the labour productivity Li^* on the Li curve (which relates the average productivity of capital to each level of labour) in the fourth quadrant.

Now suppose that the exchange seeks to exploit growth opportunities in trading values to strengthen its positioning in the competitive arena. As different platforms rub shoulders in the same markets and operate in the same business segments, the jostle for market share becomes ever more fierce. We assume the new target of production to be represented by the isoquant i_{q1}. It is reasonable to expect that the exchange will be required to increase the quantity of inputs employed: for example, due to the need to strengthen the organizational structure which may require new personnel, or because of the need to improve the efficiency of platforms.

The new equilibrium depends on the specifications for the labour/capital ratio. It is determined, in this setting, by the way in which such a ratio is affected by changes in both the output and the mix of labour and capital.[8] The equilibrium framework is substantially affected by increasing one or both of the inputs, as platforms move to higher cost frontiers.

As the ability to expand trading is largely dependent on the efficiency of platforms, all others factors – macroeconomic conditions – being equal, and assuming capital investments to be rigid in the short run, the output that can be immediately attained is represented by the isoquant i'_q. We assume labour to increase somewhat. Equilibrium is attained at the tangency with the isocost i'_c. The L/K ratio increases slightly and the l curve shifts to l'. The average productivity of capital shifts upward to v' on the $1/v$ curve (with K unchanged, the average productivity is now higher). The k curve shifts upward to k' implying that for each L/K ratio the marginal productivity of capital is lower.

In the long run, improvements in trading platforms (higher capital) may permit the output target to be reached. First of all, we consider a symmetric increase (with respect to the initial point) both in labour and capital. The exchange increases its labour force to cope with the increased needs of monitoring issuers and market integrity. Again, equilibrium is reached at the tangency point of the highest isoquant with the corresponding isocost curve. In our framework this could apply to a growing trading platform in which there still remains room for exploiting growth in trading values by expanding the number of listed companies.

Isoquants shift to the left (i_{q1}). The isocost curves move upward (see dotted i_{c1} curves in Figure 5.2). The new combination of capital and labour is attained at the (L_1*, K_1*). The technological shift due to new capital investments permits an increase in the average productivity of capital for each level of the L/K ratio. The curve shifts to $1/v^1$, and the average productivity of capital rises to v_1* and the labour intensity to Li_1*. Provided that the technology is efficient the k curve shifts downward. The increase in the marginal productivity of capital is higher than the increase in the average productivity. The new equilibrium implies a marginal productivity of capital k_1* on the curve k_1. The increase in demand for capital causes the expected return to rise (r_1 curve). Equilibrium is attained at the intersection of such a curve with the l curve that shifts to l_1.

However, we may imagine another equilibrium where the increasing in scale is labour saving (labour increases less than capital) and the platform operator may obtain the same output (i_{q1}) employing lower labour.

We assume the exchange to operate with a capital endowment K_2 and a labour force L' and obtain the same level of average productivity of capital as in the previous case ($v_2^* = v_1^*$). Equilibrium is attained at the tangency of the isocost curve, which moves to i_{c2}, with the isoquant i_{q1}. The *Li* curve moves upward (dotted line): the exchange obtains the same average productivity of capital with lower labour. The *L*/*K* ratio declines and the *k* curve moves also downward (the new technology is labour saving). Equilibrium is attained at the intersection of the r^1 curve with the l' curve which corresponds to a marginal productivity of capital k_2^*.

4 The revenue function

Delving in more detail into the economics of exchanges and other trading platforms we now discuss the main features of the revenue function. The issue is quite complex and interesting at the same time since it raises relevant concerns about the relationships with the financial industry. Of particular interest in this regard are the influences of the industry's structure for the pricing policies of exchanges.

Apart from the specific conceptualization of the revenue function, stock exchange behaviour is of paramount importance because it profoundly affects total revenues. The interplay between a variety of platform operators, in fact, poses the problem of how to react to the pricing decisions of competitors.

Broadly speaking, the revenue function depends on a wide array of macroeconomic influences, the business model and strategic choices made by platform operators. While the macroeconomic environment exerts quite obvious influences over revenues (which are mediated by the impact on market volumes), the strategic behaviour of contemporary platform operators is leading to radical changes in pricing schemes which are tied to the global competition for order flow. To be more precise, pricing structures are a concern for trading services, whereas in contrast, they appear to have less importance for listings, since issuer services have a lower incidence on exchanges' total revenues. In some exchanges they are quite marginal.

Formally, we may define revenues as a function of a vector of outputs. Considering the two typical outputs, listed companies and trading values, we have:

$$TV\left(GDP,\ yield, \frac{P}{E}\right) = (Tv_1, \ldots Tv_i, \ldots Tv_n)$$

$$L\left(GDP, yield, \frac{P}{E}\right) = (L_1, ...L_i, ...L_n)$$

where i denotes the output of *i-th* operator and the industries' aggregate output is $\sum_{i=1}^{n} Tv_i$ and $\sum_{i=1}^{n} L_i$. Given that outputs are strongly dependent on macroeconomic and financial variables, it is reasonable to assume that aggregate demand is exogenous to the exchanges. Each exchange cannot decide the quantity produced. Its share of aggregate output depends on its attractiveness in terms of prices and other attributes. The demand function is: $V_i = D(p_i)$ and $L_i = D(p_i)$. Since the exchange does not compete on quantities, it cannot strategically use quantities to limit the entry of new rivals. Broadly speaking, revenues are a function of the output of each business unit:

$$Rev = f(Sbu_1, ...Sbu_i, ...Sbu_n) \quad [5]$$

For the sake of concreteness, the *Sbus* in which platforms may be involved are listing services which we may label with *L*, cash trading services (T_C), derivatives trading services (T_D), post-trading services (*PT*), market and information services (*Info*) and *IT* services. While alternative platforms generally operate with narrow business models, traditional exchanges rely more on combinations of different services. In particular, *L* may be regarded as the number of companies listed, T_C as the trading value and T_D as the number of contracts traded. All these are measures of the output of each business unit. In general terms, the revenue function assumes the following form:

$$Rev = a + \beta_1 L + \beta_2 Tv + \beta_3 T_D + \beta_4 PT + \beta_5 info + \beta_6 IT \quad [6]$$

Given the relationships between market volumes, macroeconomic and financial variables, we may express total revenues as a function of global macroeconomic dynamics. We may therefore rewrite Equation [6] as follows:

$$Rev = a + \sum_{i=1}^{n} \beta_i Sbu_i(GDP, yield, P/E) \quad [7]$$

where Sbu_i is a vector of i outputs each expressed as functions of *GDP*, the yield curve and the price-to-earnings ratio. More precisely, we assume listing and trading business to be directly dependent on macroeconomic developments. Other business segments typically managed by exchanges may be deemed as a certain function *g(.)* of values traded.[9] Focusing, for the moment, on a two-business exchange managing listing and trading activities, herafter we provide a more precise specification of listing and trading revenues. We start with a specification of trading values:

$$TV = \alpha_1 + \beta_1 L \qquad [8]$$

We, therefore, express trading values as a function of the number of companies listed. According to Equation [8] the value of equity trading is dependent on the parameter β_1, which we can see as the marginal increase in trading value as L increases. We can think of this variable as dependent on the production technology, which we may identify with the cross-externalities that the exchange may develop across business units, and its reputation. Another factor which may impact on the coefficient is related to the type of companies listed in terms of size and liquidity. In light of the theory of network economies, we may expect high liquid companies to attract higher volumes of share trading.

The next step forward is to characterize in more detail both listing and trading revenues and the relationships among them. We model the cross-externalities between business units, and express listing services revenues as a linear relation with the number of companies listed:

$$L_{Rev}(GDP, P/E, yield) = \theta + \vartheta L \qquad [9]$$

We assume a linear function between cash trading revenues (CT_{Rev}) and trading values as well. Therefore, the function could be expressed as follows:

$$CT_{Rev}(GDP, P/E, yield) = \alpha_{TV} + \beta_{TV} TV \qquad [10]$$

In coherence with our approach to model the relations between different business units we express cash trading revenues as a function of the number of companies listed. Accordingly, we define the following linear relation between trading revenues and activity in primary markets:

$$CT_{Rev} = \alpha_L + \beta_L L \qquad [11]$$

A comment on variables θ, α_{TV} and α_L in these equations is needed. These items could be seen as fixed revenues. In particular, θ could be seen as annual fees owed to the exchange by listed exchanges whereas a_{TV} could reflect the fees paid by intermediaries for the right to use exchange platforms. In fact, the pricing schedules of exchanges set these fees in different ways. For example, security exchanges may adopt a flat trading fee based on volumes or, otherwise, a regressive pricing structure. Whatever the specific pricing schedule, such fees are variable. As for the other coefficients, a_L could be seen as a membership fee as θ and we may safely assume the two coefficients to be equal. On the other hand, β_L expresses the marginal increases in trading revenues as the number of companies listed increases. Viewed in that way, it bears conceptually the same meaning of β_1 and is dependent on the production technology and the exchange's reputation.

However, the magnitude of the two coefficients may be quite different. The increase in trading revenues as the number of companies listed increases may be subdued when the exchange faces high levels of competition. Our view is that it is reasonable to assume that β_1 and β_L will vary with volumes according to the levels of competition and the exchange's competitive (pricing) policies. For example, as competitive pressures rise, the exchange may be forced to cut fees in order to expand trading volumes. As a result the relation between trading values and revenues may substantially weaken. We will return later on to the business risk of losing revenues and its impact on the operative leverage when discussing the cost function.

For the moment we need to clarify how cross-network effects may spread across business units. According to the parameters laid down in previous discussions, network externalities between trading services and listing services may be defined in the following terms. A high sensitivity of TV on L may imply that competition on listing services is effective. If this were the case, lower marginal cash trading revenues for an increase in TV may reflect a strategic choice of the exchange to adopt aggressive pricing structures in order to deepen liquidity and attract listings. Moving the reasoning forward we now define a model for measuring cross-effects. Let us suppose that the exchange provides only cash trading services. Revenues would be defined according to Equation [10]. As the exchange adds listing services to its business model we may express cash trading revenues as follows:

$$CT_{rev}(L) = a_{TV} + \beta_{TV}(a_1 + \beta_1 L) \qquad [12]$$

We can say that cross-effects (on the cash trading side) are produced if marginal revenues are greater when combining listing and trading services compared with a mono-business exchange. Therefore, the following condition has to hold:

$$\frac{dCT_{Rev}(TV)}{dTV} < \frac{dCT_{Rev}(L)}{dL} \qquad [13]$$

which means $\beta_{TV} < \beta_1 \beta_{TV}$. We may see the right term as a measure of market power. It is clear that the greater β_1 the greater the stream of liquidity (measured by the value of equity trading) gained by the exchange. Arguably, the exchange may become the price setter as regards the pricing schedule for trades occurring on its platforms. This means that it may set β_{TV}.

The relationship between revenues and outputs is complex. Apart from the cyclical nature of total revenues, which we have already accounted for, of great concern are marginal revenues whose magnitude is strictly dependent on the pricing schemes adopted by exchanges. On the one hand, exchanges are generally used for differentiating their pricing structures, with segmentation criteria potentially embracing a variety of dimensions. Looking at the most common pricing policies, exchanges often segment traders according to the magnitude of their trading activity. The practice of applying different trading fees to traders falling in different brackets of transaction volumes is generally designated with the aim of privileging those market participants who contribute to overall market liquidity with greater activity. The design of the pricing schedule in such exchanges could vary. The exchange, for example, may charge a different flat fee to different types of participants (those engaged in, for example, high volume or low volume market trading) or a common pricing structure with regressive trading fees according to the volumes traded by participants. Often exchanges provide rebates to participants which are based on trading volumes as well, a point we will return to shortly.

Customer segmentation relies not only on the characteristics of groups of customers taken per se, but also on their true activity in the market. Therefore, we may say that an exchange's revenues are greatly dependent on customer behaviour. To this end, it is useful to recall that behaviours are influenced by exogenous factors related to the economic cycle and subjective attitudes, such as the perception and tolerance of risk.

Table 5.1 describes the relationships between revenues, GDP and the yield curve across the main listed exchanges. GDP has, generally, a positive impact on exchange revenues (with the exception of NYSE Euronext) with high significance levels. The relationship of the yield curve to revenues is, by contrast, more controversial.

Table 5.1 Exchange revenues and macroeconomic and financial variables

	Intercept	GDP	Yield curve	r-square
NASDAQ OMX	−2527.34	0.222 (***)	64.79 ('.')	0.7966
NYSE Euronext	1797.9	−0.0533 ('')	54.34 ('.')	0.2118
TMX	−788.59	0.00067 (***)	25.746 (***)	0.8789
LSEG	−1151.41	0.00352 (***)	23.2573(***)	0.6835
Deutsche Börse	−500.045	1.7138 (***)	−1277.22 ('')	0.4266
BME	−85.814	0.0006 (***)	−3.6564 ('')	0.5358

*** indicates significance at 0.1% level, '.' indicates significance at 5% level and '' indicates significance at 10% level.

Except for TMX and the LSEG the significance of the relationship is somewhat low and the sign of the relation is controversial as well.

When we focus on trading fees either in cash or derivatives markets the elasticity of revenues to increases in volumes depends on the particular pricing model that the platform adopts. As pointed out in Chapter 1, exchanges and other trading venues may design different pricing models based on transactions or access fees. In particular:

a) The transaction fees model is based on charging a flat fee on the transaction on the buyer or the seller of securities.
b) The access fees model is based on charging a fee to orders accessing the market. This model usually takes the form of the so-called maker–taker pricing scheme, which is based on a combination of fees and rebates. In particular, the liquidity provider (the maker side) is granted a rebate as compensation for bringing liquidity into the market, whereas the trader absorbing liquidity (the taker side) by trading against a standing order is charged an access fee. Actually, the model could be designed in an inverse way, that is, charging the maker and rewarding the taker (the so-called taker–maker model).[10]

Introduced first by Instinet in 1992, the maker–taker model was popular among equity markets and is now being introduced by many option markets. Although such a model may have a rationale and could be deemed to make economic sense, notwithstanding this it has been criticized in many ways. Advocates of the model maintain that it raises incentives for market makers to provide liquidity to the market by posting limit orders. According to this view, by rewarding *makers* it would benefit the entire market by raising overall liquidity and tightening spreads. Moreover, it would make sense to reward makers – since they bear the risks inherent to the orders they place – and charge the takers who, definitely, take benefits from the trade.

By contrast, critics focus on the agency problems between brokers and traders and the lack of transparency which is inherent in such a scheme (Angel, Harris and Spatt, 2010). More precisely, brokers might have the incentive to gather customers' orders to exchanges which reward them with a rebate,[11] irrespective of whether or not it quotes the best price. Therefore, a maker–taker structure would result in impaired best execution duties. Transparency concerns are, on the other hand, related to the obfuscation of the actual spreads sustained by traders. From an economic point of view true spreads are not just the difference between bid and ask quotations; rather they are net spreads comprehensive of either the access fee or the rebate. It would, therefore, be difficult for traders to properly recognize how much they are going to pay; notwithstanding, in a competitive market both takers and makers would not be better or worse off on average as an effect of the pricing structure.

The platform, by contrast, earns the difference between the access fee charged to takers and the rebate rewarded to makers. Compared to a transaction fee pricing schedule, there may not be substantial differences for platform earnings, provided that the net fee and the transaction fee are of similar magnitude, although a maker–taker model would imply externalities between the two sides of the transaction. Assuming a condition of equality between net fees in a maker–taker scheme and the transaction fee, it follows that the access fee that the taker charges is greater than that of the transaction fees.

However, how a maker–taker structure actually affects the economics of trading platforms is a difficult question to answer. The overall effect depends on the magnitude of both access fees and rebates, and the true incentives that the pricing structure exerts in attracting volumes.

Many exchanges have recently been resorting to a maker–taker model, especially in options markets. In 2007 NYSE Arca Options and the Boston Options Exchange abandoned the traditional transaction pricing model to adopt the new pricing model. Indeed, the change in pricing structure is for those exchanges nothing but part of a more complex reform of the market model, as it was accompanied by the introduction of a price–time priority rule in which orders are executed in the order they were received.[12] The combination of an appropriate price structure and the design of priority rules is an attempt to differentiate themselves from the largest options exchanges in order to gain market share. The maker–taker model was, therefore, expected to help smaller exchanges draw liquidity from the leading players who relied upon a traditional transaction pricing model that gave priority to public customers' orders over market maker orders for free.[13] Notwithstanding this development, not all exchanges adopting it actually gained benefits from a maker–taker model.

Therefore, what is happening in an increasingly competitive environment is a race to find the most suitable market model. Major transformations, in this regard, are those occurring within derivatives markets, a process which has implications for the exchange industry as a whole given the increasing convergence between cash and derivatives markets. Since it is useful for platforms to reward brokers and dealers for bringing liquidity (or absorbing it) to the market, the revenue function is shaped by the combination of trading fees and liquidity rebates, when these are foreseen.

5 The cost function

In Chapter 2 we presented the main cost items for securities exchanges, having built on WFE's aggregate data. Now we turn to a more detailed analysis of the cost function of platform operators. As we have previously noted, running a marketplace would imply relevant fixed costs linked with the implementation and development of platforms and the conduct of monitoring functions. Exchanges and other platforms, however, are generally accustomed to pay back rebates to customers.

Our purpose in this section is to model the cost function of exchanges and other trading platforms. Putting it more precisely, we aim to focus on the cost structure by modelling the effects of both fixed and variable costs. A relevant issue with costs is related to the responsiveness of costs to changes in trading volume. For the reasons that we have discussed it is reasonable to assume that the elasticity of costs to volumes traded is not constant. In an increasingly competitive framework, the impact on the elasticity of costs assumes prominent importance in affecting exchanges' behaviour and the competitive equilibrium.

In order to assess the magnitude of both fixed and variable costs we may express costs as a linear function of revenues. We start with a simple representation of the cost function employing the notations we have previously used; we then go on to refine the representation of costs. The following equation represents the cost function of platform operators.

$$C = a_c + \beta_c Rev \quad [14]$$

where the intercept a_c represents the magnitude of fixed costs and the coefficient β_c expresses the variables costs. For the reasons we have outlined, we expect a_{cT} to represent the greatest fraction of total costs.

Recalling the revenue function we presented in the previous section, we may express revenues as a function of volumes in both primary and secondary markets. Measuring the former in terms of number of companies listed and the latter in terms of value traded, and combining Equation [14] and Equation [6] we obtain the following relation of total costs as a function of market volumes.

$$C = a_C + \beta_c(a + \vartheta L + \beta_{Tv} Tv + \beta_O Oth) \quad [15]$$

where *Oth* represents the output on complementary activities. We pose $Oth = f(Tv) = \beta_{Oth} Tv$, where the output of complementary businesses is a function of trading values. Provided that the costs of jointly delivering trading and complementary services are lower than the supply of *stand-alone* services, a diversified business model spreads scope economies. The costs of engaging only on cash trading are $C = a_{cT} + \beta_c \beta_{Tv} Tv$. The costs of providing complementary services only are: $C = a_{cO} + \beta_{cO} \beta_O \beta_{Oth} Tv$.

The condition for producing scope economies is:

$$(C = a_{cT} + \beta_{cT} \beta_{Tv} Tv) + (C = a_{cO} + \beta_{cO} \beta_O \beta_{Oth} Tv) > (C = a_c + \beta_c \beta_{Tv} Tv + \beta_c \beta_O \beta_{Oth} Tv)^{14} \quad [16]$$

Scope economies might be the result of lower fixed costs when jointly supplying trading and complementary services (for example, economizing on personnel costs or fully exploiting the benefits of a single platform delivering a variety of services) or lower variable costs.

Costs, then, depend on the productive factors and the production technology employed by the platform operator. The precise specification of the cost function allows us to characterize the business of running a marketplace. To this end, the analysis should focus on relevant features of the business with reference to returns to scale and the relations between average and marginal costs.

The topic is of great importance since it is closely related to the presence of economies of scale in the exchange industry. Actually, among researchers the matter is somewhat controversial; empirical investigations have not come to a definitive solution yet. However, it seems fairly certain that the changing industry structure is substantially affecting the competitive behaviour of firms.

Following the well known 'structure-conduct-performance' paradigm exchanges react to shifts in the industry structure. In today's securities industry platform operators need to counteract increasing competitive pressures. The central point here is to gain operative efficiency by upgrading the capacity of processing trades and the data feed that originates from trades. The capital endowment is strategic within this context provided that it acts in two complementary ways. Accordingly, in our characterization of the cost function productive factors are dependent upon the structure of the exchange business, as featured by the combination of fixed costs, marginal costs and costs elasticity to trading volumes. Rather than being stable, we expect such a combination to vary with changes in the industry structure. We assume a long-run cost function where both factors are flexible and its specific features depend upon the assumptions regarding the returns to scale. Later on we develop in more detail this point.

Moreover, the competitive behaviour of platform operators (and, in particular, the consolidation process within the industry) exerts an effect on the endowment of productive factors[15] and can, at least to some extent, be expected to alter the features of the cost structure.

We suppose, in accordance with our previous analysis, the *i-th* operator providing n services employing two productive factors and, namely, capital and labour. Capital is employed in order to build up trading platforms and related IT solutions. Labour is employed to perform all the relevant monitoring functions on primary and secondary markets. Subsequently, we assume that the prices of capital and labour are θ_K and θ_l respectively, while the quantities are K and L. Next we assume that there are m_l issuers with securities listed and m_t intermediaries using the trading facilities provided by the platform operator. Both listed companies and intermediaries consume a fraction a_l and a_t of the monitoring services provided by the exchange respectively. We model the cost function assuming that the technology endowments permit the platform to admit an infinite number of companies and intermediaries. The increase in the number of companies listed and intermediaries do not require an upgrading of those endowments. This implies that the costs of using the trading facilities are fixed and we may assume it to amount to $a = a_l + a_t$.

The operator then, rewards traders with rebates which are the function of values traded. More precisely, we denote the marginal rebate as β_R, and assume the cost function not to be linear in trading values. Rather, in the model we are developing the elasticity of costs varies with trading values. This assumption may find justification in that the operator would be forced to raise the rebate rate in order to gain trading volumes in a competitive market. Therefore, the cost function may be rewritten as follows:

$$\theta_K K + \theta_l L = a + \beta_R \sum_t m_t \cdot Tv_t^h \qquad [17]$$

where h is the elasticity of costs to trading values, and Tv_t denotes the values traded by the *t-th* intermediary and, for simplicity, we assume it equals the average trading values.

By solving the equation for the endowment of physical capital, $\theta_K K$, we might obtain the amount of capital invested given the scale of the trading platform (expressed by values traded).

Building on the cost function we have just derived, we may define the average costs. Since we consider a two-business exchange, we split the total costs among the two outputs. Therefore, we derive the average costs by dividing the total fixed costs by the number of listed companies and the intermediaries and variable costs by the trading value. Formally:

$$A_C = \frac{a_l}{m_l} + \frac{a_t}{m_t} + \beta_R(h) \cdot \frac{\sum_t m_t}{TV} \cdot Tv_t^h \qquad [18]$$

where $m = m_l + m_t$.

Expressing costs as a function of values traded is useful in that it permits us to investigate scale economies in the exchange industry. With prevailing fixed costs, running markets would imply the possibility of exploiting scale economies. We should, therefore, expect the consolidation process taking place in the exchange industry to benefit major operators since it would involve the reduction of average costs.

In our model, h is crucial. Depending on the magnitude of h we obtain different configurations of the average costs. Assuming $h = 0$ and β_{Tv} are substantially low and eventually equal to zero – which implies a monopoly setting – the average costs will equal a/m. For $h:[0,1]$, the cost function is concave and the exchange operates with increasing returns to scale; both average and marginal costs, in such a setting, are decreasing. From an economic point of view, such a pattern could be justified in that as liquidity in secondary markets rise more traders are willing to access the market, pushing down average costs. We should expect that once the platform operator has built up the technological infrastructure and set up the organizational arrangements (mainly human resources), increases in output could be attained without increasing the factors of production. Should this be the case, the expansion of the production scale is a cost efficient solution (left panel in Figure 5.3).

It could be questioned whether competitive dynamics or other forces (for example, regulation) might substantially alter the production technology, causing returns to scale to decrease. Organizational factors might well result in decreasing returns to scale as complexity increases. Let us think, for example, of the complexities of overseeing transnational exchanges. Moreover, the rise of new rivals managing highly efficient trading platforms forces incumbents to devote large investments to update their technological endowments. Should the growth rate in trading values be somewhat constrained (for macroeconomic reasons, or perhaps intense competition), it would be possible for costs to increase more than the output.

Potential competition, then, works in so far as rivals adopt aggressive pricing schemes and succeed in capturing a certain fraction of liquidity. Reactivity of costs might, therefore, increase when the attempt to counteract fierce competition induces the exchange to grant higher rewards to liquidity providers, or should regulation impose some form of interlinking among market centres, causing marginal costs (β_{Tv} in our model) to increase.

Provided that the aforementioned factors produce diseconomies, we might expect the average costs curve to assume a U-shape. In that case average costs are a convex function; therefore, we may find a level of trading values which we label as Tv^* at which average costs reach a minimum before they start to rise (right panel in Figure 5.3).

Introducing transaction-based cost items would impact on marginal costs, but in the absence of such items we may assume that exchanges and other trading platforms operate with substantially low marginal costs. Moreover, it is reasonable to assume that platform operators are

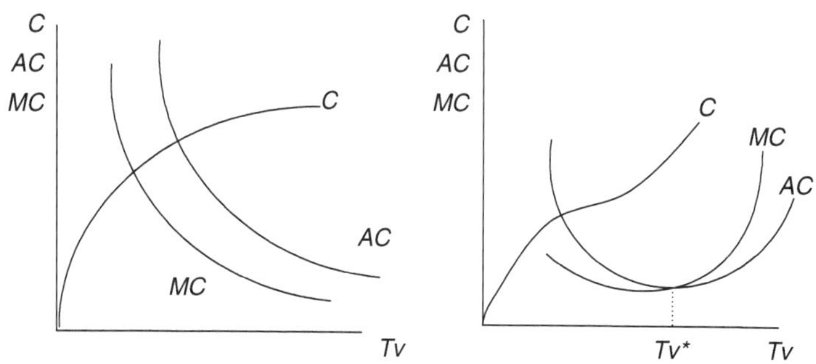

Figure 5.3 Total costs and average costs

substantially homogeneous with reference to marginal costs. Indeed, once the technical infrastructure has been set up, increases in values traded arguably do not cause costs to rise substantially, provided that the infrastructure is perfectly scalable. And with consolidation in the exchange industry continuing, alongside the harmonization of overall corporate functions, there should be a convergence in technological infrastructures, technical standards and protocols; therefore, the conditions of technical efficiency are expected to become even more homogeneous.[16]

The features of the average costs function would affect strategic decision making. Should the elasticity of costs to trading values be high, there should be a *Tv* threshold (*Tv**) which minimizes average costs. This implies that the cost function drives the optimal dimension of the platform operator. In that case, the operator chooses to expand values up to the point where it reaches the minimum average cost. Accordingly, and given the *Tv** threshold, the platform may derive the fraction, θ_K, to be invested in capital expenditures.

Consolidation strategies may be investigated in light of the aforementioned reasoning. In particular, the exchange will find it optimal to expand its scale beyond that threshold to the extent that increased dimensions would reinforce market power and thus dampen the elasticity of costs to trading volumes. It is, however, reasonable to suggest that economies of scale would become effective only for large trading volumes (Hasan and Malkamäki, 2001).

In Chapter 7, and building on the accounting data of the main listed exchanges, we estimate the cost function. We sample nine exchanges for the period from 2005 to 2011, considering quarterly accounting data.

It is, however, interesting to refine the analysis by splitting the cost function into its main constituents; we find the proportion of each cost item on total costs and then relate them with total revenues. The cost items on which we focus are personnel costs, IT costs, administrative expenses, depreciation and amortization, regulatory costs and liquidity rebates (which, in many exchanges' reports, are labelled as *costs of revenues*).

6 Objective function and profit maximization

After having analysed the supply and demand side in securities trading, we now turn to deal with the maximization problem for platform operators. We refer generally to platforms operators and not merely to securities exchanges, since this widened focus better captures the profitability of securities trading within the modern exchange industry. This is obviously true given the increasing importance of alternative platforms in the overall trading environment. Nevertheless, there is a more substantial reason for referring to platform operators in a broad sense which relates to the competitive policies of alternative platforms. It is widely acknowledged that such platforms succeed in diverting large flows of orders away from established exchanges due to their highly efficient trading platforms and their competitive fee schedules. At first sight it could be thought that they can support lower tariffs due to their more flexible business model and lower structure costs. Given the peculiar ownership structure of alternative platforms dominated by large intermediaries, however, we have good reasons for wondering if they really act in such a way to maximize profits.

We define the objective function of operators and model their behaviour under different assumptions over the industry structure and the ownership structure of operators. More precisely, given the nature of platform operators with reference to the relationships between owners and users, we may think of platform operators as entities whose behavioural models are shaped by different combinations of the prevailing industrial competitive paradigms and vested interests at company level.

Platforms are nowadays largely run by for-profit companies, although large differences still remain. Within this basic scenario varying competitive models and heterogeneous vested interests sharply affect the objective function of platform operators.

In principle, we may identify the following combinations of industry structure and ownership arrangements; we will address the theoretical ramifications of these models in more detail throughout this section:

a) A pure competitive industry with fully outside ownership.
b) A pure competitive industry with prevailing inside ownership.
c) An oligopolistic competition with fully outside ownership.
d) An oligopolistic competition with inside ownership.
e) An oligopolistic competition with informal coalitions.

In a perfectly competitive industry, the platform operator maximizes his profits acting as price-taker on both the listing and trading side. The ownership structure impacts on the constraints of profit maximization. Fully outside ownership implies that the behaviour of the operator is not constrained, whereas prevailing inside ownership would, arguably, constrain profit maximization to a certain maximum level of trading costs. Looking at the actual structure of the exchange industry, the pure competitive setting is not appropriate to describe the interaction among platform operators. Consolidation and links among platforms (both at trading and post-trading level) confer on large conglomerates a form of oligopolistic power.

Assuming an oligopolistic setting for the industry, exchanges are expected to have power in setting fees. However, the competitive jostle between large conglomerates and mounting competition from new rivals requires each player to take into account the reaction of competitors to its decisions.[17]

Even where the objective function of incorporated – and especially listed – exchanges is profit maximization, the ownership structure may still have an impact on the specific design of the function.

For platform operators largely owned by shareholders that are involved in trading activity (in other words members of the exchange or institutional investors) it is reasonable to assume that the objective function of the operator is profit maximization, subject to the constraint of the trading costs not exceeding a certain threshold. We think this is plausible given that shareholders do retain an interest in running as cheap a marketplace as possible.[18]

We start by considering a simple setting where the platform focuses on trading services, with no involvement in listing or other complementary businesses, and does not take into account competitors' reactions to its decisions. It sets trading fees that maximize profits subject to the constraint noted. We assume the value of share trading (the output) as the base to which to apply trading fees, in line with the fee schedules adopted by almost all exchanges. The operator bears fixed costs that we may refer to as the trading infrastructures. We assume that the operator also bears variable costs, which mainly include the rebates that it will eventually award to traders. The maximization problem, therefore, becomes as follows:

$$\underset{Tf}{max}\left[(T_f \cdot V)-(R_f \cdot V)-F\right] \qquad [19]$$

$$sub\ (T_f - R_f) \leq \overline{f}$$

where T_f are the trading fees, R_f denotes the rebates awarded to traders, V is the trading value and F denotes the fixed costs and is $\overline{f}$ is the maximum net trading costs acceptable for traders, defined as trading fees net of rebates. We may think of $\overline{f}$ as such level of net trading costs which is coherent with shareholders' profit maximization.

The problem of the operator, therefore, is to set the level of trading fees and rebates in such a way that it jointly maximizes the operator's profit and minimizes the overall costs sustained by customers.[19]

A more realistic methodological approach, however, requires consideration of interactions between platforms. The interaction between firms in the exchange industry may be described in light of a sequential games hypothesis with conjectural variations. In particular, such a setting seems to be appropriate, taking into account the nature of the relationships between traditional exchanges and new rivals. The latter (at least certainly large ECNs) succeed in capturing large flows of orders by adopting aggressive pricing schemes, the process forcing leaders to react. Ease of access, enhanced by technological innovations, makes the access of new rivals a credible threat.[20] Therefore, exchange leaders should take into account the behaviour of followers. On the other hand, a follower has some power to set its prices. We feel that the sequential games setting with homogeneous product is inappropriate here. Indeed, followers have the ability to somewhat differentiate their services through faster and innovative platforms or strategic routing services.

To start, we assume that there are n platform operators that operate with a cost function, which we may express as $C\ (M, Inf)$ where M denotes monitoring costs (both on listed companies and trading on the marketplace) and *Inf* denotes investments in infrastructures. We may deem these costs as being fixed. The operator bears then, variable costs as a function of trading volumes. In fact, variable costs may have a different nature; as previously noted, we may think of those costs as rebates awarded to brokers and label them as $C\ (TV)$. In such a case, the cost items are strictly dependent on the competitive policies of the exchange, with the pricing schemes being a manifestation of such policies. However, transaction-based costs may be connected to fees or other considerations that the exchange owes to other trading platforms when executing upon it the order received from a member.[21]

The maximization problem for the exchange is dependent on the assumptions made on the type of competition (quantities or prices) and the nature of the interaction among firms. Given the nature of the exchange industry, it is reasonable to assume the price as the strategic variable. In a simple setting, where platforms perform trading business only, the profit function would be:

$$\pi = [(T_f \cdot V) - (R_f + Ro_f) \cdot V - F] \qquad [20]$$

where T_f are the trading fees, R_f denotes the rebates to brokers, Ro_f denotes routing fees charged by other venues, V is the trading value and

F denotes the fixed costs. If we introduce the hypothesis of sequential games with conjectural variations, each trading venue assumes its pricing decisions affects those of its rivals. Assuming an exchange leader and a follower (we may think of it as an ECN), the former maximizes its profit conjecturing the reaction function of the follower ($T_{f2} = R_2(T_{f1})$) with a demand function $V_1 = D_1(T_{f1}, T_{f2})$. Therefore, the profit function for the leader becomes:

$$\pi_1 = T_{f1} \cdot D_1(T_{f1}, T_{f2}) - (R_{f1} + Ro_{f1}) \cdot D_1(T_{f1}, T_{f2}) - F_1 \qquad [21]$$

Denoting variable costs with C, the first order condition of the leader differentiating by T_f becomes:

$$\frac{\partial \pi_1(T_{f1}, T_{f2})}{\partial T_{f1}} = D_1(T_{f1}, T_{f2}) + \left(T_{f1} - \frac{\partial C_1}{\partial V_1}\right) \cdot \left[\frac{\partial D_1}{\partial T_{f1}} + \frac{\partial D_1}{\partial T_{f1}} \frac{\partial T_{f2}}{\partial T_{f1}}\right] = 0 \qquad [22]$$

where $\frac{\partial T_{f2}}{\partial T_{f1}} = cv_1$ is the price conjectural variation of exchange leader. In contrast, we assume the standard hypothesis of industrial organization models with conjectural variations that $cv_2 = 0$. Therefore, the follower sets its fees without conjecture and the leader will vary its price accordingly. The first order condition of the follower becomes:

$$\frac{\partial \pi_2(T_{f1}, T_{f2})}{\partial T_{f2}} = D_1(T_{f1}, T_{f2}) + \left(T_{f2} - \frac{\partial C_2}{\partial V_2}\right) \cdot \left[\frac{\partial D_2}{\partial T_{f2}}\right] = 0 \qquad [23]$$

Given T^*_{f1} and $T^*_{f2} = R(T^*_{f1})$ as the optimal strategies and assuming a quadratic cost function $a + \beta_{Tv} V_i^2$ and a linear demand function $V_i = a - bT_{fi} + cT_{fj}$, the first order condition for the leader becomes:

$$a + T^*_{f1}(c - 2b) + cT^*_{f2} + \beta_{Tv} V_1 \left(c \frac{\partial T_{f2}}{\partial T_{f1}} - b\right) = 0 \qquad [24]$$

and

$$T^*_{f1} = \frac{-\left[a + cT^*_{f2} + \beta_{Tv} V_1 \left(c \frac{\partial T^*_{f2}}{\partial T^*_{f1}} - b\right)\right]}{(c - 2b)}.$$

Solving by V_1 we obtain the production level (the trading value). Given that a large part of costs are fixed, the exchange should capture trading demand above a minimum threshold for recovering unit costs. Given that unit costs are $\overline{F_1} = \frac{F_1}{V_1}$, the minimum output level is

$V_1^* = \frac{F}{(T_{f1} - C_1)}$. Moreover, it represents the minimum scale in consolidation deals involving two or more exchange leaders in their market, facing increasing competition from new entrants.

Things change when we consider multi-business exchanges. For the sake of simplicity we consider an exchange managing listing and trading services, although our reasoning can be extended to a more general case of exchanges investing in diverse business areas. According to the two-sided platforms theory, the value that customers receive on one side depends on the number of customers (and their level of consumption) on the other side (indirect externalities). Therefore, the profit function is affected by two types of effects, one deriving from external competition and the other related to the intra-exchange relations between the two sides (elasticity of demand on both sides and indirect network effects). For a two-business exchange managing listing and trading business the demand function on each side can be expressed as $V_i = D_i(T_{fi}, T_{fj}, L_i)$ and $L_i = D_i(L_{fi}, L_{fj}, V_i)$, where V_i and L_i are the trading values and the number of listed companies for platform i and T_{fi}, T_{fj}, L_{fi}, and L_{fj} are the trading and listing fees charged by platform i and j respectively. The profit function for platform i becomes:

$$\begin{aligned} \pi_i = {} & T_{fi} \cdot D_{Ti}(T_{fi}, T_{fj}, L_i) + L_{fi} \cdot D_{Li}(L_{fi}, L_{fj}, V_i) - C \cdot D_{Ti}(T_{fi}, T_{fj}, L_i) \\ & - C \cdot D_{Li}(L_{fj}, L_{fi}, V_i) - F \end{aligned} \qquad [25]$$

Profit maximization requires determining the first order condition differentiating by the trading and listing fees respectively. The system becomes as follows:

$$\begin{cases} \frac{\partial \pi_i}{\partial T_{fi}} = D_{Ti} + (T_{fi} - C)\left[\frac{\partial D_T}{\partial T_{fi}} + \frac{\partial D_T}{\partial T_{fj}}\frac{\partial T_{fj}}{\partial T_{fi}} + \frac{\partial D_T}{\partial L_i}\frac{\partial T_{Li}}{\partial T_{fi}}\right] + (L_{fi} - C)\left[\frac{\partial D_L}{\partial V_i}\frac{\partial V_T}{\partial T_{fi}} + \frac{\partial D_L}{\partial L_{fi}}\frac{\partial L_{fi}}{\partial T_{fi}} + \frac{\partial D_L}{\partial T_{fj}}\frac{\partial L_{fj}}{\partial T_{fi}}\right] \\ \frac{\partial \pi_i}{\partial L_{fi}} = D_{Li} + (L_{fi} - C)\left[\frac{\partial DL}{\partial L_{fi}} + \frac{\partial D_L}{\partial T_{fj}}\frac{\partial L_{fj}}{\partial L_{fi}} + \frac{\partial D_L}{\partial V_i}\frac{\partial V_i}{\partial L_{fi}}\right] + (T_{fi} - C)\left[\frac{\partial D_T}{\partial T_{fi}}\frac{\partial T_{fi}}{\partial L_{fi}} + \frac{\partial D_T}{\partial L_{fj}}\frac{\partial T_{fj}}{\partial T_{fi}} + \frac{\partial D_T}{\partial T_i}\frac{\partial L_i}{\partial T_{fi}}\right] \end{cases}$$

[26]

Pricing on both sides is influenced by different forces, apart from the reaction function of the rival. Focusing on the trading side, the fees that the *i-th* platform charge depends on:

a) The conjectures on the reaction function of platform *j* on both sides.[22]
b) The strengths of the externalities connecting the two groups of participants (listed companies and traders) within the platform.[23]

c) The cross-effects between two sides across exchanges, that is, the elasticity of trading values for *i-th* platform with respect to listing fees of *j-th* platform, and the elasticity of listings for *i-th* platform with respect to trading fees of platform *j-th*.[24]

The first order conditions above elicit some considerations related to the ability of the exchange to differentiate its products and services and to build up its market power. Despite the importance of scale economies in the exchange industry, this type of barrier hardly prevents the entrance of new rivals in today's exchange industry. Neither do we think that exchanges would be able to exclude rivals by setting a limit price, as in the limit-pricing models (Bain, 1956; Sylos-Labini, 1962; Modigliani, 1958). Rather, platform operators may try to retain order flow by differentiating themselves in the eyes of their customers.

Differentiation is primarily attainable by providing different kinds of services or addressing different needs. Cross-network externalities have the potential to differentiate the exchange among its peers as well. In these circumstances, the differentiating factor is the liquidity advantage of large pools. Obviously, such pools do not shield exchanges from competition at all;[25] notwithstanding the competitive arena being the same, the greater the cross-externalities effect the greater the retention capabilities of platform operators. Arguably, in such a case one might imagine that the conjectural variations will fade away.

As the operator moves towards a diversified business model – as is the case for most listed exchanges – the maximization function becomes more complex since it explicitly takes into consideration all the cross-selling opportunities across different business lines. Indeed it is the case that the possibility of exploiting cross-selling opportunities is one of the main reasons driving exchanges to merge. The wider the business model of the operator, the more difficult it becomes to model cross-selling opportunities, as they would in turn link together complex relationships and a wide array of business lines.[26]

Some interesting conclusions may be drawn from the aggregations between platform operators, both formal (mergers) or informal (clusters of exchanges). In particular, a peculiar ownership structure, with a model of common ownership, is emerging. It appears, therefore, reasonable to assume that some form of coordination between platforms is occurring.

By consolidating profits, such aggregations result in an internalization of cross-externalities among the exchanges in the cluster. In that sense, each exchange (or other platform) forming the group constitutes a single access point to an agglomerate, which from an economic perspective can be regarded as a unique entity.

In such a setting, each exchange is an access node to the cluster. Assuming the controlling shareholders as being interested in the consolidated profit, the relevant cross-effects are, therefore, those between each node and competitors outside the cluster. Should the cross-effects between a specific exchange in the cluster and outside competitors be weak, strategic pricing becomes feasible. In such a case, one might expect the cluster to raise fees where the cross-effects with outside platforms are low and adopt an aggressive pricing policy at those nodes where external cross-effects are higher.

7 Conclusions

In this chapter we have provided a general framework for contextualizing value creation in the exchange industry. We have defined, in particular, the objective function and the production technology of platform operators, and have derived a microeconomic model which describes the demand for capital and labour at different levels of output. Our model may be useful for driving managerial decisions regarding the scale of production and the allocation of productive factors in a rapidly changing environment. Put succinctly, changes in the industry structure and mounting competition may alter the conditions of doing business (the cost structure, the technological paradigms) and, therefore, heavily impact on strategic choices.

Building on this framework we have characterized the cost and revenue functions of exchanges and other platforms, which is the base for describing the demand and supply side. Our analysis provides an insight into the maximization problem in light of the developments occurring in the exchange industry, developments that we have accounted for in detail in previous chapters. The institutionalization of ownership arguably has an impact on the incentives driving strategic decision making, whilst the speeding up of the consolidation process has led to the rise of large conglomerates. The global securities industry is, therefore, generally characterized by mounting competition between large conglomerates and new rivals. The aforementioned developments also affect the interaction among players. In turn, this requires us to delve in more detail into the maximization problem of exchanges, explicitly considering the externalities connecting different groups of participants within each platform, the conjectures on the reaction function of the rivals and the cross-effects between different types of customers across exchanges. In this regard, structural changes in the morphology of the industry are expected to widely affect the elasticity of each output to changes in listing and trading fees charged by the other platforms.

6
A Risk-Adjusted Model for Peformance Measurement

1 Introduction

This chapter outlines the foundations of a risk-adjusted performance (RAP) measure for calibrating performance in the exchange industry. As previously noted, it has only been with the demutualization and listing of securities exchanges that the emerging *firm view* has elicited renewed attention with regard to performance measurement in the industry. However, both academic researchers and industry practitioners have so far only focused on standard measures of operative performances such as *return on equity* (or the *return on tangible equity*) or the *return on assets* (ROE and ROA, respectively).

By contrast, the idea of measuring performance taking explicitly into account risks has been neglected. The role of capital, in particular, has not been exhaustively investigated. During the years immediately preceding the financial crisis there was rising optimism on the prospects of the industry and, in particular, with regard to the benefits of the consolidation process. Such optimism was mirrored in the sharp upward movements in exchanges' stock prices. In comparison, the perception of risks was subdued. The risks associated with growing intangibles for exchanges expanding through sizeable acquisitions are particularly relevant to our analysis, as sharp declines in revenues may give rise to significant impairments. In an environment of growing revenues and margins this risk was neglected.

Since the beginning of the financial crisis the profitability of the industry has sharply declined. However, declines in performances do not simply reflect the mere contingencies of the crisis. Rather, the compression of profits is structural and it is to be attributed to increasing competition within the industry. We may note in passing, though, that the crisis could create new opportunities for exchanges. This suggests that refining the entire framework of performance measurement by introducing the risk dimension would be useful. The area of capital management should be expected to become of paramount importance within the strategic decision-making process of exchanges.

The chapter will develop as follows. In section 2 we provide the rationale for a RAP approach for measuring performances in the industry, outlining, in particular, the purposes it may serve. Then, section 3, we define the basic constituents of a measure of operative performance. Here, in particular, the role of capital for platform operators will be discussed. In section 4 the main risks for trading venues, both at corporate and Strategic Business Unit (SBU) level, are discussed, and in section 5 we define a model for measuring the cost of capital. The purpose is to build on the peculiar features of exchanges and other venues for identifying the determinants of the cost of capital. Given the multi-business architecture of modern exchanges, which, arguably, are exposed to different risks, we discuss the cost-of-capital issue with reference to different business units. Finally, in section 6 we set down the basic RAP-measure framework. Section 7 concludes.

2 The conceptual framework

In light of the most recent transformations in the securities and exchange industry, a RAP approach for measuring performances may find plenty of practical applications which resemble those commonly adopted in other sectors of the financial industry, especially the banking and insurance sectors.

Nowadays, most of the world's largest financial institutions have adopted highly sophisticated risk-management systems for managing the risk-return trade-off related to their investments. The use of risk-adjusted metrics in financial institutions falls within capital management processes. It is, then, a matter of fact that the regulators themselves stimulate financial institutions to resort to capital allocation policies.[1]

The securities industry regulations do not lay down a minimum capital requirement as for banks and insurance companies, if we except certain segments of the industry (post-trading entities, for example) which may perform banking activities and, therefore, fall within the capital regulation framework. Notwithstanding this, managing uncertainty requires an efficient and comprehensive framework for capital management. Such a framework should consist in a balanced set of targets (for performances) and limits, conceived for reducing the risk exposure to earnings volatility, which is particularly compelling in light of increasing competitive strains. Rather than managing credit risks platform operators are mainly concerned with the earnings at risk implied by their business model.

Table 6.1 describes the framework by clarifying the rationale of both targets and limits with reference to each driver of performance. To lay down the framework, the profitability of platform operators is driven by the combination of three forces, which we may label as *strategy, risk management* and *corporate governance*.

Within this framework strategic decision making and corporate governance are the areas that mainly may benefit from an established and formalized process of measuring risk-adjusted performances. The corporate processes involved in these areas have a relevant impact on economic performances.

Corporate strategy identifies a far-reaching process encompassing the choice of business model and, eventually, expansion strategies via mergers, joint ventures or informal alliances. In every case, the exchange faces a typical *capital budgeting* problem where the choice among a *bouquet* of potential investment projects is to be made according to a minimum threshold for the return and the risk tolerance defined by the management with the ultimate goal of supporting value creation policies. The path, in this regard, has already been traced and is embodied in an array of theoretical contributions dealing with the relationship between value theory and RAP value metrics.

Risk management and corporate governance are strictly related and are responsible for creating value by properly controlling exposure to risks, setting limits to risk taking, checking deviations from those limits

Table 6.1 The framework

	Drivers of performance		
	Strategy	**Risk management**	**Corporate governance**
Targets of performance	Capital budgeting, expansion strategies (mergers, alliances)	Pricing risk according to the targets	Remuneration policies, bonuses
Limits to risk taking	Defining the acceptable level of risk	Controlling risk taking at SBU level, reporting, risk management	Reporting to top management

and defining an efficient and long-term oriented system of incentives in order to preserve the viability of the business.

The corporate strategy is of paramount importance in an environment of increasing competition, and encompasses a wide array of decisions spanning several dimensions such as *horizontal* and *vertical integration*, *geographical expansion* and alliances, both formal (*mergers*, *joint ventures*) or informal. All of these dimensions qualify the business diversification strategies of exchanges and elicit considerations on the contribution to overall economic performances. When deciding upon the addition of a new product line or business unit the management faces a typical portfolio problem. It is worth emphasizing that the firm view prompts consideration of the exchange (but analogous considerations may apply for other trading platforms) as a portfolio of different business activities. The portfolio perspective is quite common in the management of exchanges. Business plans and periodic reports obviously dwell on the contribution of each business unit to overall corporate revenues. Moreover, the breakdown of the business model into its constituent business units is functional to the representation of the competitive positioning of the exchange in each area.

According to the theory, business diversification (on product lines and at a market level) should help exchanges and other trading platforms to stabilize revenues and margins. The cyclicality of trading activity which we documented in Chapter 2 is supportive of strategies targeted to smooth the impact of macroeconomic developments on the economic figures. As noted, such strategies generally lead to the integration of derivatives trading with cash markets, assuming that derivatives trading is less dependent on the cycle if not countercyclical at all.

Standard corporate finance theory has it that undergoing an investment project entails a capital budgeting problem targeted to select those projects that better contribute to value creation. However, a *lego approach* to exchange business requires an in-depth analysis of the contribution of each business unit to the overall level of profitability. Therefore, the traditional segment reporting is not completely satisfactory. In fact, while showing the revenues and margins attributable to each business unit it fails to support the strategic decision-making process since it does not measure their contributions to the expected yield of the portfolio.

Capital-based performance metrics are a key tool for business management in financial institutions; they may serve a variety of purposes (Zaik et al., 1996), including the management of corporate leverage in order to find a minimizing-cost-of-funding financial structure and risk–return assessment. The goal of optimizing the capital structure addresses the trade-offs between the benefits of debt (the tax shield connected to tax-deducible interests) and the risks of financial distress, and helps optimize the proportion of equity on total assets. The risk–return trade-off requires that attention be paid to the relation between risk exposure and the performance of different business lines or products across the financial institution. The ultimate goal is to help the management in strategic decision making, remuneration policies and the pricing of products. More synthetically, therefore, the ultimate goal is to support the broad value creation strategies.

The aforementioned approach allows us to treat a financial institution as a portfolio of business units in order to estimate the contribution of each unit to the overall portfolio risk, measure the corresponding required capital at corporate level and allocate it to the different units (Zaik et al., 1996). Capital assignment is thought of here as part of a system of computing a risk-adjusted rate of return for different businesses with the aim of measuring their contribution to value creation. An interesting extension of the problem relates to performance measurement for corporate investments in the presence of growth opportunities. While standard measures of performance have been extended to address this specific topic (Hirst et al., 2008), the same has not been done for risk-adjusted performance measures.

Theoretically, capital budgeting decisions could be assumed using standard models (such as those based on the *net present value* (NPV)). These models, however, fail to take into account the effects of earnings volatility, which, for risk-adverse institutions, is a compelling issue. In the literature it has been pointed out (Froot and Stein, 1998) that the volatility of earnings bears relevant managerial implications with reference to several profiles, apart from capital allocation. In particular, capital structure and earnings risk hedging require a proper understanding of the contribution of each business unit to the aggregate earnings volatility.

The study by Froot and Stein is relevant in that it provides solid theoretical ground for the adoption of risk-adjusted performance measures for capital budgeting and risk management purposes, as opposed to standard corporate finance approaches. Provided that the Modigliani–Miller theorem holds and risks can be traded without friction in the market, caring about risk management becomes a matter of little consequence. By contrast, the authors set down a framework in which not all risks are tradable in the market and where risk-management concerns have to be factored within capital budgeting techniques. Although their model may be applied to any company facing risks associated with illiquid assets, it is mainly focused on financial institutions and, in particular, on banking loans.

The basic idea that lies behind Froot and Stein's model[2] is that there are increasing costs to rising external funds. Therefore, the costs associated with rebuilding capital encourage banks to behave in a risk-averse manner. Building on a two-period model and assuming convex costs of recapitalization they derive a hurdle rate for investments. In particular, by using a two-factor pricing model they demonstrate that a hurdle rate such as this derives from two distinct sources of risk: the covariance of the return with the market and with the risks of the existing portfolio.

In banking literature the costs associated with finding external funds (in particular, non-deposit external finance) are widely recognized and modelled (see, among others, Kashyap and Stein, 1994; Froot and Stein, 1995; Greenwald, Levinson and Stiglitz, 1991). The same concerns, however, are common to other financial institutions. Financial exchanges had long neglected the costs of raising finance for a variety of reasons, mainly stemming from their traditional governance models and the prevailing industry structure. Mutual exchanges operating as natural monopolies were not concerned about competition, innovation and growth opportunities. With the demutualization of securities exchanges the structure of incentives remained largely unchanged, at least for those exchanges that continued to be dominated by trading intermediaries and substantially shielded from competition. In fact, the need to raise new external capital was not perceived as the main reason leading exchanges to demutualize. It is only with the beginning of the consolidation process that expansion financing becomes a concern for exchanges.

The consolidation process involving major exchanges has, at least in some cases, led to substantial increases in the leverage, introducing new constraints in exchange management. Within this framework, the mandate of an adequate capital management strategy goes far beyond the goal of preserving a sound financial structure. In fact, it should be conceived as a means to provide the exchange with the endowments which are indispensable for exploiting growth opportunities and supporting value creation policies.

The growth options embedded in expansion strategies and business combinations have an impact on value creation. Indeed, the risks associated with them might heavily impact on the viability of the business and, ultimately, on the exchange capital base. Shocks in the industry may be associated with such options losing their value, and result in deep depreciations of goodwill in such a way as to compromise the viability of the business. Should such a scenario take place, it would be very difficult for the platform operator to rebuild the capital base given, in particular, the value associated with its reputational capital. An operator behaving in a risk-adverse fashion should hedge, or otherwise manage risks. Large exchanges embody a bouquet of heterogeneous risks. While standard market risks (such as interest rate risk and currency risks) can be easily traded and transferred through capital markets, business risks are more difficult to hedge.

As we discuss in more detail throughout this chapter (see in particular sections 4, 5 and 6), business risks are strictly related to the projects in which the exchange invests. Although the exchange may well disinvest by selling certain assets or entire business units to other players, their degree of liquidity may depend on their intrinsic characteristics and the specific design of the buyer's business model. At least to some extent, exchanges and other platforms make corporate-specific investments. The specific contribution of each business line to value creation depends on the ability to effectively exploit all the potential synergies when combining it with the other activities in the portfolio. It implies that such synergies might not be easily replicated within another organization, impairing, therefore, the ability to transfer risk in the market.

Of course, events of risk may cause exchanges' earnings to drop, thereby adversely affecting shareholders value. While business diversification may help to flatten earnings volatility, it brings new risks within the exchange. What emerges, therefore, is the need to properly measure performances and risks across different business units. Assuming a managerial perspective, a risk-based framework would be useful for managers seeking to assess the contribution of each unit to enterprise value and drive the strategic decision-making process; it might also help them to design an efficient system of performance based rewards.

A complex but interesting issue is, then, related to the construction of an appropriate risk-adjusted performance measure and its relations to value creation for shareholders. A widely used metric is the *risk adjusted return on capital* (RAROC). Despite its conceptual simplicity, it requires the adoption of a coherent measure of risk, which might have consequences for the significance of the measure. RAROC metrics are generally grounded on a *value at risk* (VAR) measure which, despite being widely adopted, is subject to criticism. The drawback of a VAR measure is that it violates the axiom of sub-additivity and, therefore, fails to recognize the benefits of diversification within a combined portfolio.[3] The viability of such a measure is dependent on the specific application as implied in Milne and Onorato (2012).[4]

As we have noted, major exchanges have been transformed into large conglomerates performing a great variety of activities, mainly through mergers and alliances. Business diversification finds its rationale in the need to flatten revenue volatility. Specific to the exchange industry are the cross-selling opportunities from combining cash trading with related activities; in fact in many combination agreements the possible exploitation of relevant cross-selling opportunities was one of the determinants of the merger.

We should add that the specific nature of risks has an impact on the process of measuring them and on capital allocation as well. While in credit risk the distribution of losses is decidedly asymmetric, trading platforms are mainly subject to market risks for which we may assume a normal distribution. In many exchanges intangibles (and, in particular, goodwill) represent a relevant part of assets, the value of which is strictly dependent on the ability of the exchange to generate earnings. Financial investments (see the discussion in section 3) generally have a lower incidence.

The capital allocation across business units is primarily targeted to back the exchange against the volatility of earnings. The most appropriate metric should be, therefore, an *earning at risk measure*, which should be constructed in order to take into account the effects of synergies implied by business combinations.

Despite its wide diffusion among banks and practitioners, the use of RAROC measures suffers from drawbacks and it has stimulated considerable debate in academic circles. The most interesting issue, apart from an intellectual curiosity about the relations between such measures and traditional financial theory, pertains to its effectiveness for value creation purposes. This is a point which has recently been addressed by prominent research.

The main criticism that has been moved of the RAROC is grounded on the basic argument that representing both contribution to default risk and required shareholders return at the same time may entail substantial losses of value (Milne and Onorato, 2010).[5] This implies that these two aspects of risk should be distinguished and treated separately.

Another problem arises with setting a RAROC hurdle rate for strategic decision making. Putting it in simple terms, performance measurement in financial institutions is based on an economic value added (EVA) measure for calculating the contribution of each project to the value added for shareholders. More precisely, the approach of financial institutions to value creation is based on a margin measure of the RAROC over the hurdle rate.

$$V = (RAROC - \overline{RAROC}) \cdot Risk\ capital$$

where $\overline{RAROC}$ represents an appropriate hurdle rate for the RAROC. In financial literature a widespread debate has emerged on how to determine an appropriate measure for the hurdle rate. Crouhy et al. (1999), assuming arithmetic and log-normally distributed returns, show that there is a single appropriate hurdle rate which (in cases of log-normally distributed returns) rises with the volatility. By contrast, Milne and Onorato (2010 and 2012) show that the appropriate hurdle rate may differ substantially for different types of exposures; the rate in their model is particularly conditioned on the shape of the distribution. Their findings provide the conceptual ground for assuming exposure-specific hurdle rates, with credit portfolios requiring far lower rates of return than market portfolios.

Such findings have practical implications, apart from the relevance of their theoretical implications. In fact, they admit either finer distinctions (for instance, distinguishing among different classes of credit exposures) or, on the contrary, cluster-like applications for capital budgeting purposes. Multi-business firms, therefore, may be valued by applying different hurdles for the RAROC according to their specific risk exposures.

A RAP approach, as widely employed by banks, may then, have relevant and significant applications for corporate governance purposes. Performance measures, in this way, may serve to design an efficient system of incentives and delegation of decision making along different management levels. As regards incentives, the RAP measure may be used for evaluating performance of business units and to compensate line managers. The objective here is to determine the value added by a particular division or business unit and use it as a basis for designing incentive-based compensations for line managers. As for decision delegation there is a wide body of literature on capital decisions in financial corporations. Part of this literature addresses the trade-off between central management and managers bearing responsibilities for investment decisions building on the information asymmetries paradigm (Stoughton and Zechner, 2003). As divisional managers are better informed than central managers, a RAROC measure may be effectively employed in order to coordinate delegated decision making and control managerial behaviours.

Despite the limits that a RAP measure may entail – and that have been widely recognized in the literature – we are going to develop a risk-adjusted metric for strategic decision making, measuring performances and value creation purposes. We build, in particular, on a RAROC approach. While it has been criticized for melding together different concepts and, in the ultimate analysis, for lacking a sound theoretical framework, we still think that we may take it as a useful starting point for applying a RAP approach in the context of platform management. We contend that those criticisms that have been levelled at the calculation of capital at risk (CaR) on the basis of a normal distribution have minor implications with reference to the typical risks entailed by running platforms. Since those risks are essentially associated with the dynamics of capital markets we may rely on standard assumptions for CaR calculations. In any case, the debate on RAROC has not yet come up with any well-defined and viable alternative measures.

3 An operative performance measure: the constituents

In this section we introduce the constituents of an operative performance measure. We start measuring performances by employing standard measures of operative performance. As with other firms, the basic measures of operative performance are based on the ROE and the ROA. Methodologically, we operate in a sequential way. We first define the elementary measures of operative performance; then we combine such measures in order to show the contribution of different value drivers to the overall performance.

Traditionally, exchanges were valued by invoking other indicators constructed on volumes (or contracts) traded, or on measures of market efficiency (spreads, trading costs). Corporatization, and subsequent listing, of major exchanges requires that they now take care over the profitability of their own funds. As competitive strains are becoming an even greater concern for platform operators, the need to support expansion strategies may induce firms to resort to capital markets to raise new funds.

We start by building on the ROE as a simple measure of operative performance. Accounting figures show that large conglomerate groups that have resulted from mergers, operate with high levels of goodwill. Therefore, it has become common among exchanges, financial analysts and rating agencies to refer to the return on tangible equity (ROTE) in order to measure the profitability of an institution's own funds. Functionally, by removing the most uncertain and subjective components of valuation the ROTE would come to a more appropriate calculus of what the underlying worth of the firm is.

Thus, corporate finance provides the conceptual basis for analysing the returns on own funds as a function of the main levers of value.

The standard formulation breaks down the ROTE into the ROA and the excess return on the cost of debt. Formally:

$$ROTE = ROA + \left[ROA - K_d\right] \cdot Fl \qquad [1]$$

In this work, we prefer to restate the standard formulation by taking into consideration the *return on capital employed* ((*ROCE=(EBIT/CE)*)) rather than the ROA. While the latter is calculated using total assets as the denominator, the former is based on the concept of capital employed (that is, the total capital that the firm utilizes in order to produce profits). Platform operators generally invest in fixed assets which generate utility for long periods. In our framework the exchange makes investments in long-term maturity options: it seeks to extract revenues by exploiting growth opportunities that disclose their potential only over long periods.

Equation [1] may be adapted in order to take into account the specificities of exchanges; the value drivers in the exchange industry can be made more explicit by breaking down the ROA into the *trading margin* and *trading intensity*. More precisely:

a) The *trading margin* (the ratio of earnings before interest and taxes (EBIT) on trading value) is a measure of the profitability of trading, and measures the margin that the exchange is able to extract from a unit of trading value.
b) The *trading intensity* (the ratio of trading value on the capital employed) measures the productivity of the capital employed. By relating the output to the investments of the exchange, it could be seen as a measure of technical efficiency.

Exchanges, therefore, may improve the profitability of capital employed by improving the operative margin or by leveraging on the efficiency of its platforms. Formally:

$$ROCE = \frac{EBIT}{CE} = \frac{EBIT}{Trading\ value} \cdot \frac{Trading\ value}{CE}$$

Therefore we have: $ROCE = \left(\frac{EBIT}{Tv}\right) \cdot \left(\frac{Tv}{CE}\right)$.

A discussion is needed in relation to the capital employed. As is generally known, capital employed is calculated by subtracting current liabilities from total assets and, therefore, it equals equity plus total long-term liabilities (all long-term funds employed by the company).

Many securities exchanges manage post-trading services from which they collect margins from clearing participants (reported as liabilities in the balance sheet); these are then invested in special short-term assets. For exchanges operating post-trading activities such liabilities constitute a very large part of current liabilities, while trade and receivables and other current liabilities are, in most cases, marginal compared with long-term sources of financing. Since the corresponding investments are intended to serve (and match) the exchange's liabilities in relation to clearing margins, total assets should more correctly be intended net of the above-mentioned investments.

Expressing costs as a linear function of revenues, $C = a - \beta Rev$, we may define EBIT as $EBIT = (1-\beta)Rev - a$ and the ROCE becomes:

$$ROCE = \frac{(1-\beta)Rev - a}{CE} \quad [2]$$

Seeking to express revenues as the sum of listing and trading revenues (here, for the sake of simplicity, we do not consider other business areas) we obtain:

$$Rev_{tot} = \theta + \vartheta L + a_{Tv} + \beta_{TV} TV = \theta + \vartheta L + a_{Tv} + \beta_{Tv}(a_1 + \beta_1 L) \quad [3]$$

where notations have the same meaning that we introduced in the preceding chapters. Rearranging, we obtain $Rev_{Tot} = \theta + a_{Tv} + \beta_{Tv}a_1 + (\vartheta + \beta_{Tv}\beta_1)L$ or simply $Rev_{Tot} = \tau + \omega L$, where $\tau = \theta + a_{Tv} + \beta_{Tv}a_1$ and $\omega = [(\vartheta + \beta_{Tv}\beta_1)]$ is the sum of variables factors.

Therefore, ROCE in Equation [2] may be expressed as $ROCE = \frac{(1-\beta)[\tau + \omega L] - a}{CE}$ or, rearranging, $ROCE = \frac{(\tau - a) + \omega L(1-\beta) - \beta\tau}{CE}$. Focusing on the numerator, ROCE is a function of three terms. The first, $(\tau - a)$, is the difference between fixed revenues and fixed costs; the second expresses variable revenues net of variable costs. The third is a residual item. Given τ and a and neglecting β (which for several exchanges assumes low values), ROCE is an increasing function of L and ω which, as noted, can be assumed as a measure of market power for the exchange.

The profitability of securities exchanges then, depends on the firm's leverage, both operational and financial. Broadly speaking, operational leverage may be expressed in different ways. A useful measure is the contribution margin (revenues net of variable costs) which measures how fast profits increase with sales. Alternatively, operational leverage may be measured by calculating the change in operative income for a given change in revenues. As is well known, operational leverage is a direct function of fixed costs. Apart from the specific formulation of the leverage, it is eminently industry specific with those businesses operating with high fixed costs (for instance, those relying on high investments in R&D) being more exposed to the volatility of operative income. Apart from the specific features of the business, the firm's pricing policies themselves may have the effect of modifying its operational leverage.

For exchanges and other platform operators almost all business units entail fixed costs. Conglomerate exchanges generally cover all the typical business lines involved in the exchange industry. Both trading (on cash and derivatives markets) and post-trading activities are capital intensive as they entail heavy investments in platforms for processing trades. Information dissemination itself, which is a source of revenues for many exchanges, presupposes efficient platforms for distributing information on prices and quantities. Consequently, most exchanges run an IT business which is aimed at developing their software and hardware in-house. We expect an IT business unit to operate with a fraction of fixed costs as well – directly related to investments in R&D. Alternative trading platforms, by contrast, generally focus on cash trading businesses only, without performing admission-to-listing functions. Their competitive policies, moreover, are grounded on granting large rebates to brokers in order to gain higher trading flows. Generally reported as costs of revenues in financial statements, these rebates vary with trading volumes. High rebates may have the effect of substantially altering the cost structure of platform operators, reducing the incidence of fixed costs and, therefore, the operational leverage.

The specific formulation of operational leverage is a point worth discussing. In particular, it is interesting to express it as a function of volumes traded. We recall that operational leverage is $Ol = \frac{(Rev - \beta Rev)}{(1-\beta)Rev - a}$ or $Ol = \frac{(1-\beta)Rev}{(1-\beta)Rev - a}$. Given the formulation of our revenue function, the operational leverage is a function of market volumes on both primary and secondary markets, $Ol = f(L, Tv)$, and is decreasing as the number of listed companies and trading volumes increases. All things being equal, we may expect exchanges to reduce their operational leverage during the upward phases of the cycle and, by contrast, expand it during downturns. Volatility of margins would also be reduced in favourable times and increased in bad times. Building on Equation [2], and recalling our definition of operational leverage, we obtain: $ROCE = \frac{(Rev - \beta)}{CE} \cdot \frac{1}{Ol}$ which, rearranging and recalling the definitions of *trading margin* and *trading intensity*, yields:

$$Ol = \frac{(Rev - \beta)}{CE} \cdot \frac{Tv}{EBIT} \cdot \frac{CE}{Tv} = \frac{(Rev - \beta)}{CE} \cdot \frac{1}{Tr\_mar} \cdot \frac{1}{Tr\_Int} \quad [4]$$

Such a formulation is particularly useful as, with the appropriate adjustments, it may explicitly show the contribution of the operative structure (that is, the *operational leverage*) to the profitability of the firm.

On the other hand, we may express financial leverage as $\frac{EBIT}{Net\ Income}$. Financial leverage seemingly poses particular concerns for those exchanges that are moving forward through sizeable acquisitions, as the recent consolidation process showed.

The combination of operational leverage with financial leverage gives rise to the total corporate leverage which measures the volatility of earnings per share to total revenues (meaning the percentage change in a firm's earnings per share (EPS) given a 1 per cent change in corporate total revenues).

By making reference to this indicator we are able to express performance as a function of capital, business risk and financial structure.

Rearranging the terms on the right side we may come to a modified version of Equation [1], which will be useful in order to capture the effects on performances of main financial risks and, in particular, the operational leverage and the financial leverage.

$$ROTE = \frac{Rev - \beta}{CE} \cdot \frac{1}{Ol} + \frac{Rev - \beta}{CE} \cdot \frac{Fl}{Ol} - Kd \cdot Fl \quad [5]$$

We, therefore, obtain a formulation in which the return on tangible equity is a function of the main drivers of performance, namely the return on assets, the operational leverage and the financial structure.

Equation [5] expresses the profitability of exchanges in terms of three main strategic areas: business structure, financial structure and capital management. To be more precise, business structure is dependent on costs and revenues functions and defines operational leverage. At this level the main risks are related to the effects stemming from declining market activity and losses in the number of companies listed, which, in turn, put pressures on revenues. Moreover, changes in the industry's structure may play an important role, possibly having an impact on the marginal revenues through changes in those variables (θ, β_L, β_{TV}) that convert a marginal increase in L or TV in revenues. For example, the success of alternative systems in drawing large flows of liquidity from established exchanges may force widespread price cuts. All other things being equal (in particular, the cost structure of the exchange), the operational leverage would increase.

4 Managing trading platforms: a map of risks

In this section we lay down the framework of risk management, and depict a map of the main risks that are incurred in managing trading platforms; we also assess the impact of risk on profitability. Every business that manages risk has a fundamental part in generating shareholder value. Likewise, exchanges need a framework which should cover the major risk areas that we may identify as *operational risk, financial risk* and *strategic risk*. Operational risk is related to the efficiency and reliability of trading platforms; financial risk is connected with the sustainability of revenues and the entire financial structure; whilst strategic risk is related to the viability of the firm's competitive policies.

Overall risk management falls within the system of corporate governance. As we pointed out in Chapter 4, it is part of a corporate philosophy that is aimed at ensuring the sustainability of the business. We may put it thus: this objective requires a risk management approach that should monitor all sources of risk across all business areas or functions.

It is possible to draw a map of risks within the entire corporate organization (Table 6.2), which consists of the single business units and the wider corporate level. In particular, Table 6.2 synthesizes the main issues entailed by each source of risk, the risks and opportunities that are implied and the strategic business units which are mainly involved in generating overall risks.

The matter of risk in the exchange industry is complex since it depends on the prevailing business models. Within an ideal continuum, ranging from a mono-business exchange to a *conglomerate exchange*, the exposure to risk increases correspondingly, thus spanning a wide array of risk factors.

The extension of the business model invariably exposes an exchange to the aforementioned sources of risk, and with largely diversified portfolios of activities actually managing strategic risks becomes more challenging. In these circumstances exchanges choose to compete in multiple markets with different characteristics of demand (in terms of elasticity and objectives), and which may be differently exposed to competitive threats or economic downturns. The assessment of risks and opportunities requires the factoring in of a wide array of variables

Table 6.2 The risk framework

Risk areas	Issues	Risks and opportunities	Corporate level
Strategic risk	Remaining competitive in a changing environment Ensuring an up-to-date offer of products and services against competitors Ensuring a viable and efficient technological infrastructure Ensuring compliance with rules and regulations and prime monitoring standards which impact on reputational capital	*Opportunities* Improving the competitiveness of the exchange on an ongoing basis Creating value and attracting investors which will lead to transformations in the exchange industry *Risks* Poor strategic risk management Failures in assessing and pricing the risks assumed by the exchange Losses in value	Overall corporate level (top management) for alliance, joint ventures, mergers, capital budgeting decisions Single business units (innovations in products and services offered)
Operational risk	Maintaining efficiency in procedures and preserving integrity of directors Preserving high-level monitoring standards on issuers and conduct of trading	*Opportunities* Set up of efficient and scalable platforms Increasing the pool of liquidity *Risks* Losses in reputational capital Margin erosion due to legal fines and other losses	IT division for the development of technology infrastructure Single business units for oversight at unit level Risk control for monitoring overall risks
Financial risk	Maintaining a balanced financial structure Controlling leverage (both financial and operational leverage) Improving profitability at both corporate and unit level	*Opportunities* Balanced risk taking which ensures stability of the business on an ongoing basis *Risks* Uncontrolled expansion of financial risk posing a threat to the continuity of the business on an ongoing basis	Overall corporate level (top management) for setting limits on risk taking and checking remuneration of risks Risk control for monitoring overall risks Single business units (commercial choices impacting on both unit and firm's profitability)

regarding: the volatility of revenues both at SBU and portfolio level; the effective exploitation of cross-selling opportunities and innovations in product lines and commercial policies; potential revenue and cost (with particualr reference to the impact on administrative expenses) synergies.

Another relevant issue is the complexity of procedures and controls which may become difficult to cope with as the business model becomes widely diversified (eventually, both on product and geographical level). When diversification is the result of the combination of different entities, the most challenging issues pertain to the adoption of common platforms and protocols, the harmonization of different cultures and the design of a viable system of controls and reporting.

Exchanges and other platforms are exposed both to endogenous and exogenous sources of risks, the former depending on the internal processes and operations performed by the platforms, and the latter stemming from the environment in which the platform operates. In order to provide an exhaustive representation of risk exposure in the exchange industry we use the value chain approach (Table 6.3), where for each stage of the chain we explicitly state the risks (both endogenous and exogenous) to which the platform operator is exposed.

Each source of risk, although stemming from risk factors of a different nature, entails potential losses in revenues.

Endogenous risk factors are spread across all business units. Their sources are weak monitoring procedures and policies, along with disruptions in operations (stemming, for example, from faults in trading and post-trading platforms). In that way, endogenous factors are linked to the perception that the financial industry and market operators have of the trading platform. Such factors, therefore, have a direct impact on the reputational capital of the platform.

Table 6.3 A map of risks

	Listing	**Trading**	**Post-trading**
Endogenous	Poor admission (monitoring) standards, losses in reputational capital	Poor monitoring standards, disruption in operations	Disruption in operations, services offered (i.e. securities lending, novation)
Exogenous	Competition, economic downturns, falls in new issues	Competition, economic downturns, falls in trading volumes	Competition, regulation, credit and liquidity risks

Listing, trading (both on cash and derivatives markets) and data dissemination are subsequently exposed to exogenous risks that are directly related to adverse conditions in capital markets. Here, we may recall the discussion developed in Chapter 2 as to the cyclical nature of exchange business on primary and secondary markets. We found a positive correlation between new capital raised and trading volumes and the dynamics in GDP and corporate earnings (which are themselves positively related to economic activity), and the same holds for data dissemination business as falls in trading lead to a contraction in the selling of data. The impact of derivatives trading is an open question. Despite being traditionally seen as a countercyclical business, in certain markets derivatives show trends that are quite close to those of cash trading. The contribution to business diversification of derivatives trading is, therefore, quite ambiguous. More generally speaking, the market is becoming ever more concentrated around a very few large players and smaller derivatives exchanges are increasingly suffering from competition.

The sources of risk at post-trading level are partially different in nature. While at this stage the platform operator is exposed to the risk of market downturns (the lower the volumes traded the lower the transaction processes at post-trading level) it may bear counterparty credit and liquidity risks as well, depending on the business model and services offered. Provided that post-trading activities span all the services typically involved in custody, clearing and services, the operator is exposed to counterparty risks within both the CCP business (mainly risks related to buy-in and sell-out procedures or margin calls) and settlement activities (when, for example, it manages a securities lending service acting as lender). Certain post-trading entities are then incorporated as banks.

The manifestation of endogenous and exogenous risk factors gives rise to losses in revenue during downturns which may hamper profitability both at business unit level and corporate-wide level. The financial structure, as is well known, may sharply influence the volatility of earnings. Arguably, exchanges working with a high operational and/or financial leverage are particularly exposed to the risk of losing revenues.

However, the responsiveness of revenues to changes in trading activity may not be proportional. In fact, it is the function of pricing policies as well; actually cutting fees as a result of increasing competitive pressures may give rise to drops in revenue even if volumes traded hold.

According to modern portfolio theory, the risk borne by the portfolio is a combination of single risks and correlations between the assets in which the portfolio is invested. The discussion we have developed here underlies the criticalities in treating covariance in the exchange industry. However, while traditional industry-related businesses are to a large extent connected to the economic cycle, diversification opportunities may still develop on a geographical basis. Large conglomerate exchanges may actually be intended as combinations of products and markets. Even though diversification may be difficult to achieve across product lines, business expansion over various markets with different positioning in the economic cycle may help to smooth fluctuations in economic performances.

Treating the exchange as a portfolio of business units, the risk of the portfolio (its variance) is the sum of variances plus the covariance of each SBU with the others. Given the *i-th* and the *j-th* business unit, the variances are σ_i and σ_j respectively.

$$\sigma p = \sum_{i,j} x_i x_j \sigma_{i,j} \quad [6]$$

where $\sigma_{i,j}$ is the standard deviation of the *i-th* business activity in *j-th* jurisdiction. Diversified business models across product lines or jurisdictions allow for cross-selling opportunities. Theoretically, cross-selling may spread across different business lines (either located in the same or different countries) or within the same business line operated in different countries. The impact of cross-selling opportunities on the overall risk depends on their effects on the volatility of earnings at SBU level and the correlations among business units.

For a conglomerate firm, therefore, we may build an earnings' variance and covariance matrix of the different business units. Following a similar approach we may build a matrix of cross-selling opportunities between business lines operating in different jurisdictions. Table 6.4 presents the building blocks of total portfolio variance. The left side represents the variances and covariance matrix attributable to the stand-alone business units, while the right side depicts the matrix of cross-selling effects.

Table 6.4 The matrix of correlations and cross-selling effects

$$\begin{bmatrix} \sigma_{1,1:1,1} & \cdots & \\ \vdots & \ddots & \vdots \\ & \cdots & \sigma_{i,i:i,i} \end{bmatrix} \begin{bmatrix} \gamma_{1,1:1,1} & \cdots & \\ \vdots & \ddots & \vdots \\ & \cdots & \gamma_{i,i:i,i} \end{bmatrix}$$

Where $\sigma_{i,j;j,i}$ represents the correlation between the *i-th* business line in the *j-th* country and the *j-th* business line in the *i-th* country. Similar to the notations we have previously employed, we will denote with $\gamma_{i,j:j,i}$ cross-selling opportunities between the *i-th* business line in the *j-th* country and the *j-th* business line in the *i-th* country.

Provided that the combination of different business lines yields greater revenues than the sum of stand-alone businesses, cross-selling opportunities result in dampening the overall volatility of the firm. Cross-selling opportunities may be derived as the cross derivative of *i-th* business unit's revenues to volumes traded with the *i-th* and *j-th* SBU respectively.

$$\frac{\partial Rev_i}{\partial Vol_i \partial Vol_j} \qquad [7]$$

Therefore, revenues attributable to the *i-th* business unit equal the stand-alone *i-th* SBU's revenues plus the increase in *i-th* SBU's revenues due to the joint effect with the *j-th* business unit. Total revenues may be expressed as the sum of *stand-alone* revenues plus cross-selling effects: $Rev_i = \sum_{i=1}^{n} Rev_i + \sum_{i,j} Rev_{ij}$, where Rev_i denotes the revenues of the *i-th* SBU and Rev_{ij} are the additional revenues coming from cross-selling. Expected revenues for the *i*-th business unit are $E(Rev_i + Rev_{ij}) = E(Rev_i) + E(Rev_{ij})$.

Since cross-selling entails that the combined revenues are greater than the sum of the *stand-alone* revenues attributable to the two units, we expect their revenue distributions to be affected to some extent.

Adjusted for the effect of cross-selling opportunities, the variance of the *i-th* SBU may be expressed as $\sigma_i^2 = \frac{\Sigma_n \left(Rev_i^n + Rev_{ij}^n - E(Rev)\right)^2}{n}$, where Rev_i^n denotes the *n-th* observation of the *i-th* business unit and Rev_{ij}^n is the increase in revenues due to cross-selling effects. On the one hand, therefore, the effects of cross-selling impact on SBU's revenue volatility. One might expect them to increase revenues for *i-th* business units during favourable economic conditions and smooth declines during downturns. Should this be the case, business diversification would be effective in dampening volatility. On the other hand, however, cross-effects might turn out to increase the correlation among business units.

To the extent that it effectively discloses cross-selling opportunities, the combination of two or more business lines, therefore, would result in a modification of the distribution. However, it is important to note that the overall effect depends on the volatility of cross-effects. Provided that the latter operate even during downturns, we may expect the overall effect to result in a skewed distribution with a shorter left tail.

Incidentally, by factoring in the total portfolio variance of both the contribution of correlations and cross-selling opportunities, the management may have a useful support in strategic decision making. In designing the optimal portfolio combination the matrix of covariance and cross-selling opportunities may act as a map for locating the combinations which minimize the overall volatility. From a practical standpoint, and to the extent that the exploitation of cross-selling opportunities modifies the overall volatility of the portfolio, this would be relevant for the systematic risk attributable to each business unit and to the overall portfolio. When calculating the cost of capital for capital budgeting purposes, or within the process of controlling (and rewarding) risk taking, the interaction between different business lines (or jurisdictions) becomes of particular interest.

5 The cost of capital

The cost of capital calculation represents a key topic in corporate finance for corporate and asset valuation purposes. The standard measure which is largely used in corporate finance is based on the capital asset pricing model (CAPM) where risks are priced against the market and are the function of the non-diversifiable risk. As previously noted, major listed exchanges have in the past experienced high values of the β. The bourgeoning empirical evidence on the CAPM gathered over the last 40 years raises some questions on the model's explanatory power.

The appraisal of the systematic risk is particularly challenging for firms that have large investments in intangibles. When determining the cost of capital of trading platforms, therefore, the equity β derived by the simple regression of the share price over the market trends, may not fully apprise the value embedded in the intangibles which, in the context of the exchange industry, constitute a large part of the total assets.

The simple derivation of the cost of capital on the basis of the CAPM model may actually lead to biased results. Whilst the average stock return appears to be lineally and positively linked to its beta, evidence suggests that there remain areas of variability that the β fails to account for. Such results have practical implications, requiring an investigation relating to the nature and the determinants of the β. In this regard, a large body of literature relates equity β to factors such as financial leverage, debt maturity, operational leverage, income volatility, dividends or the dynamics in the economic cycle (see, among others, Hamada, 1972; Galai and Masulis, 1976; Beaver and Manegold, 1975; Gahlon and

Gentry, 1982). Other factors that may have an impact on the systematic risk and its variability are the firm's size and its equity-to-market ratio (Fama and French, 1992; Kothari et al., 1995). Explanatory factors such as the '*book-to-market*' ratio should be deemed of particular relevance as proxies for the weight of growth options on the firm's market value.

Companies may disclose growth opportunities which have a relevant impact on corporate valuation (and this point may be extended to single business units). A biased equity beta, depending on specific industry characteristics, may arise because it fails to properly mirror all the options on future cash flows embedded in the company's assets. The magnitude of growth options is, obviously, industry specific. In the context of the exchange industry the valuation of such options is particularly compelling in the event of business combinations. Intangibles are claims on expected cash flows which are conditional on the returns that capital investments aim to yield in the positive scenario.

When valuing a firm (or a business unit) we should distinguish the present value of cash flows deriving from assets-in-place from the present value of cash flows attributable to growth opportunities. The former reflects the cash flows that the firm could expect to extract from the allocation of resources which it has already undertaken, while the latter is expressive of expected returns stemming from the allocations that the firm might undertake. Growth opportunities, therefore, arise when the firm has the right to decide upon the allocation of resources and the investment in capabilities which, when not abandoned, may impact upon future cash flows. As a firm's value could be seen as a weighted average of value of the assets-in-place and the value of growth opportunities, any changes in the distribution of weights may impact on the risks and return of the stock.

In industries undergoing structural changes the issue turns out to be of particular interest, especially when new investments give rise to the formation of large intangibles. In cases where the embedded growth opportunities fail to fully manifest, firms would undergo substantial losses. As previously noted, the industry has undergone great change over the last decade with exchanges and other platforms largely investing in future growth through M&As. The features of this transformation are mirrored in deep structural change: radically altered business models, the emergence of a network-like system of relations between exchanges and trading platforms and increases in financial leverage. The expectations accompanying such changes are shown by the huge increases in the equity market values of major listed exchanges in the pre-crisis period (see Chapter 7) relative to their book value, revealing keen anticipation of growth opportunities.

The aforementioned developments give rise to relevant questions in regard to the valuation of trading platforms. In turn, this requires us to draw on corporate finance literature in order to gain in-depth understanding of the cost of capital in the industry. We need, therefore, a model for deriving the cost of capital in the industry linking it with its determinants and appraising the growth opportunities.

To this end, we build on the literature by taking into account the specificities of the industry. We relate the cost of capital to the main economic and financial variables that the existing literature assumes as being explicatory, but also consider industry-specific market variables. From a strategic point of view, knowing the drivers of the cost of capital is useful for gaining an in-depth understanding of how the risk factors may impact on the economics of exchanges. Putting it in different terms, understanding the relation between cost of capital and risk factors, the exchange management would be able to infer how its business, through its economic and financial structure, is sensitive to changes in the competitive environment. Methodologically, we model the cost of capital building on a multivariate regression analysis in which the k_e is explained through certain independent variables which we expect to play a relevant role in determining the overall risk profile of the exchange.

The cost of capital is, generally speaking, sensitive to the main economic and financial variables which capture the business structure of the trading platform. More precisely, we may use certain measures of profitability, such as the EBIT, the EPS and ROE, along with the operational and financial leverage. Revenues and profit margins are the function of the volumes attracted to primary markets (number of companies listed or new capital raised) and secondary markets (trading volumes). If revenues and profits were subdued, even though market activity is strong, certain opportunities would remain to be exploited; the uncertainty which surrounds them should be factored in the calculation of the cost of capital.

Financial leverage becomes an issue of concern for exchanges involved in M&As when mergers are financed recurring to debt issues. Most of the main deals in the past have been closed with a mix of debt and equity exchange; however, it is a matter of fact that exchanges involved in M&As have experienced increases in leverage (see Chapter 7). Indeed, in an even more competitive environment putting pressure on revenues and margins a higher debt service may raise concerns about the sustainability of debt.

While financial leverage expresses the risks associated with the sustainability of the financial structure, operational leverage is a measure of how revenue growth translates into growth in operational income. It is also a measure of how volatile the operational income is. Logically, therefore, operational leverage may be deemed as a measure of the business risk of the firm. *Earnings at risk* (EaR) would be particularly high for highly leveraged trading platforms facing significant downturns in volumes traded and revenues. We will endeavour, in section 6, to examine in more detail the relationship between the volatility of revenues and corporate performances. Here we limit ourselves to stressing the determinants of the operational leverage and the role of business structure in driving operational performances.

The cost of capital may, therefore, be estimated through a linear model. Using a multivariate regression on a sample of exchanges one will find the value of the estimators for each explanatory variable. Building on the estimators for a sample of comparable exchanges, it would be possible to come to an estimate of the cost of capital for different exchanges, other trading platforms or business units. The following relation describes the model.

$$k_e = a + b_1 prof + b_2 oplev + b_3 finlev + b_4 market + b_5 rgrowth \qquad [8]$$

where '*prof*' denotes the selected performance measure, '*oplev*' and '*finlev*' indicate the operational and financial leverage respectively and '*market*' denotes the selected market variable. Finally, '*rgrowth*' denotes the risks associated with the growth opportunities embedded in the firm's assets. In sum, Equation [8] captures the uncertainty underlying the future exploitation of such opportunities which could be estimated using the volatility implied in the option component as a proxy.

The *market* and *growth* variables capture the competitive positioning of the trading platform and the growth opportunities embedded in its business model. The competitive positioning is reflected in the platform's market share in listings and trading volumes. Since the attractiveness of the exchange on both primary and secondary markets mirrors its reputational capital, a well-positioned trading platform may be rewarded with a lower cost of capital compared to competitors despite poor economic results due to contingent downturns or to increased competition. In contrast, we expect growth opportunities to be negatively related to the cost of capital as they mirror potential increases in value which are quite uncertain.

From a methodological point of view, recognizing the contribution of growth opportunities to the cost of capital poses the problem of measuring such opportunities and the risks associated with them.

The issue was initially raised by Myers and Turnbull (1977). The authors point out how the growth component of share value presents an option-like feature, which implies some criticalities in valuing the option embedded in the firm's assets. The most challenging issue related to growth options concerns the magnitude of the systematic risk of the firm. The basic argument may be summarized in two strictly related points. The first is that the risk of an option is greater than the risk of the firm's assets. Thus, for firms having large growth opportunities – the value of the option is large compared with that of the assets – the β is expected to be an underestimate of the true risk of the firm, and, conversely, the rate of return based on common β overestimates the appropriate rate of return. Secondly, these distortions in risk and return estimates have implications for the calculation of the appropriate hurdle rate for a certain investment. Valuing the options embedded in the firm's assets is, therefore, of crucial relevance when making coherent capital budgeting decisions.

Hereafter we propose a model for adjusting the equity beta for exchanges in order to capture the contribution of growth opportunities to systematic risk. We refine somewhat Hirst's model by disentangling growth opportunities in two components, namely those embedded in assets-in-place (in other words we recognize the possibility that assets-in-place themselves present latent growth opportunities), and those related to new capital investments. The following model measures growth opportunities starting from the value of intangibles.

In capital budgeting applications the firm's management may be engaged in investing in assets (SBUs, exchanges or other trading platforms) which do not have a market price. For instance, the acquisition of an unlisted ECN that has quickly rising trading volumes but low margins (that is, a situation in which all future growth opportunities have not been disclosed) entails the problem of determining an appropriate cost of capital. The well-established methodologies in corporate finance would suggest taking the β of a similar company (with its own level of financial leverage), deleveraging it and then leveraging it again using the specific financial leverage of the acquired asset.

Finding comparables in the exchange industry can be difficult, given the vast heterogeneity of business models, the range of markets covered, the array of product lines and growth rates in trading volumes. Instead, it may be useful to set up a model for appraising the value of growth opportunities and its weight over the total firm's value; this could then be deemed as a measure of risk exposure.

The literature on corporate finance deals with the formal assessment of the β in the presence of growth opportunities. Prevalent models attempt to disentangle the share price of firms into the value of assets-in-place and the value attributable to growth opportunities. To this end, Kester (1984) derives the price due to growth opportunities as the difference between the market price and the price attributable to assets-in-place. In turn, the latter is calculated by simply using an earnings discount model where the discount rate is the cost of equity capital based on the firm's β.

Kester's model has recently been criticized (Hirst et al., 2008). The basic argument is that with growth opportunities it is not methodologically appropriate to discount cash flows at equity β; rather, it would be necessary to generate the beta values associated with each component (asset-in-place and growth opportunities). Hirst and his co-authors propose a formal model for deriving the two betas. The conceptual foundation of the model lies in the consideration that the β of assets-in-place is the weighted average of the β attributable to the growth opportunities and the β of the cash required to finance those opportunities, which is null. The β of growth opportunities is weighted by the difference between the value of the assets-in-place and the book value of the company divided by the value of the assets-in-place, which is similar to the *Tobin-q*.

A similar approach is that followed by De Andrés et al. (2008), where the firm's beta is the weighted average of the beta of its assets-in-place and its growth options. Formally:

$$\beta_f = \beta_{Aip} \frac{V_{Aip}}{V} + \beta_G \frac{V_G}{V} \qquad [9]$$

where β_f is the beta of the firm, β_{Aip} and β_G are the betas of assets-in-place and growth opportunities respectively. Similarly, V is the value of the firm and V_{Aip} and V_G are the values of assets-in-place and growth opportunities respectively. Recalling that the systematic risk is a linear function of the beta of the firm's stock and debt and assuming the systematic risk of the debt to be zero, the authors derive the equity beta for firms belonging to the same risk class (k) as a linear function of the level of leverage and the weight of the value of its growth options: $\beta_e = a_k \frac{V}{E} + b_k \frac{V_G}{E}$. In turn, the firm's value, V, is the market value of equity (E) less the book value of equity plus the book value of assets.

The value of growth opportunities could be seen as the firm's value (V) less the value of its assets-in-place which, in turn, are an expression of the present value of current earnings before interest, expenses and after income taxes. De Andrés and his co-authors derive the beta of assets-in-place as the covariance of the firm's ROE with the average ROE of the firms in the sample (market ROE) divided by the variance of the market ROE. Since many exchanges operate with high levels of intangibles and, therefore, are differently exposed to the volatility of ROE, we propose a modified version of the beta of assets-in-place. Given the average beta of comparables, $\bar{\beta}$ we calculate a beta referred only to tangible assets as $\beta_T = \frac{\bar{\beta}}{\left(1 + \frac{\overline{TA}}{\overline{A}}\right)}$ where $\overline{TA}/\overline{A}$ is the average ratio of tangible assets (TA) on total assets (A) for the exchanges in the sample. The beta of assets in place for the specific exchange becomes $\beta_{Aip} = \beta_T\left(1 + \frac{TA}{A}\right)$.

Applying this model to the exchange industry poses the problem of coherently identifying the appropriate risk classes. Platform operators widely differ when it comes to the extension of their business model, markets covered, financial structure and revenue growth rates. Many of the conglomerate exchanges that have resulted from widespread mergers operate with high levels of intangibles, and thus are largely exposed to impairment risks compared with small exchanges. Definitively, conglomerate exchanges, in particular transnational ones, are arguably differently exposed to risks rather than small national exchanges. Similarly, alternative trading platforms that are largely focused on cash markets may be differently exposed to risk compared with conglomerate exchanges.

In order to run our model for estimating the cost of capital we need to estimate the risks associated with growth opportunities. As such opportunities bear an option feature, we may estimate them using established option pricing models, taking V_G as the option value and deriving the implied volatility of the underlying assets. Formally, *rgrowth = implied volatility*.

On balance, the evolution of beta is symptomatic of risks perceived. In the exchange industry the issue has come to the forefront with reference to the listing of many exchanges and the supposed incentive of listed exchanges to engage in risky business activities. However, empirical results (see Worthington and Higgs, 2005) show that despite presenting high volatility over time, exchange's beta are covariance stationary and mean reverting. These results suggest that there has been no significant change in financial risk after listing.

6 The model

Moving forward with our thesis, we now define a capital management framework for exchanges. We think of this metric as a useful decision tool for managing risks and measuring performances among different SBUs. Correlatively, it would be helpful in supporting capital allocation to each business unit. And a third application of a RAP measure is for pricing purposes where the cost of capital allocated is factored into a simple pricing formula.

We accomplish the task by modelling a RAP metric for stock exchanges' performances. This is a new approach in stock exchange management, although some exchanges adopt certain metrics for measuring risk. Considering the exchange as a portfolio of different business units, we first derive a RAP metric at business unit level, and then we calculate a RAP measure at corporate level.

We previously pointed out that the most appropriate measure of risk is given by the volatility of earnings. For a multi-business exchange, the determination of such a measure at SBU level would help the management to gain a better insight into the economics of each business unit; this would help drive the relevant strategic choices. We express risk adjusted earnings as $EBIT_i - n\sigma(EBIT_i)$, where i denotes the *i-th* business unit and $n\sigma EBIT$ is the EaR. Assuming a normal distribution for the *EBIT* and n=3, this means covering potential losses up to 99.7 per cent of cases. Further, we may derive the exchange's CaR by calculating the present value of such a rent at an appropriate *risk-free* rate. Formally: $CaR = \frac{n\sigma(EBIT)}{i}$.

For multi-business exchanges it becomes compelling to measure the capital absorbed at corporate level. When deriving the cost of capital at a corporate level we have, obviously, to take into consideration the effect of correlations between SBUs. According to the conventional explanation, business diversification would reduce overall risk assuming a reduced correlation between cash trading and other businesses (mainly derivatives trading). Formally, we may express the EaR at a corporate level as follows:

$$EaR_C = \sum_{i=1}^{n} EaR_i + \sigma(EaR)_{i,j} \quad [10]$$

where $\sigma(EaR)_{i,j}$ is the covariance between EaRs of the *i-th* and *j-th* business unit. From Equation [10] we obtain the CaR at a corporate level:

$$[CaR]_C = \frac{[EaR]_C}{i} = \frac{\left(\sum_{(i=1)}^{n}[[n\sigma(EBIT)]_i + [\sigma(EBIT)]_{i,j}]\right)}{i}$$

A proper knowledge of the CaR, either at a business unit or corporate level, will help the management in the strategic decision making process, allowing monitoring of risks and the capital absorbed and setting targets in terms of risk-adjusted return. However, we may think of capital management according to two possible options. The first is to measure the capital absorbed by the business and the return on that capital; the second is to assign an explicit limit to the capital absorbed by each unit.

We are now able to derive a risk-adjusted performance measure. We can define it in terms of risk adjusted return on risk adjusted capital (RARORAC). Like other financial institutions, the exchange business absorbs resources which should find an adequate remuneration. Resources comprise human capital, intangibles and the capital allocated against business risk. Therefore, the price schedule should be defined in order to remunerate the production inputs but also the cost of the economic capital.

More precisely, we express this metric for the *i-th* business unit in terms of expected return and CaR. Formally:

$$\overline{RARORAC_i} = \frac{E(R_i)}{CaR_i} \qquad [11]$$

where $E(R_i)$ is the expected return for the *i-th* business unit and CaR_i is the CaR of that SBU.

In more detail, we may express the minimum expected return in terms of the cost of capital Ke_i for the *i-th* business unit: $\overline{RARORAC_i} = \frac{Ke_i CaR}{CaR_i}$. Therefore, the $\overline{RARORAC}$ expresses the minimum threshold level of a risk-adjusted return coherent with the aim of creating value for shareholders.

Posing the problem in these terms, a business unit becomes profitable when it yields a return which is at least equal to the opportunity cost of the capital allocated to that unit. In particular, we may think of the cost of capital as a function of a combination of different economic and market variables (for example, EPS, number of listed companies, value of share trading and the leverage).

An obvious extension of the model is to apply the portfolio theory to the strategic management of exchanges. Treating the exchange as a portfolio of different strategic business units implies that we should consider the contribution of each unit to both the yield and risk of the portfolio. Formally, we may define a RAP measure at a corporate level as a linear function of each business unit's performance and the cross selling opportunities. Formally:

$$[RARORAC]_C = \frac{\left(\sum_{(i=1)}^{n}[x_i E(R_i)]\right)}{\left(\frac{\left(\sum_{(i=1)}^{n}[n\sigma[(EBIT)]_i + \sigma[(EBIT)]_{(i,j)}]\right)}{i}\right)} + \gamma_{i,j} \qquad [12]$$

where $RARORAC_C$ is the firm's *RARORAC*, $E(R_i)$ is the expected return for the *i-th* business unit, x_i is its weight (which, for reference, may represent the capital invested on that unit). Combining different activities might impact on the RARORAC in different ways. It could dampen the volatility of revenues (and thus the CaR) provided the exchange invests in weakly correlated business, or spur economies of scope by offering a variety of services building on the same platform (which implies an increase in the expected return).

Finally, $\gamma_{i,j}$ is a term expressing the return from cross-selling opportunities between the two business units, *i* and *j*. This return could be viewed as the ratio between cross-selling opportunities and the CaR. Indeed, it would reflect the synergies that stem from combining different business units.

Moving on with our reasoning, the model we propose represents a different way of assessing the consolidation process in the securities industry, which, as we have consistently argued, has resulted, in almost all cases, in large conglomerate groups with a diversified business model and diversified geographical extension.

So far, the prevailing theoretical contributions have addressed the problem of assessing efficiency for diversified exchanges by adopting either a concept of *technical efficiency* or economic efficiency grounded on a simple measure of the EBIT. In contrast, we express the economics of exchanges in a slightly different way. In particular, we define the performance of the exchange (or of each business unit) in terms of *value added* (*VA*), which might be expressed as follows:

$$VA = (\overline{RARORAC} - K_e) \cdot CaR \qquad [13]$$

When RARORAC equals the cost of capital the value added becomes, clearly, null. At SBU level it represents, therefore, a cut-off value for the acceptability of an investment project (such as adding a new business unit). However, the management may define a certain minimum threshold for the *value added* attributable to a particular unit. In this case, expanding the business model by adding a new SBU becomes a rational choice in as far as the value added exceeds this threshold.

If we imagine a value added target at a corporate level, it will carry implications with regard to the exchange's behaviour. Let us suppose that the management set a minimum target $\overline{VA}$ for the value added. Therefore, the exchange has to obtain a RARORAC which satisfies: $VA = (RARORAC - Ke) \cdot CaR > \overline{VA} = (\overline{RARORAC} - Ke) \cdot CaR$. Hence, given the CaR and the VA target, we can derive the minimum expected return (which we label as $\overline{E(R)}$) which is coherent with that target.

So the following will have to hold:

$$RARORAC > \frac{\overline{VA}}{CaR} + Ke \qquad [14]$$

Since *RARORAC* is the expected return divided by *CaR*, if we multiply each member by *CaR* Equation [14] yields $E(R) > \overline{VA} + Ke \cdot CaR$.

As discussed in Chapter 5, the cost of capital is increasing in capital investments. Therefore, we expect exchanges that expand investments in trading platforms to be required to yield a greater risk-adjusted return in order to obtain a given value added.

Defining the value creation problem in terms of a RARORAC measure requires that we focus on two related issues. The first is the definition of an appropriate measure for the cost of capital. The second relates to the pricing policies of exchanges.

To measure the cost of capital we should take into consideration the entire business structure of the exchange. Our hypothesis is that the cost of capital is dependent on variables capturing economic performance (for example, total revenues, EBIT and EPS), risks and some market variables.

Our model requires an in-depth analysis of pricing behaviour displayed by exchanges. Broadly speaking, the price (both for listing services and trading services) should cover fixed costs, marginal costs and the cost of economic capital. As we have seen, marginal costs for an additional unit of output are expected to be negligible once the exchange has set up all of the infrastructures (rules, standards and trading platforms) needed to perform the business. Therefore, we can express revenues as follows:

$$\tau + \beta_{Tv}(\alpha_1 + \beta_1 L) = \alpha_c + \beta_c[\tau + \beta_{Tv}(\alpha_1 + \beta_1 L)] + Ke \cdot CaR \qquad [15]$$

Posing $E(R) = Rev - Costs = Ke \cdot CaR$, in order to satisfy Equation [14] the following must hold: $(Rev - Costs) > \overline{VA} + Ke \cdot CaR$. Building on Equation [15] it means:

$$\tau + \beta_{Tv}(a_1 + \beta_1 L) - a_c - \beta_c[\tau + \beta_{Tv}(a_1 + \beta_1 L)] > \overline{VA} + KeCaR \qquad [16]$$

The notations are those that we introduced in Chapter 5, and subsequently employed in section 3 of the present chapter. Equation [16] is useful insofar as it permits us to define both revenues and costs as a function of the number of companies listed. In turn, we may derive the pricing policies of the exchange in order to satisfy Equation [16]. To this end, we assume as given the cost structure of the exchange and, therefore, the weight of both fixed and variable costs. As for revenues, we might also assume them as given fixed items, such as the fees paid by intermediaries for the right to use trading platforms and the annual fees paid by issuers. Finally, we assume β_1 as a variable not directly under the control of the exchange. We can think of that variable as being dependent on the production technology of the exchange and, to a considerable extent, on the reputation of the exchange. Therefore, the exchange chooses β_{Tv}, which reflects the pricing schedule for the trades occurring on its platforms. We derive the value of such variable in order to satisfy Equation [16]:

$$\beta^*_{Tv} > \frac{\overline{E(R)} + Ke \cdot CaR + a_C - (1 - \beta_C)(\theta + \vartheta L + a_{Tv})}{(a_1 + \beta_1 L)(1 - \beta_C)}$$

Assuming a broader perspective, a RAP metric might be used for other purposes, perhaps within the internal control function or when managing business combinations between exchanges.

With this latter point specifically in mind, the metrics we have presented may be useful for defining the *fair value* of the exchange on the occasion of an eventual business combination. More precisely, from a RAP measure we may derive the value that a bidder would be willing to pay for acquiring a portfolio of activities given the yield and risks of that portfolio. This is a different way in assessing the value of exchanges. Thus far in the literature, the issue of exchange value in mergers was addressed by observing the implied multiples in merger agreements and comparing those multiples with market multiples. In a business combination, however, the RARORAC should not be calculated by assuming the exchange target as stand-alone. Building on our previous analysis we derive the RARORAC for the exchange target as if it were combined with the exchange bidder. In other words, it represents the risk-adjusted performance that the target company would yield to the bidder taking into account the synergies between the two parts. Provided that the merger is value accretive, we expect the RARORAC attributable to the target being greater than the stand-alone RARORAC.

$$RARORAC_{Tc} = RARORAC_T + \gamma_{T,B}$$

Where $RARORAC_{Tc}$ is the risk-adjusted performance of the exchange target assuming the combination with the bidder, $RARORAC_T$ is the performance of the exchange target considered as being *stand-alone* and $\gamma_{T,B}$ are the synergies potentially stemming from the combination. We may, then, derive the cost of capital for the exchange target under the combination agreement. More precisely, this would reflect the risks of the exchange for the bidder; it is also a function of the correlation with the other value generating activities of the enlarged group. Formally:

$$Ke_{Tc} = RARORAC_{Tc} \cdot CaR_{Tc}$$

where Ke_{Tc} is the cost of capital for the exchange target assuming the perspective of the bidder and $\overline{VA}$ is the capital absorbed by the exchange under the combination agreement. It is the function of the contribution of the exchange to target the overall risk for the entire group. Defining the cost of capital for the exchange target from the bidder's point of view, we may derive the value that the bidder would be willing to pay by discounting expected earnings (comprising the effect of synergies) at that cost of capital.

7 Conclusions

Value creation for securities exchanges is a far from well-established field of research. The theoretical literature focuses on the main features of the economics of exchanges and, in particular, the presence of relevant network externalities. Other contributions deal with efficiency matters in relation to conglomerate exchanges. However, there is a lack of knowledge about the main drivers of value for exchanges. This chapter has tried to bridge the gap.

Increasing competition requires the management of uncertainty which, in turn, needs an efficient and comprehensive framework for capital management. Such a framework should consist of a balanced set of targets (for performances) and limits conceived to restrict the risk exposure to earnings volatility, which is particularly compelling in light of increasing competitive strains within the industry. In particular, platform operators are concerned with EaR implied by their business model. The profitability of platform operators is driven by the combination of four forces, which we have labelled as *strategy, regulation, risk management* and *corporate governance*.

Building on this framework, we have developed a basic model for measuring performances in the industry. In particular, we have proposed a performance measure which is a function of both operational and financial leverage – the two factors we have identified as the main sources of business risk. We then moved forward by developing a risk-adjusted approach for measuring performances of exchanges. We represented the exchange as a portfolio of activities (SBUs); for each of them we formalized a risk-adjusted performance measure which is a function of the cost of capital and the CaR. Finally, we have argued that a risk-adjusted approach for measuring performances would be useful for managerial purposes, driving capital allocation across business units, the definition of performance targets and the pricing of services provided by the exchange.

7
The Economics of the Exchange Industry: An Empirical Overview

1 Introduction

The aim of this chapter is to carry on an empirical analysis of the economics of the exchange industry. In Chapter 2 we provided a part-overview of the main aggregate performance measures, and focused on a comparison of performances across exchanges belonging to different legal statuses. Now our purpose is to provide more insight into economic performances.

The chapter builds on the analysis we have carried out throughout the book, providing a detailed investigation of prevailing business models in the exchange industry. The focus of the investigation is all the listed exchanges around the world. Despite the financial data span, in certain cases, a rather more limited time frame of the analysis will, however, provide some interesting insights. In most cases the available data cover the years immediately preceding the financial crisis (which were characterized by fast growing volumes and revenues) and the crisis period. Therefore, we can investigate revenue and cost structures over a complete economic cycle. This will permit us to gain a clear understanding of the relations between the economics of exchanges and market dynamics. We then extend the analysis to alternative platforms, a necessary step given their increasing relevance within the exchange industry.

It is important to stress that the competitive jostle among trading platforms mirrors quite different competitive policies; differences in the business structure emerge between exchanges and other platforms. In the first instance, the prevailing business models are substantially different, with major exchanges being widely diversified and other platforms tending to focus on a narrower array of product lines although covering the main international marketplaces. On the other hand, cost structures are quite different as well. Perhaps, however, the most interesting issue pertains to the impact of different ownership structures on economic performances. We expect listed exchanges to have a clearer profit-oriented objective function compared to other platforms which have a more concentrated ownership structure, substantially dominated by large banks.

Another interesting topic concerns the relationship between the share prices of listed exchanges and their economic performances. A relevant stream of the literature regards share performances as a proxy of value creation for shareholders. However, market developments that have occurred during the last few years raise deep concerns over the sustainability of past performances.

The chapter is organized as follows. In section 2 we perform an analysis of the financial position of listed exchanges. In section 3 we shed light on their economics, and in particular we focus on the revenues and the cost structure of listed exchanges and provide a comparison with other trading platforms, evidencing differences in competitive policies. Then, section 4, we provide an in-depth overview of the operational performances of trading platforms. Section 5 provides an insight into exchanges' value, investigating market multiples and comparing them with those observed in M&As. Then, section 6 investigates share performances of listed exchanges and the risk profile expressed by the beta. Section 7 draws some conclusions.

2 A financial analysis

When measuring the dimensions of an exchange one should identify the appropriate variables to take into account. As for other businesses we may measure the dimensions of the exchanges by referring both to the total assets and the volume of outputs. We apply, in particular, a concept of capital employed and the trading values as a measure of outputs. We start our analysis by representing the dimensions of the exchanges comprising our sample, since the aforementioned variable will play a role in the investigation of the economics of exchanges that will follow.

Before analysing the operational performances of exchanges, it will be useful to give a better insight into the financial structure of exchanges. Figure 7.1 depicts the relationship between the ratio of total equity on total assets (leverage) and the ratio of total intangible assets on total assets (left side panel). It provides, therefore, a picture of the risks that exchanges are exposed to as it shows both the leverage of exchanges

Table 7.1 Financial flexibility

	2011	Average for the period
NYSE Euronext	51.8%	51.2%
NASDAQ OMX	56.9%	54.4%
TMX	58.0%	32.9%
CME	58.0%	51.1%
ICE	11.2%	44.5%
CBOE	72.0%	69.4%
BM&FBOVESPA	97.9%	61.5%
Bolsa Mexicana	93.4%	93.7%
Bolsa de Colombia	82.2%	79.1%
LSEG	41.8%	81.6%
Deutsche Börse	14.6%	23.7%
BME	82.8%	76.1%
HKECH	83.8%	69.9%
Singapore Stock Exchange	89.4%	72.5%
Osaka Stock Exchange	90.3%	90.6%
ASX	94.2%	86.0%
Johannesburg Stock Exchange	86.1%	84.3%

and the incidence of intangible assets on the book value. The right side panel of Figure 7.1 depicts the ratio of tangible equity on tangible assets with the ratio of financial debt on equity.

Figure 7.1 elicits a few considerations about risks across exchanges. Concerns may emerge with reference to a few exchanges (NYSE Euronext, LSEG, CME, the Australian Exchange – ASX – and the BM&FBOVESPA) operating with a high incidence of intangible assets (mainly software and goodwill) on total assets. Since goodwill normally constitutes a large fraction of intangibles, such exchanges are widely exposed to risk of impairments as any sharp cuts in earnings would result in a substantial devaluation of assets. We should add that goodwill is strictly related to mergers and acquisitions, but not all exchanges involved in M&As present a high level of intangibles on total assets. However, there are a few exchanges (for example, Deutsche Börse, NASDAQ, ICE, TMX and the Johannesburg Stock Exchange) that despite having a lower incidence of intangibles on total assets, nevertheless operate with a weak financial position as they have a negligible, or sometimes negative, tangible equity. Looking at financial debt an astonishing difference emerges between the largest exchanges operating with high ratios of financial debt on equity (where debt is mainly contracted to fund expansion programmes) and other exchanges where this ratio is substantially lower. On balance, while business expansion is expected to benefit exchanges (by permitting product

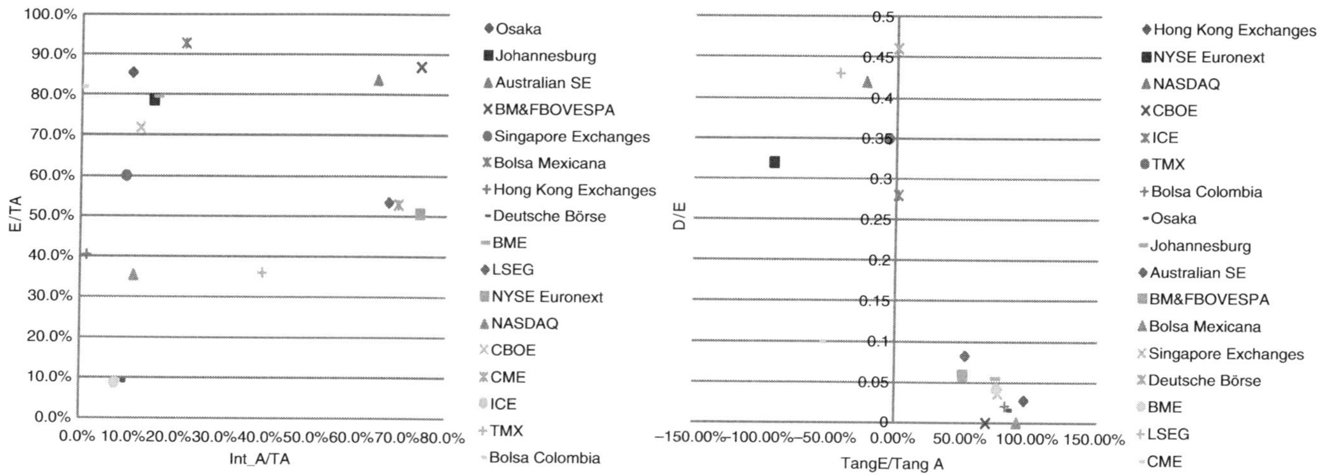

Figure 7.1 Equity, leverage and assets

and geographical diversification and the pooling of liquidity), nevertheless it is a source of instability for large conglomerates.

When investigating the financial structure of an exchange it is, then, useful to analyse the degree of financial flexibility as measured by the incidence of stable funds (long-term liabilities and equity) on total assets. Table 7.1 depicts the ratio for listed exchanges.

Apart from Deutsche Börse and ICE, which operate with a fragile financial structure, all the exchanges present a high incidence of the long-term funds. Financial flexibility, therefore, is seemingly not a concern for listed exchanges.

3 Revenue and cost functions

This section provides some empirical evidence on the cost and revenue functions for listed exchanges and the main ECNs. The objective is to show the patterns of costs and revenues focusing, in particular, on the connections with trading volumes.

We start by highlighting some of the dynamics in revenues. In previous chapters we modelled a linear relationship between revenues and outputs. Hereafter we test such relations by examining three models (Table 7.2): the first relates total revenues with trading values and listed companies; the second looks at the incidence of revenues other than cash market revenues; and the third model relates total revenues with trading values and the fraction of other revenues. As the results tell us, all the explanatory variables appear to be significant in explaining total revenues. Moreover, the models we investigated appear to fit well with our data set, according to the chi-square value. The second, however, have a greater r-square within. R-square between are negligible in all the three models. Focusing on a timeframe spanning the period 2005–11 revenues have shown quite different patterns among securities exchanges across the world. We analyse in great detail all listed exchanges belonging to the WFE.

To start with, Figure 7.2 relates the standard deviation and the compound annual growth rate (CAGR) of revenues for listed exchanges and for Chi-X Europe, one of the major ECNs. For comparability the figures are derived from data expressed in US dollars. It is worth recalling that for a few exchanges we only have data for a shorter time span due to the M&As that have occurred during the last few years. A few exchanges, moreover, only recently became public and do not report figures for the years preceding the IPO.

From these results we may derive the following conclusions about exchanges' performances. The figures evidence a clear positive relationship between revenue growth and volatility. Managing securities

Table 7.2 Revenues regressed on outputs proxies

	Model 1	Model 2	Model 3
Tv	0.4430	0.4631	0.4783
	(0.000)	(0.000)	(0.000)
L	0.2856	0.3415	
	(0.002)	(0.000)	
%Oth_Rev		0.6739	0.6639
		(0.000)	(0.000)
Intercept	2.5227	1.7282	2.5852
χ^2	0.000	0.000	0.000
R^2 within	0.28	0.39	0.3489
R^2 between	0.02	0.0003	0.080
Number of groups	15	14	14
Number of observations	383	355	355

Source: our elaborations on exchanges' annual reports (for revenues) and WFE statistics (for trading values and listed companies). Within brackets, under the estimates, we report the significance coefficients for each explanatory variable.

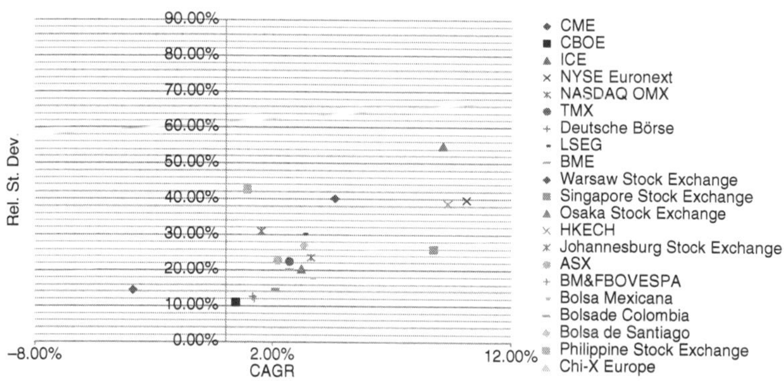

Figure 7.2 Revenue growth and relative standard deviation
Source: Our elaborations on exchanges' reports and Bloomberg database.

exchanges is normally, with a few exceptions, a highly volatile business in operational revenues.

It is interesting to note that the largest derivatives markets, with the exception of the CBOE, operate with a higher volatility of revenues than other exchanges. Among the high-growth and high-volatile exchanges we find those located in fast growing countries, such as the Singapore Stock Exchange and the Hong Kong Exchanges and Clearing Houses (HKECH). We have already accounted for the positive relationship between the economic cycle and the typical output of securities exchanges (namely, listed companies and trading volumes).

The increasing relevance of capital markets in such countries mirrors, therefore, the dynamism of their economies; and it also arguably marks the path for future developments in the industry.

Diverging patterns emerge with reference to well-established exchanges such as the LSEG, Deutsche Börse, NASDAQ OMX and NYSE Euronext. Deutsche Börse operates with both a lower revenue compound annual growth rate (CAGR) and volatility. By contrast, NYSE Euronext has the highest revenue CAGR and is among the exchanges with the highest levels of revenue volatility, somewhat surprising given the widely diversified business model both on a product and geographical basis.

The data presented in Figure 7.2 allow a comparison between established exchanges and main ECNs. Despite the fact that ECNs are a very recent phenomena, at least in Europe, they are growing at a fast pace. Chi-X Europe, which succeeded in attracting large parts of the order flow from the biggest exchanges, operates with higher revenues' CAGR than other exchanges, and a higher volatility as well, something which seems quite normal for fast growing trading platforms.[1]

Turning to a more detailed analysis of revenues, we relate the total revenues for our sample of listed exchanges to both costs and market data (trading values and number of listed companies). We build on the discussions in Chapters 2 and 5,[2] and in the Appendix we summarize the corresponding estimators for each exchange.

Turning to an analysis of costs, we start by examining the prevailing cost items for our sample. Then we investigate the relation between costs and outputs. In line with our discussions in Chapter 5, we assume the trading value and the number of companies listed as proxies of an exchange's outputs.[3]

Table 7.3 provides the composition of total costs, showing the major cost items, for the sample group of listed exchanges. These figures show certain patterns in operational expenses which are somewhat expected, although there a few notable exceptions. The common pattern which emerges after looking at operational expenses is the predominance of personnel expenses. In most exchanges such expenses count for a little less than 50 per cent of total operational revenues. We may assume such revenues as substantially fixed. In almost all exchanges the volatility of personnel expenses is subdued. Considering also the investments in technology (technology and software development, in particular, absorb a high fraction of total operational expenses for certain exchanges), fixed costs are predominant across almost all exchanges. Other relevant cost items are those related to investment depreciation and

Table 7.3 Exchange costs: a breakdown

	Personnel costs	Technology development	Depreciation	Administration and marketing	Transaction related
NYSE Euronext	17.1%	4.8%	7.5%	6.7%	36.7%
NASDAQ OMX	17.3%	2.3%	4.1%	1.9%	63.9%
CME	33.5%	6.9%	20.6%	n.a.	–
CBOE	38.4%	6.6%	12.7%	n.a.	23.1%
ICE	47.7%	9.1%	25.2%	6.9%	–
TMX	49.5%	18.6%	9.3%	25.1%	–
BM&FBOVESPA	29.7%	12.8%	7.5%	2.7%	–
Bolsa Mexicana	56.5%	18.1%	3.0%	n.a.	–
Bolsa de Colombia	n.a.	n.a.	n.a.	n.a.	n.a.
Bolsa de Santiago	n.a.	n.a.	n.a.	n.a.	n.a.
Deutsche Börse	37.3%	27.5%	8.9%	7.8%	24.6%
BME	56.9%	9.2%	9.6%	n.a.	–
LSEG	39.0%	19.3%	10.7%	n.a.	11.5%
HKECH	53.8%	18.1%	4.5%	11.3%	–
Singapore Stock Exchange	37.0%	17.9%	1.5%	2.0%	–
Osaka Stock Exchange	24.1%	n.a.	30.2%	27.9%	–
ASX	57.4%	11.3%	14.5%	15.7%	
Johannesburg Stock Exchange	38.5%	6.2%	6.4%	4.4%	4.3%

Source: Our elaborations on annual reports.

amortization; the magnitude of these items, however, substantially varies across exchanges.

The exceptions to the above-mentioned patterns are those represented by the American exchanges, specifically their transaction-related expenses. This is particularly the case of NYSE Euronext and NASDAQ OMX, with the latter spending some 64 per cent of its costs on such items. We would emphasize here that transaction-related costs are a by-product of regulation and the system of linkages among exchanges in the US. The combination of regulation and links substantially alters the structure of costs, as transaction-related expenses are a function of trading volumes and are, therefore, essentially variable.

Managing exchanges and trading platforms is commonly regarded as a fixed-cost business. To test this hypothesis we relate total costs with the main outputs of exchanges (trading value on cash markets and the number of companies listed). We would expect exchanges to economize on expenses with increases in trading values. The presence of economies of scale would imply a negative relation between operational expenses and trading values. Theoretically, such a relation should be expected to hold for the number of companies listed as well. Since listings are, normally, less volatile than trading volumes we may expect a weaker relation of operational expenses with listings.

While continuing to represent their traditional business areas, securities exchanges are increasingly operating as conglomerate entities. As we have noted, the traditional sphere of business does not represent the predominant source of revenues for certain exchanges. So, arguably, for such exchanges trading values and number of companies listed may not fully explain total costs.

We employ a cross-section analysis to test the behaviour of operational costs for 16[4] securities exchanges embracing a timeframe spanning the period 2005–11. We employ data drawn from exchange quarterly reports for operational expenses, and look to WFE statistics for the quarterly trading values and number of companies listed.

The methodology employed tests three models. Model 1 regresses the operational expenses against the trading value and the number of companies listed. More precisely, we take the logs of the above-mentioned variables. Model 2 controls for the weight of revenues other than listing and cash trading revenues on total revenues. Model 3 regresses operational expenses against trading value and the weight of other revenues.

We capture the contribution of other businesses through a variable representing their weight on total revenues (the variable, here, is *%Oth_Rev*).

In the full model (Model 2), we use the following regression to describe costs:

$$logC_{it} = \alpha + \beta_1 \cdot logTv_{it} + \beta_2 \cdot logL_{it} + \beta_3 \cdot \%Oth\_Rev_{it}$$

Table 7.4 summarizes the results of the longitudinal regression for each of the three models.

Our results elicit some interesting considerations that we may summarize as follows. In each of the three models we have tested, the trading value is not significant in explaining operational expenses. On the one hand, this result is to some extent not surprising since the main cost items for securities exchanges are, normally, salaries and wages. An increase in trades, once the technology infrastructure has been built, has arguably little effect on operational expenses. On the other hand, the trading value depends not only on the number of trades but also on the market prices for each security traded on the exchange's platforms.

By contrast, the number of companies listed is more significant in explaining operational expenses. The close relation between listing-related activities (admission to listing and oversight of issuers) and operational expenses (a relevant part of which are labour costs) should not be surprising given that the former are substantially labour intensive. However, the significance of listed companies in Model 1 is weak. By contrast, it is greater in Model 2, which controls for revenues spurring from business units other than cash markets. The weight of other business units is strongly significant. Moreover, looking at the estimates, operational expenses are more sensitive to engagement in other

Table 7.4 Expenses regressed on output proxies

	Model 1	Model 2	Model 3
Tv	0.003	0.015	0.019
	(0.932)	(0.705)	(0.635)
L	0.2	0.233	
	(0.062)	(0.025)	
%Oth_Rev		0.547	0.545
		(0.000)	(0.000)
Intercept	7.756	7.275	7.916
χ^2	0.1694	0.000	0.000
R^2	0.2097	0.1613	0.0305
Number of groups	16	16	16
Number of observations	410	410	410

Note: Within brackets, under the estimates, we report the significance coefficients for each explanatory variable.

business units than listings and trading values. While expanding typical outputs the exchange may exploit to some extent scale economies, a widely diversified business may introduce complexity in exchange management, and thus impact on total costs. From a managerial point of view, this may have significance: when choosing whether to diversify the business model or just focus on trading on cash markets a firm's management should take particular care to note the profitability of related businesses.

Overall, the model that seems to better explain operational costs is the second, which has an *r-square* that equals 0.16. The first model has a greater *r-square* and *chi-square* statistic as well. When looking at Model 3, the r-square is insignificant, confirming that we cannot properly explain operational expenses without taking into account companies listed. If we exclude the trading value and just regress expenses against listings and revenues on other businesses, the results do not change significantly compared to Model 2, which confirms the greater relevance of primary markets and the overall business model in explaining operational expenses.

Figure 7.3 relates unit operational expenses with trading value (left panel) and number of companies listed (right panel). To be more precise, the panel on the right relates the log of the ratio of expenses on trading value with the log of trading value; the left side panel relates the log of the ratio of expenses on the number of companies listed with the log of listings.

The results summarized in Figure 7.3 do not clearly support the hypothesis of reduction in unit costs with increases in outputs, despite the largest exchanges seeming to benefit, at least to some extent, from increases in trading values and listings.

When looking at the right panel in Figure 7.3 we observe that the largest exchanges in terms of trading values (namely, NYSE Euronext

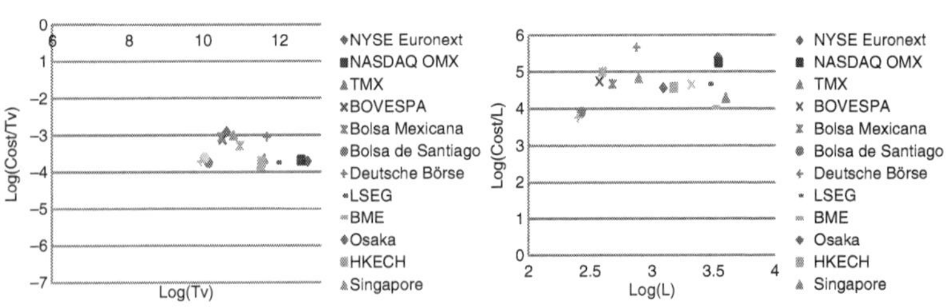

Figure 7.3 Operational expenses, trading values and listed companies

and NASDAQ OMX) are among those exchanges operating with the lower ratio of operational expenses on trading values. However, we also note that certain small exchanges, such as the Bolsa de Santiago, operate with similar unit operational expenses. The LSEG itself operates with similar unit operational expenses to NYSE Euronext and NASDAQ OMX despite having lower trading values and a similar business model. The two large American exchanges function with the highest incidence of operating expenses on listed companies as well. The transformation of the exchange industry and, in particular, transatlantic expansion (which hardly involved the large American exchanges) may have introduced complexity in managing different entities. Finally, the figures for Deutsche Börse may cause some concerns about far-reaching diversification strategies. The German Exchange operates with the highest unit operational expenses against both trading value and listed companies.

4 A performance analysis

This section analyses the economic performance of exchanges and the main ECNs. As noted in Chapter 6, we focus in particular on the earnings before interest, taxes, depreciation and amortization (EBITDA) margin and measures of operational performance such as the *return on tangible equity* (ROTE) and the *return on capital employed* (ROCE).

Turning to the analysis of operating measures of performances, we focus on the EBITDA margin, ROE, ROTE and ROCE. Table A.2 in the Appendix reports the average values and the relative standard deviations on a quarterly basis from 2005 to 2011, for the listed exchanges in the sample. We rank exchanges according to the weight of cash market revenues on total revenues.

The figures in Table A.2 provide evidence of huge differences across exchanges around the world. On average, margins are sustained by almost all exchanges, although there are divergences which prompt considerations of both the business model and the geographical area of influence. As a first instance, exchanges predominantly (or exclusively) engaging in business activities other than cash markets seemingly operate with higher margins. Pure derivatives exchanges (with the exception of CBOE) are among those exchanges with higher margins. Deutsche Börse itself, where cash market revenues are marginal, falls among the more profitable exchanges.

When reading the results in Table A.2 according to a geographical point of view we observe that exchanges (such as the Singapore Stock Exchange, HKECH and the BM&FBOVESPA) operating in fast-growing areas operate with higher margins than other exchanges. On balance, Asian–Pacific exchanges seemingly operate on a lower locus of the risk-return frontier. While having returns that are similar to those of the large American derivatives exchanges they have, generally, lower levels of volatility.

Large exchanges – in terms of trading values – do not necessarily produce high margins. The largest exchanges (that is, NYSE Euronext, NASDAQ OMX and LSEG) have far lower EBITDA margins compared to other exchanges in the sample, and higher levels of volatility. Moreover, returns are markedly subdued for the exchanges as well. When looking in particular at the ROTE, major concerns may arise as to the sustainability of their businesses. Negative values for the metric are the consequence of negative values of the tangible equity, as we explained in section 2.

The Spanish Exchange is among those better positioned in terms of average margins and returns and with the lowest levels of volatility. The BME represents an interesting case: despite formally operating as a regional exchange, it has a relevant international dimension in particular when considering its close relations with Latin America.

We now turn our focus to the return on capital employed; we measure the ROCE as the ratio of the operational margin on the capital employed.[5] We then break the ratio in order to show the contribution of the *trading margin* and the *trading intensity*. More precisely:

a) The *trading margin* (the ratio of EBIT on trading value) is a measure of the profitability of trading and expresses the margin that the exchange is able to extract from a unit of trading value.
b) The *trading intensity* (the ratio of trading value on the capital employed) expresses the productivity of the capital employed. By relating the output to the investments of the exchange, it can be seen as a measure of technical efficiency.

An exchange, therefore, may improve the profitability of capital employed by improving the operational margin or by leveraging on the efficiency of its platforms. Figure 7.4 depicts the contribution to the ROCE of the aforementioned basic constituents: it shows that exchanges across the world follow different patterns of development. Fast-growing exchanges, such as Hong Kong and Singapore, are those experiencing the highest returns on capital employed, together with the BME.

Table 7.5 reports the main results for our sample of listed exchanges: the figures illustrate very different patterns in generating margins. While the Singapore Stock Exchange succeeds in extracting high margins from

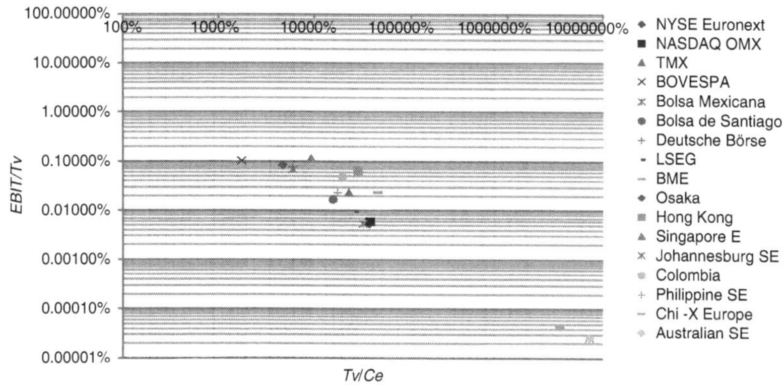

Figure 7.4 ROCE analysis

Table 7.5 Trading margin and trading intensity

	EBIT/Tv	Tv/Ce
NYSE Euronext	0.00547%	37264%
NASDAQ OMX	0.00602%	37728%
TMX	0.02390%	22679%
BM&FBOVESPA	0.10492%	1720%
Bolsa Mexicana	0.06973%	5897%
Bolsa de Santiago	0.01721%	15461%
Deutsche Börse	0.07760%	5814%
LSEG	0.00967%	26333%
BME	0.02426%	45251%
Osaka Stock Exchange	0.08476%	4611%
HKECH	0.06642%	28239%
Singapore Stock Exchange	0.11669%	9112%
ASX	0.00003%	7251567%
Johannesburg Stock Exchange	0.00541%	32057%
Bolsa de Colombia	0.04953%	19557%
Philippine Stock Exchange	0.02380%	17330%
Chi-X Europe	0.00004%	3550186%

trading activity (it has the highest *EBIT*/*Tv* ratio) while operating with a low trading intensity, the HKECH has a more balanced contribution of trading margin and trading intensity to the return on capital employed. The two largest exchanges (NYSE Euronext and NASDAQ OMX) are among those exchanges with the lowest trading margins. Their model of development is substantially based on expanding quantities.

By contrast, Chi-X Europe, while experiencing fast growth in trading activity during the last few years, operates with the lowest returns on capital employed. It competes on quantities; its trading intensity is exceptionally high whereas the trading margin is negligible.

5 Earnings and multiples

In this section we start to delve into the problem of valuation for securities exchanges. The topic is of paramount importance in light of the intense consolidation process that occurred during the pre-crisis period and the most recent mergers. Traditionally, mergers have been seen as a means to improve efficiency and cope with competitive threats, and spurring, therefore, a battle for the control of major players. It is, therefore, interesting to compare the multiples attached to exchanges

Table 7.6 Multiples and earnings

	P/E			EV/EBITDA			EPS	
	2005–11	I SP	II SP	2005–11	I SP	II SP	$	CAGR
NYSE Euronext	22.5	48.1	12.9	12.5	26	11.4	0.27	2.5%
NASDAQ OMX	21.3	33.7	11.9	10.7	15	9	0.43	4.7%
TSX	18.7	27.4	12.1	6.3	8.3	4.8	0.52	2.7%
CME	29.2	41.3	20.1	16.2	23	14.2	3.64	6.5%
CBOE	17.1	-	17.1	17.1	-	9.8	0.31	2.4%
ICE	30.4	45.6	21.9	16.6	29.3	12	0.93	8.9%
Bolsa Mexicana	58.1	-	58.1	13	-	13	0.01	4.3%
BM&FBOVESPA	22.6	-	22.6	17.1	-	17.1	0.01	−2.4%
Bolsa de Colombia	28	25.2	28.7	19.3	24.8	17.9	0.0001	1%
Bolsa de Santiago	21.7	11.2	28	8.9	6.9	11.3	44756	1.1%
LSEG	22.4	27.1	17.6	10.3	14	7.5	0.08	0.6%
Deutsche Börse	18.3	21.6	16.2	10	12.1	8.4	1.60	−0.7%
BME	12	19.9	10.5	7.1	12.3	5.8	0.66	0.5%
ASX	20.2	22.4	18.6	24.5	70.9	12.9	0.38	1.8%
Johannesburg Stock Exchange	22.7	49.6	12.6	25.9	68	9.6	10.2	1%
Singapore Stock Exchange	22.5	21.1	23.6	17.6	17.1	17.9	0.05	4.3%
HKECH	28.3	30.3	28.9	23.6	28.1	20.3	0.13	6.2%
Osaka Stock Exchange	18.7	16.5	20.1	5.8	3.5	6.9	0.05	3.5%

in M&As with market multiples and M&As' multiples at different points in time.

We start by providing an overview of the evolution of market multiples and earnings for listed exchanges in the period 2005–11. We focus on quarterly data. As for multiples we take into account the P/E and EV/EBITDA multiples, showing the averages for the period and the averages for the sub-periods 2005–7 (I sub-period) and 2008–11 (II sub-period). For earnings we report the average earning per share and the compound growth rate.

At first glance (Table 7.6), we observe significantly high multiples, at least for a few exchanges, in particular the largest derivatives exchanges and Hong Kong. Certain smaller exchanges (the Colombia and Santiago exchanges) show high multiples as well. In the first sub-period figures show generally high P/E and EV/EBTDA multiples, with some minor exceptions.[6] In the second sub-period, multiples sharply decline with a few exceptions where multiples remain at high levels (we note, in particular, CME, ICE, ASX, the Hong Kong and Singapore exchanges). Seemingly, the exchanges performing better are those experiencing the higher earnings growth during our timespan. As for the largest European markets earnings growth was poorer and multiples suffered.

Hereafter we provide an overview of the M&As' multiples. Methodologically, we have collected the EV/EBITDA multiples for the main mergers that occurred (or were proposed) starting from 2005.[7]

Table 7.7 EV/EBITDA multiples in major M&A deals

Bidder	Target	Year	EV/EBITDA
NYSE	Archipelago	2005	37
NASDAQ	LSE	2006	19.5
NYSE Group	Euronext	2006	23.5
ICE	NYBOT	2006	37.2
LSE	Borsa Italiana	2007	14.3
Deutsche Börse	ISE	2007	27.6
CME	CBOT	2007	36
LSEG[8]	TMX*	2011	10.4
Deutsche Börse	NYSE Euronext*	2011	11.2
NASDAQ OMX	NYSE Euronext*	2011	13
BATS	Chi-X	2011	465
Tokyo Stock Exchange	Osaka Stock Exchange	2012	31.7
LSEG	LCH	2012	57
ICE	NYSE Euronext	2012	13.2

Source: Our elaborations on annual reports and prospectuses.
* Not finalized.

For the sake of completeness (and for comparitive purposes), we include in the analysis those deals which have not yet been finalized. Table 7.7 presents the main results.

Pre-crisis mergers occurred within a framework of increasing market valuations across the US and Europe, although with a degree of volatility which was greater for the American exchanges. The aforementioned mergers were closed at far higher multiples than market multiples. It can be seen that on average the values for US markets are higher than those for European markets. Polato and Floreani (2010) found that pre-crisis mergers were settled at EV/EBITDA multiples averaging 27x. American exchanges were valued more than European ones – an average EV/EBITDA multiple of 28.5x compared with an average multiple of 25.3x. Moreover, since most of the deals in the US market involved derivatives management companies, it can be deduced that the highest values refer to that particular market.

More recently, a new wave of consolidation has occurred with the offer of LSEG for the Canadian TMX and the battle for NYSE Euronext between Deutsche Börse and the consortium NASDAQ OMX–ICE. What we can observe is a substantial cut in M&As' multiples compared to the pre-crisis period; which is not surprising given that financial crisis gave rise to uncertainty as regards the cycle, dampened investment programmes by issuers and lowered investors' appetite for risk. Notwithstanding this, they appear in line with average market multiples during the period 2002–10. This would suggest that the joint effects of the crisis and increasing competition did not affect long-term profit expectations in a substantial way.

While pre-crisis mergers seemingly differentiated exchanges by business model or geographical location, such differences are apparently flattened in the most recent deals. For example, similar valuations in recent merger agreements were attached to LSEG and NYSE Euronext, despite their operating with partially different business models. It is worth noting that formal valuations do not seem to be the only criteria driving deals. NYSE Euronext, for example, accepted the Deutsche Börse offer despite receiving a lower valuation than that implied in the NASDAQ OMX–ICE offer.[9]

A new step in the consolidation process is the merger between ECNs. The takeover of BATS on Chi-X is of particular interest in light of the straightforward valuation that was given for the target company.[10] Such platforms support rapidly growing trading volumes with aggressive pricing schedules, which put pressures on margins. It is important to note, however, that ECNs operate with a unique and more flexible business model than traditional exchanges. In fact, by offering trading facilities over a wide array of international blue-chips they operate like an international exchange but with a thinner structure given that they do not perform certain functions that are typical of exchanges (for example, admissions to listing).

More recently, the merger between the Osaka Stock Exchange and Tokyo Stock Exchange, and the NASDAQ OMX offer for NYSE Euronext witnessed a sharp recovery in multiples. In 2012 the LSEG made a €15[11] offer for a 60 per cent stake in the London Clearing House which corresponds to a 57x multiple of the EV on the EBITDA.

6 Securities exchanges: shareholder value and risk profile

6.1 Share returns and shareholder value

As is well known, value creation is a multifaceted issue. Broadly speaking, several indicators or metrics may be regarded as proxies of value for shareholders. Prominent research focuses on share performance as a measure of value creation. During the years immediately preceding the crisis major listed exchanges experienced sharp increases in share prices reflecting high expectations of growth in revenues and margins stemming from the ongoing consolidation process. In this section we explore in more detail the share performances of listed exchanges during the recent past. We start by presenting some basic statistics. We investigate the returns on share prices and compare them with the returns of the reference index. Then we explore the relations between share values and major economic and financial data.

Starting with a simple representation of share performances, the raw data employed in the study are the daily share prices for listed exchanges and the daily values of the reference index, assuming the timeframe spanning from 2005 to 2011 (although obviously with the exception of exchanges with a shorter track record). Table A.3 in the Appendix reports the mean and median daily returns on share prices and the reference index and explores the characteristics of the distribution as well, as identified by the skewness and the kurtosis. Our analysis extends that of Higgs and Worthington (2005) who focused on four exchanges (Deutsche Börse, LSE, ASX and the Singapore Stock Exchange) and considered share and index performances up to June 2005.

At first sight, almost all listed exchanges experienced greater daily returns than the reference index, with Asian exchanges performing far better than the others. Among Western markets, the best performances were those of ICE and, to a lesser extent, NYSE Euronext and

NASDAQ OMX. The exchanges performing better were generally those experiencing the greater growth in earnings, although there are some exceptions.[12] Figures reveal differences in volatility as well. A common pattern is the greater volatility in exchanges' share performance compared with the reference index. There is, however, no clear evidence that the best share performances are associated with greater volatility in prices, as could be seen by looking at the figures for ICE and HKECH.

Looking at the characteristics of the distribution, and similarly to Higgs and Worthington, we find that all of the returns are positively skewed (except TMX)[13] while index returns are negatively skewed (with the exceptions of the BME, LSEG, Deutsche Börse, Bolsa Mexicana, BM&FBOVESPA and HKECH). The figures, therefore, indicate a greater likelihood of large increases in share returns than falls, while the inverse holds for index returns.[14] The kurtosis is also large for all exchanges. On balance, share returns across listed exchanges do not resemble a normal distribution.

In order to gain more insight into shareholder value, we focus on a selected sub-sample of listed exchanges. In particular, we focus on three measures of value. We first use the Tobin's q for expressing corporate valuation. We express the Tobin's q as the ratio of market value of common equity on total asset value where the numerator is expressed as total assets minus book value plus the market value of equity capital.

We then consider two relative measures of value. The first is based on the performance of exchanges' shares relative to the performance of the index. In particular, we compute on quarterly bases the ratio between the quarterly variation of the share and the variation of the index. We assign the ratio a negative sign when the share does worse than the index (in other words a lower positive performance, a greater negative performance or a negative performance when the index has a positive performance) and a positive sign in the opposite case. The second is based on the ratio of the exchange price-to-earnings ratio (P/E) and the average P/E of the index on quarterly bases. We compute the P/E of the exchange as the ratio of the average share price and the earnings per share on each quarter.

We expect the yield curve to affect the exchange's valuation through the standard impact on discounted cash flows and its relation with the economic cycle. For example, an inverted yield curve is generally associated with expectations of economic downturn which, in turn, would have a negative impact on an exchange's turnover, as evidence shows, and, therefore, on expected revenues.

Table 7.8 Performance measures: descriptive statistics

	Tobin's q		Relative share performance		Relative P/E	
	Average	St. Dev.	Average	St. Dev.	Average	St. Dev.
NASDAQ OMX	1.39	0.52	1.68	13.22	1.09	0.75
NYSE Euronext	1.52	1.03	3.67	17.06	1.38	1.29
TMX	2.23	0.84	1.90	4.70	1.05	0.49
LSEG	4.19	4.84	2.16	7.97	1.75	0.59
Deutsche Börse	1.06	0.06	2.19	6.33	1.38	0.48
BME	1.11	0.39	0.63	4.30	1.14	0.17
CME	0.52	0.13	3.71	9.40	1.44	0.79
ICE	0.64	0.30	5.26	15.63	1.49	0.90
HKECH	0.84	0.03	38.24	155.02	2.12	0.56
Singapore Stock Exchange	4.01	1.17	−2.17	154.95	2.20	0.85
ASX	2.525889	2.1737589	0.700115	10.55328	1.227138	0.47
Osaka Stock Exchange	0.867927	0.0217674	1.108935	18.33946	1.237224	0.77
Johannesburg Stock Exchange	1.964007	0.5528329	3.464406	10.45371	1.773314	0.89

Source: Our elaborations on exchanges' accounting data as for company assets and Bloomberg database for share and index performances and P/E measures.

Our sub-sample is restricted to 13 exchanges that are listed from at least 2006 for reasons of significance of the results. Hereafter we present the results of our analysis. We start by providing a broad overview of the performance measures across the exchanges we sampled. Table 7.8 summarizes the mean and standard deviation of the Tobin's q, the relative share performance[15] and the relative P/E ratio for the exchanges in the sample.

On average, and looking at Western markets, the American exchanges and LSEG are the best performers when considering the Tobin's q; they exhibit higher standard deviations as well. It is interesting to see the exception of the two large derivatives markets (CME and ICE) for which the measure is the lowest among the sample we considered. Expanding the analysis to the other market centres, performances are quite heterogeneous: the Singapore Stock Exchange and ASX (and, to a lesser extent, the Johannesburg Stock Exchange) present a high Tobin's q with higher volatility.

As for the two relative measures of value (the relative share performance index and relative P/E), the evidence is mixed. On average, HKECH has a far higher share performance index among all the exchanges in the sample and is followed by the two large derivatives exchanges, NYSE Euronext and the Johannesburg Stock Exchange. The Singapore Stock Exchange is an interesting case, the only exchange having, on average, a negative value for the index but with high levels of volatility as well. The Hong Kong and Singapore exchanges have the highest relative P/E values as well. On balance, such figures are consistent with their character of fast-growing markets.

Among Western exchanges, LSEG and Deutsche Börse are the best performers in terms of the relative P/E compared to the American exchanges. The Spanish BME has performances which are somewhat subdued.

Generally, the three measures of performance we considered are positively correlated, with a few exceptions. The most important is the ICE, for which the Tobin's q is negatively correlated with the other two measures. NYSE Euronext is the only case of negative correlation between the Tobin's q and the relative share performance. There are, then, a few cases of negative correlation between the Tobin's q and the relative P/E or between the relative share index and the relative P/E. Table A.4 in the Appendix presents the correlation matrix between the three measures of performance.

We now take a step forward in investigating the determinants of exchange performances. In particular, we focus on the Tobin's q and the P/E ratio of each exchange in our sub-sample and relate them to a set of industry-specific and financial variables.

The industry-specific variable comprises the degree of liquidity of the stock exchange that we measure by the market turnover (trading value on market capitalization).[16] In exchange industry studies liquidity is the main attribute of securities exchanges to the extent that it affects the efficiency of price discovery. Besides this, we expect liquidity to have a positive impact on an exchange's valuation for at least two reasons. First, we expect highly liquid exchanges to attract more customers (listed companies and traders) due to the well known externality effects. Moreover, since an exchange's trading revenues are a function of trading values, the higher the turnover the higher the trading fees should be. We have accounted for a positive correlation between trading value and listed companies, so there is no case for considering total listed companies in the analysis. Rather, we consider the ratio of foreign listings on total listings, which is deemed to capture the competitive positioning of the exchange. Financial variables comprise the variation of the EPS and the P/E of the index. Governance, however, may have an impact on performances as well, affecting investor protection and the incentives to expropriate minority shareholders.

Table 7.9 Results

	Tobin's q	P/E	Tobin's q (controlling for governance)	P/E (controlling for governance)
Constant	2.9032'***'	23.3201'***'	1.5661'***'	15.485'***'
FListings	−0.0033'**'	−0.0089' '	−0.0004' '	0.0038' '
Turnover	−0.2135' '	−0.4078' '	−0.3378'*'	−0.1078' '
Var. EPS	0.2333'*'	1.1228'.'	0.2029' '	1.2895'*'
ROCE	−5.2100'***'	−1.4986' '	−6.0455'***'	0.2515' '
P/E Index	−0.0054' '	−0.0891'*'	−0.0145'.'	−0.0749'.'
Inst. Own.			1.5371'.'	5.9552' '
χ^2 (6)	0.0000	0.0555	0.0000	0.0172
r-sq within	0.2350	0.0559	0.2474	0.0234
r-sq between	0.1051	0.0114	0.5034	0.9336
r-sq overall	0.0246	0.0106	0.2998	0.0973
Number of observations	286	271	153	150

Note: Significance codes: 0 '***' 0.001 '**' 0.01 '*' 0.05 '.' 0.1 ' ' 1. χ^2 test: within brackets, the degrees of freedom.

We test two models – a Tobin's q model and a P/E model – with industry specific and financial variables as explanatory variables, and then the same models including a governance variable which we identify in the percentage of institutional ownership.[17] We use a pooled model. Table 7.9 summarizes the main results.

The models we investigated appear to fit well with our data set, especially the Tobin's q model (either when including or excluding the governance variable), according to the chi-square value. The r-squares, however, are low. Within effects are greater for the Tobin's q model but negligible for the P/E model. The inclusion of the governance variable raises, however, the r-square (in particular, the r-square between and overall) in the Tobin's q model.

Seemingly, the Tobin's q is better explained by the variables included in the model. It is interesting to note that the sign of the coefficients are generally negative, with the exception of the EPS variation and the institutional ownership, which may appear somewhat counterintuitive. One would expect the competitive positioning (measured by the number of foreign listings) and the liquidity levels to positively affect performances. As competitive positioning and liquidity improve, the overall risk of the exchange might be expected to decline. However, as we have noted, higher levels of the Tobin's q metric are associated with greater degrees of volatility. Downward revisions in the appraisal of risk would, therefore, sustain market prices. A possible explanation of the pattern we observe is that attracting issuers and rising turnovers would require the adoption of aggressive pricing policies to cope with increasing competition, thus putting pressures on earnings. However, the crisis and the transformations that the industry is undergoing have, arguably, played a relevant role. Share prices experienced a sharp decline after rising in the pre-crisis period. By contrast, foreign listings remained more stable,[18] and trading volumes generally recovered. Differences, however, emerge from the data as regards the significance of the explanatory variables. In addition, foreign listings present a high degree of significance. By contrast, turnover is not significant in explaining the Tobin's q. The return on capital employed itself has a negative sign (and a high level of significance). During the last few years exchanges have experienced increases in returns associated with increases in the capital employed, the latter being related, in many cases, to the consolidation process. Mergers are aimed at improving efficiency and finding new sources of revenues, but often result in an expansion of capital invested.

6.2 The risk profile of listed exchanges: an analysis of the beta

We now turn our attentions to the analysis of the risk profile of exchanges by investigating their betas. We employ quarterly data in the time span 2005–10 for beta calculation.[19] We start by providing the basic statistics. In the Appendix (Table A.5) we provide an overview of the betas for each exchange showing the mean, median, standard deviation, minimum and maximum.[20] Looking at mean and median values, we observe that American exchanges, comprising the CME and ICE derivatives markets, have the highest levels of beta and the greatest volatility as well. The Hong Kong and Singapore exchanges, despite being classifiable as aggressive securities, present lower levels for their respective betas. At least for NYSE Euronext and NASDAQ OMX, the dynamics of the beta are, arguably, related to the movements surrounding the overall exchange industry. As has been noted, both of these exchanges assumed a central position in the industry-wide consolidation process, either as a result of the mergers that occurred during the last few years or because they are leading participants in the battle that is still taking place for supremacy in the exchange industry. In this regard the movements over NYSE Euronext involving the German exchange and, more recently, the ICE should be recalled, together with the attempts of NASDAQ to gain control over the LSEG. Such movements, while obviously conferring on these

Table 7.10 Beta of assets in place and growth opportunities

	β_{Aip}	EV/E	VG/E
NYSE Euronext	0.0538	1.944815	−1.49301
NASDAQ OMX	−0.3478	3.098263	−5.64678
TMX	0.0624	1.679944	−0.9622
CME	0.5707	5734.743	5733.433
ICE	0.856	3729.868	3728.889
Deutsche Börse	−0.0234	28.97654	24.43446
LSEG	12.2075	0.455079	0.450466
BME	−0.2857	18.97112	16.54784
Osaka Stock Exchange	−0.0429	5189.806	−2593.75
HKECH	−0.0673	626.2401	−2445.74
Singapore Stock Exchange	−0.4443	1.094426	−4.42157
ASX	0.5234	1.664782	0.802931
Johannesburg Stock Exchange	−0.0975	1.601405	1.172305

exchanges a substantially speculative character, elicit the questions of which equilibrium will be attained and when the industry will come to a stable position.

On the basis of the equity betas we have calculated we proceed to investigate the betas of assets in place and the growth opportunities (V_G) embedded in major exchanges. We employ, in this regard, the methodology of De Andrés et al.[21] (see Chapter 6). The value of growth opportunities is calculated by subtracting from the enterprise value the value of assets in place.[22]

Evidence largely differs across exchanges. The London-based exchange presents a high value of the beta of assets in place. The other markets have low betas, and for some of them the beta is negative. Seemingly, therefore, there are exchanges that behave in a countercyclical manner as for the ROA. The estimated value of growth opportunities largely diverges as well, ranging from absolutely large values for the CME and ICE to the negative values of other exchanges (in particular, the other American exchanges and Asian market centres); the total market value, therefore, does not capture the full values embedded in assets in place.

Taking another theoretical step forward, it is interesting to investigate whether there is some relation between the relevant industry-specific and financial measures. According to the model set forth in Chapter 6,

Table 7.11 The variables

	Investments
$Tech_{i,t}$/Total expenses	Expenditures in technology and software applications on total expenses for exchange *i* on time *t*
$Tang\_Assets_{i,t}$/ Total expenses	Tangible assets on total assets for exchange *i* on time *t*
	Financial Flexibility
$Lt\_funds_{i,t}$	Long-term funds (equity and long-term liabilities) on total assets for exchange *i* on time *t*
	Competitive positioning
$\Delta\ Turnover_{i,t}$	Trading volumes on market capitalization for exchange *i* on time *t*
$TValue_{i,t}$	Trading value for exchange *i* in the period *t*−1, *t*
$FListings_{i,t}$	Foreign listed companies on total listed companies for exchange *i* in the period *t*−*1*, *t*
	Governance
$Inst_{i,t}$	Institutional investors' ownership for exchange *i* in the period *t*
$Own\%_{,it}$	Total ownership of institutional investors with stakes > 5% for exchange *i* in the period *t*
	Financial structure
$Op\_lev_{i,t}$	Operational leverage
$Fin\_lev_{i,t}$	Financial leverage for exchange *i* in the period *t*[23]
	Economic performances
$\Delta\ earnings_{i,t}$	% change in earnings per share for exchange *i* in the period *t*−*1*, *t*
$ROCE_{i,t}$	Return on capital employed for exchange *i* in the period *t*−*1*, *t*
	Risks
$\%TangA_{i,t}$/ Av%TangA	Ratio of tangible assets on total assets for exchange in the period t on the average TangA/TA

we investigate beta of exchanges in relation to a set of variables expressing the investment strategies, the financial flexibility, the competitive positioning, the financial structure, the economic performances and the risk exposure. Table 7.11 summarizes the explanatory variables we employ.

In the Appendix (Table A.6) we present the matrix of correlations for the selected variables. Methodologically, we employ a pooled model across 16 listed exchanges[24] (in particular we use a random effect-GLS model) together with a time series analysis for a selected sample of exchanges (based on an OLS regression). Table A.7 in the Appendix provides the results.

On balance, the pooled model we investigated seemingly fits our data set well, according to the chi-square value. The r-square overall equals 0.3275 (for within and between effects the r-square is 0.3142 and 0.8749). Looking at the signs of the coefficients, we have in particular a negative sign for the variables expressing financial flexibility, the incidence of tangible assets on total assets, foreign listings, turnover, operational leverage and institutional ownership. The signs for foreign listings, turnover and long-term funds are consistent with what one would expect. As the firm reinforces its competitive positioning and improves its financial flexibility, overall risk tends to decline. By contrast, the sign of the operational leverage is somewhat surprising. The behaviour of governance variables is interesting. While institutional ownership is negatively related with the beta, which seems consistent with the hypothesis of institutional investors promoting better governance, the concentration measure (stakes which exceed 5 per cent) have a positive relation. However, only trading value appears to be strongly significant in explaining betas. Its sign is positive, which may appear to be somewhat counterintuitive; for possible explanations we recall what we have observed when commenting on share performances. Seemingly, the ROCE is positively related with the beta; here the sign could reflect the risks entailed by consolidation and engagement in risky activities.[25]

Finally, when looking at the results for the single exchanges the outcomes are controversial. Looking at the F-value, the model fits only in very few cases the population across all exchanges. The r-square values vary substantially. In fact, the explanatory variables seemingly have (with very few exceptions) low levels of significance.

7 Implications and expected future developments

The global exchange industry is undergoing a continuing and substantial transformation following two paths. The first is the increasing competition between trading platforms (exchanges and other platforms). The second is the deep consolidation process which is reshaping the morphology of the industry. As we have noted, the aforementioned developments are being driven by the strategic decisions of large institutional investors who are the main shareholders of the major groups. The new competitive environment has radically changed the long-established paradigms of managing exchanges with important implications for the governance mechanisms. Those vested interests that currently prevail strongly act in a way to promote value creation for

Table 7.12 Ranking analysis

	Financial Flexibility	EBITDA %	ROE	ROCE	EBIT/TV	TV/CE	Total	Average	Inv	Total Rank
NYSE Euronext	14	17	16	15	12	4	78	13	−13	16
NASDAQ OMX	13	16	8	13	11	3	64	11	−11	14
TMX	11	9	4	12	9	8	53	9	−9	8
CME	11	5	12	5	–	–	33	8	−8	6
ICE	17	6	10	10	–	–	43	11	−11	15
CBOE	10	11	3	2	–	–	26	7	−7	4
BM&FBOVESPA	1	7	15	15	2	14	54	9	−9	9
Bolsa Mexicana	3	13	14	13	5	11	59	10	−10	13
Bolsa de Colombia	9	14	6	6	7	9	51	9	−9	7
LSEG	15	12	17	17	10	7	78	13	−13	16
Deutsche Börse	16	8	7	7	4	12	54	9	−9	9
BME	8	3	5	4	8	2	30	5	−5	3
HKECH	7	2	1	1	6	6	23	4	−4	2
Singapore Stock Exchange	5	1	2	3	1	10	22	4	−4	1
Osaka Stock Exchange	4	10	13	11	3	13	54	9	−9	9
ASX	2	4	11	8	14	1	40	7	−7	5
Johannesburg Stock Exchange	6	15	8	9	13	5	56	9	−9	12

shareholders, whereas in the past the promoters of exchange strategies were the platform users. It is certainly true that large shareholders of listed exchanges are interested in the functioning of trading platforms. Arguably, however, their interests as shareholders tend to prevail over their utility as platform users.

On balance, these developments require an in-depth analysis of the economics of exchanges. Table 7.12 performs a ranking analysis of listed exchanges with reference to a selected panel of financial and performance measures. As we can see, Asian exchanges are at the top of the total rank metric constructed on our selected performance measures. The largest exchanges, in particular the American exchanges which were at the forefront of the widespread consolidation process that affected the industry, are on the bottom side.

The problem of value becomes of paramount importance in the context of an ongoing consolidation process for the very practical reason of determining the relative values of merging entities and establishing a fair determination of the considerations owed to shareholders of acquired firms. Moving the reasoning onto a strategic ground, value creation is important in order to determine who will lead the next stages in the consolidation process. Relative values mirror the success in competitive strategies and those exchanges realizing the better outcomes will take an active role in defining the competitive paradigms. So far, the consolidation process has largely interested Western markets, but recently the Asian landscape has started to show movements with the merger between the two Japanese exchanges. It is to be expected, however, that the process will expand further, bridging Asian and Western markets. And we would also note that the strategic implications of consolidation are mirrored by the recovering multiples (following the declines observed during the crisis) in the most recent mergers.

Appendix

Table A.1 Estimates

	a	β	a_1	β_1	θ	ϑ	a_{Tv}	β_{Tv}
NYSE Euronext	0.5290	0.9327	11.7374	0.2899	11.7752	0.2795	−3.096	0.9078
NASDAQ OMX	2.9497	0.4422	0.4168	3.4253	3.3391	1.2742	2.9497	0.4422
TMX	−1.4673	1.1380	0.1592	3.1899	0.2117	2.0818	−1.1539	0.7471
CME	70.382	0.4111	–	–	–	–	–	–
ICE	−11.72	0.4402	–	–	–	–	–	–
BM&FBOVESPA	4.7856	0.3956	13.599	−0.7955	25.0787	−6.9998	−2.5272	0.9341
Bolsa Mexicana	−7.7871	1.8788	18.0561	−2.4898	4.6720	1.2566	2.4640	0.4441
Bolsa de Santiago	12.7931	0.5847	n.a	n.a	n.a	n.a	n.a	n.a
Deutsche Börse	6.4742	0.2262	8.5478	1.0374	13.5781	−2.3233	−1.1378	0.7744
LSEG	7.0088	0.0981	−0.4193	3.4419	2.3040	1.4106	−0.6176	0.7122
BME	5.1375	0.2903	0.9516	2.9669	−2.5546	2.6465	1.9319	0.4916
Osaka Stock Exchange	−0.9456	1.0759	11.9297	0.2337	8.7495	−0.0302	11.4457	−0.1663
HKECH	5.7645	0.3062	1.3074	3.5426	−1.8445	3.2479	−3.1948	0.9528
Singapore Stock Exchange	3.2972	0.5463	2.1993	3.0379	−0.6718	2.7395	−1.8294	0.8847
ASX	5.9980	0.1996	11.8651	0.7848	0.6904	2.0626	2.5153	0.8761
Johannesburg Stock Exchange	2.6257	0.6713	5.3	2.4566	7.3951	−0.0485	−0.5204	0.7057
Bolsa de Colombia	10.1401	−0.0215	22.8426	−5.0435	8.0293	0.9245	8.8874	0.1213

Table A.2 Performance measures

	EBITDA %		ROE		ROTE		ROCE	
	Average	**Rel. St. Dev**	**Average**	**Rel. St. Dev**	**Average**	**Rel. St. Dev**	**Average**	**Rel. St. Dev**
NYSE Euronext	17.5%	164%	0.9%	556.1%	−1.1%	960.6%	1.3%	233.6%
NASDAQ OMX	23.2%	53.4%	5.5%	151.7%	−3.15%	800.3%	3.0%	126.8%
TMX	56.1%	19.5%	10.3%	60.3%	6.9%	454.8%	3.04%	35.9%
CME	69.6%	11.2%	3.6%	84.4%	−0.6%	1247.7%	6.6%	101.3%
CBOE	48.1%	11.6%	10.6%	37.2%	12.8%	41.4%	15.0%	36.8%
ICE	65.3%	19.3%	5.3%	55.4%	−114.4%	366.8%	4.3%	122.1%
BM&FBOVESPA	61.7%	22.5%	1.1%	50.25%	5.7%	60.1%	1.3%	39.6%
Bolsa Mexicana	41.4%	13.6%	2%	131.8%	2.7%	132.4%	3.0%	30.8%
Bolsa de Santiago	34.4%	19.1%	6.15%	36.6%	6.15%	36.6%	4.0%	23.8%
Deutsche Börse	58.1%	12.7%	6.5%	32.5%	389.45%	375.1%	5.8%	34.2%
LSEG	41.7%	104.7%	−0.8%	973.3%	−3%	474.8%	−6.5%	701.9%
BME	70.7%	10.3%	7.9%	35%	9.8%	34.9%	11.0%	22.7%
Osaka Stock Exchange	55.4%	15.6%	3.4%	41.6%	4.2%	40.4%	4.0%	26.2%
HKECH	71.5%	14.3%	14.4%	38.8%	14.4%	38.8%	9.15	35.5%
Singapore Stock Exchange	62.65	14.9%	11.5%	29.6%	13%	25.7%	13.5%	29.0%
ASX	69.9%	15.6%	4.9%	80.8%	15.5%	22.0%	5.6%	79.0%
Johannesburg Stock Exchange	30.6%	46.3%	5.5%	40.2%	6.4%	41.5%	4.8%	57.1%
Bolsa de Colombia	40%	46.4%	7.8%	56.3%	7.8%	56.3%	6.2%	60.7%

Table A.3 Share and index performance

	NYSE Euronext		NASDAQ OMX		TMX		BME		Japan SE		Johannesburg Stock Exchange		Singapore Stock Exchange	
	Share	**Index**	**Share**	**Index**	**Share**	**Index**	**Share**	**Index**	**Share**	**Index**	**Share**	**Index**	**Share**	**Index**
Obs.	1824	1824	1824	1824	1824	1824	1425	1425	1899	1899	1401	1401	1755	1755
Start date	04/01/05	04/01/05	04/01/05	04/01/05	04/01/05	04/01/05	17/07/06	17/07/06	5/4/04	5/4/04	06/06/06	06/06/06	04/01/05	04/01/05
End Date	30/12/11	30/12/11	30/12/11	30/12/11	30/12/11	30/12/11	30/12/11	30/12/11	30/12/11	30/12/11	30/12/11	30/12/11	30/12/11	30/12/11
Mean	0.0765	0.0127	0.0988	0.0127	0.0433	0.0228	−0.0030	-0.0040	0.1149	0.0144	0.1413	0	0.0991	0.0194
Median	−0.0323	0.0544	0	0.0544	0	0.0590	−0.0441	0.0139	0.1123	0.0248	0	0.1019	0	0.0929
St. Dev.	3.6350	1.4346	3.1943	1.4346	1.9571	1.3236	2.10273	1.7369	3.368	1.4917	2.6217	2.1510	2.4023	1.2983
Skewness	2.9146	−0.0436	0.6078	−0.0436	−0.2335	−0.4603	0.1987	0.4217	0.7923	−0.1784	8.8084	−13.5704	0.5067	−0.1796
Kurtosis	47.7206	12.6268	8.7204	12.6268	9.1711	11.7116	5.1641	10.1815	6.938	11.464	198.0359	364.1386	6.6204	7.9760

	CME		ICE		CBOE		LSEG		Deutsche Börse		ASX		Bolsa Mexicana	
	Share	**Index**	**Share**	**Index**	**Share**	**Index**	**Share**	**Index**	**Share**	**Index**	**Share**	**Index**	**Share**	**Index**
Obs.	1824	1824	1598	1598	404	404	1824	1824	1824	1824	1825	1825	895	895
Start date	04/01/05	04/01/05	16/11/05	16/11/05	15/06/10	15/06/10	04/01/05	04/01/05	04/01/05	04/01/05	04/01/05	04/01/05	13/06/08	13/06/08
End Date	30/12/11	30/12/11	30/12/11	30/12/11	30/12/11	30/12/11	30/12/11	30/12/11	30/12/11	30/12/11	30/12/11	30/12/11	30/12/11	30/12/11
Mean	0.0479	0.0127	0.1715	0.0128	−0.0041	0.0439	0.0524	0.0169	0.0672	0.0285	0.0283	-0.0302	0.0585	0.0350
Median	0	0.0544	0	0.0600	0	0.0529	0	0	0	0.0726	0	0.0020	0	0.0879
St. Dev.	2.8907	1.4346	3.9623	1.5128	2.2099	1.300	2.6856	1.3366	2.5015	1.4936	1.9703	2.0350	2.2046	1.6278
Skewness	0.1068	−0.0436	2.0314	−0.0428	0.3708	−0.4003	1.2896	0.0614	0.3653	0.2860	0.4496	−21.2695	0.5007	0.4461
Kurtosis	10.0924	12.6268	29.4436	11.6456	6.2486	6.3299	17.6066	10.8930	8.2134	10.6359	17.8673	719.0109	6.4910	9.4171

	BM&FBOVESPA		HKECH	
	Share	Index	Share	Index
Obs.	1065	1065	1728	1728
Start date	03/12/07	03/12/07	04/01/05	04/01/05
End Date	30/12/11	30/12/11	30/12/11	30/12/11
Mean	−0.0209	−0.0127	0.1366	0.0311
Median	0	0	0	0.0753
St. Dev.	3.6099	2.6596	2.6039	1.8045
Skewness	0.4815	0.3356	0.7349	0.3260
Kurtosis	8.3325	7.4422	8.8590	11.4079

Table A.4 Correlation matrix

NASDAQ OMX	**Tobin's q**	**Rel. Sh. P.**	**Rel P/E**	**NYSE E.**	**Tobin's q**	**Rel. Sh. P.**	**Rel P/E**
Tobin's q	1			Tobin's q	1		
Rel. Sh. P	0.5055	1		Rel. Sh. P	−0.2622	1	
Rel P/E	0.8523	0.3130	1	Rel P/E	0.9063	−0.1235	1
TMX	**Tobin's q**	**Rel. Sh. P.**	**Rel P/E**	**LSEG**	**Tobin's q**	**Rel. Sh. P.**	**Rel P/E**
Tobin's q	1			Tobin's q	1		
Rel. Sh. P	0.2327	1		Rel. Sh. P	0.1019	1	
Rel P/E	0.7976	0.5100	1	Rel P/E	0.6100	0.2649	1
Deutsche Börse	**Tobin's q**	**Rel. Sh. P.**	**Rel P/E**	**BME**	**Tobin's q**	**Rel. Sh. P.**	**Rel P/E**
Tobin's q	1			Tobin's q	1		
Rel. Sh. P	0.3178	1		Rel. Sh. P	0.3092	1	
Rel P/E	0.2312	0.5204	1	Rel P/E	0.0733	0.3910	1
CME	**Tobin's q**	**Rel. Sh. P.**	**Rel P/E**	**ICE**	**Tobin's q**	**Rel. Sh. P.**	**Rel P/E**
Tobin's q	1			Tobin's q	1		
Rel. Sh. P	0.3533	1		Rel. Sh. P	−0.2633	1	
Rel P/E	0.4796	0.3939	1	Rel P/E	−0.7961	0.4011	1
HKECH	**Tobin's q**	**Rel. Sh. P.**	**Rel P/E**	**Singapore Stock Exchange**	**Tobin's q**	**Rel. Sh. P.**	**Rel P/E**
Tobin's q	1			Tobin's q	1		
Rel. Sh. P	0.3488	1		Rel. Sh. P	0.0543	1	
Rel P/E	−0.5211	−0.025	1	Rel P/E	0.0324	−0.5388	1
ASX	**Tobin's q**	**Rel. Sh. P.**	**Rel P/E**	**Osaka Stock Exchange**	**Tobin's q**	**Rel. Sh. P.**	**Rel P/E**
Tobin's q	1			Tobin's q	1		
Rel. Sh. P	0.1987	1		Rel. Sh. P	0.0285	1	
Rel P/E	0.0315	−0.0601	1	Rel P/E	N.A.	N.A.	1
Johannesburg Stock Exchange	**Tobin's q**	**Rel. Sh. P.**	**Rel P/E**				
Tobin's q	1						
Rel. Sh. P	0.1643	1					
Rel P/E	0.3744	−0.1149	1				

Table A.5 Beta

	β					β_{Aip}
	Median	**Mean**	**Min**	**Max**	**St.Dev.**	
NYSE Euronext	1.735	1.671	1.185	2.182	0.287	0.0538
NASDAQ OMX	1.403	1.439	0.958	2.472	0.387	−0.3478
TMX	0.686	0.724	0.360	1.101	0.188	0.0624
CME	1.246	1.261	1.051	1.776	0.165	0.5707
CBOE	0.655	0.796	0.539	1.642	0.385	4.1798
ICE	1.553	1.595	1.093	2.389	0.385	0.8560
BM&FBOVESPA	0.460	0.472	0.223	0.685	0.125	0.1035
Bolsa Mexicana	0.716	0.754	0.576	1.110	0.168	0.2615
Bolsa de Colombia	0.785	0.774	0.660	0.893	0.085	0.1551
Deutsche Börse	1.046	1.035	0.613	1.502	0.210	−0.0234
LSEG	1.039	0.978	0.564	1.394	0.278	12.2075
BME	0.759	0.776	0.497	1.178	0.219	−0.2857
Osaka Stock Exchange	0.751	0.867	0.549	1.563	0.276	−0.0429
HKECH	1.106	1.163	0.882	1.578	0.185	−0.0673
Singapore Stock Exchange	1.170	1.315	0.909	1.863	0.346	−0.4443
ASX	0.921	0.951	0.708	1.300	0.154	0.5234
Johannesburg Stock Exchange	0.495	0.567	0.255	1.114	0.246	−0.0975

Table A.6 Selected variables for beta analysis: matrix of correlations (pooled)

	1	2	3	4	5	6	7	8	9	10	11	12	13
1 $Tech_{i,t}$/*Total expenses*	1												
2 $Tang\_Assets_{i,t}$/*Total Assets*	0.420	1											
3 $Lt\_funds_{i,t}$	0.228	0.388	1										
4 $\Delta TValue_{i,t}$	−0.033	0.082	−0.086	1									
5 $FListings_{i,t}$	−0.045	−0.801	−0.411	−0.027	1								
6 $Turnover_{i,t}$	−0.429	−0.471	−0.372	0.128	0.243	1							
7 $Op\_lev_{i,t}$	−0.229	−0.145	0.028	0.121	−0.142	0.544	1						
8 $Fin\_lev_{i,t}$	−0.250	−0.608	−0.483	0.151	0.703	0.348	−0.051	1					
9 $Inst_{i,t}$	0.073	0.095	−0.207	0.039	−0.050	−0.079	0.011	0.097	1				
10 $Own\%_{,it}$	−0.102	−0.354	−0.437	0.087	0.401	0.250	0.083	0.420	0.641	1			
11 Δ $earnings_{i,t}$	0.066	0.128	0.142	0.176	−0.109	0.114	0.072	−0.107	−0.022	−0.024	1		
12 $Roce_{i,t}$	0.475	0.730	0.382	0.038	−0.498	−0.302	−0.242	−0.515	−0.045	−0.353	0.423	1	
13 $\%TangA_{i,t}/Av\%TangA$	0.258	0.864	0.306	0.046	−0.697	−0.394	−0.138	−0.540	0.056	−0.291	0.085	0.633	1

Table A.7 Beta analysis: results

	Pooled model	NYSE Euronext	NASDAQ OMX	TMG	CME	ICE	LSEG	Deutsche Börse	BME	Singapore Stock Exchange	HKECH	Osaka Stock Exchange	ASX
Const	12.419 ‘ ’	−3691‘ ’	20.6509‘ ’	−270.13‘ ’	−2374.5‘ ’	n.s.	−804.09‘ ’	−294.6‘ ’	−1075.4‘ ’	−21.89‘ ’	1454.6‘ ’	−29.41‘ ’	1387‘ ’
$Tech_{i,t}$/Tot exp	222.55‘ ’	−4997.1‘ ’	1656.8‘ ’	−28.87‘ ’	586.5‘ ’	n.s.		−20.11‘ ’	2219.1‘ ’	5.567‘ ’	−1502‘ ’		−1385.6‘ ’
$Tang\_Assets_{i,t}$/TA	−114.37 ‘ ’	−1556.6‘ ’	−28.520‘ ’	−6.510‘ ’	1627.5‘ ’	n.s.	−474.65‘ ’	214.2‘ ’	1130.9‘ ’	23.24‘ ’	Omitted	−4.30‘ ’	128.9‘ ’
$Lt\_funds_{i,t}$	−47.469‘ ’	9457.1‘ ’	−430.3‘ ’	−89.03''	2171.8‘ ’	n.s.	−179.87‘ ’	96.86‘ ’	81.67‘ ’	−5.95‘ ’	−610.03‘ ’	30.95‘ ’	323.77‘ ’
$\Delta TValue_{i,t}$	0.0003‘*** ’	401.8‘ ’	6.135‘ ’	−4.013‘ ’	316.3‘ ’	n.s.	1100.7‘. ’	−28.8‘ ’	−96.93‘ ’	0.995‘ ’	129.6‘ ’	1.563‘ ’	−50.06‘ ’
$FListings_{i,t}$	−0.1004‘ ’	2.108‘ ’	−0.455‘*’	1.796‘ ’		n.s.	0.731‘ ’	0.015‘ ’	−2.981‘ ’	−0.009‘ ’	−11.64‘ ’	Omitted	−25.70‘ ’
$Turnover_{i,t}$	−24.238‘.’	−359.6‘ ’	−1.234‘ ’	11.804‘ ’		n.s.	535.4‘ ’	25.56‘ ’	−155.04‘ ’	−39.8‘ ’	−384‘ ’	7.759‘ ’	5.260‘ ’
$Op\_lev_{i,t}$	−7.695‘*’	−153437‘ ’	18.063‘.’	49.394‘ ’	186.3‘ ’	n.s.	153.6‘ ’	16.14‘ ’	199.75‘ ’	−0.381‘ ’	−179.3‘ ’	−0.709‘ ’	−97.77‘ ’
$Fin\_lev_{i,t}$	60.068‘ ’	2897.4‘ ’	−36.850‘ ’	25.10‘ ’	2121.6‘ ’	n.s.	−29.53‘ ’	−32.7‘ ’	−513.4‘ ’	−10.5‘ ’	−607.6‘ ’	12.36‘ ’	−162.4‘ ’
Own%	−122.74‘ ’	−4528.8‘. ’	196.18‘. ’	391.03‘ ’	21.22‘ ’	n.s.	1546.8‘ ’	88.578‘ ’	−1191.1‘ ’				
$\%Inst_{,it}$	216.494‘ ’	2896.6‘ ’	57.55‘ ’	−60.403‘ ’	690.9‘ ’	n.s.	−2189.2‘ ’	−197.4‘. ’	Omitted				
$\Delta\ earnings_{i,t}$	18.672‘ ’	30.69‘ ’	−5.221‘ ’	−5.255‘ ’	18.83''	n.s.	71.189‘ ’	8.719‘ ’	54.45‘ ’	−1.93‘ ’	23.63‘ ’	0.357‘ ’	1088.7‘ ’
$Roce_{i,t}$	1116.7‘*’	−2025‘ ’	5046.3‘ ***’	−28.23‘ ’	−7838.05''	n.s.	199.02‘ ’	684.7‘ ’	1611.6‘ ’	108.1‘ ***’	−276.4‘ ’	23.38‘ ’	−2522.7‘ ’
$\%TangA_{i,t}$/ Av%TangA	8.380‘ ’	−119.84‘ ’	−29.488‘ ’	21.72‘ ’	−165.02‘ ’	n.s.	−354.74‘ ’	1.38‘ ’	−66.413‘ ’	1.85‘ ’	−90.58‘ ’	1.14‘ ’	−186.4‘ ’
r-sq within	0.3142												
r-sq between	0.8749												
r-sq overall	0.3275	0.6085	0.9955	0.462	0.2709		0.4733	0.5887	0.6494	0.810	0.2757	0.3637	0.1474
Wald $\chi^2(13)$	53.57												
Prob > χ^2	0.0000												
Prob >F (13,6)		0.7118	0.000	0.8091	0.8705		0.4611	0.318	0.6714	0.0004	0.7849	0.4246	0.9899
D Watson			2.5586	2.3366	2.1834		2.7839	2.5292	1.8313	2.989	2.358	2.2362	2.1126
Number of groups	6												

Significance codes: 0 ‘***’ 0.001 ‘**’ 0.01 ‘*’ 0.05 ‘.’ 0.1 ‘ ’ 1. Wald Chi-square: within brackets the degrees of freedom

Notes

1 Securities Industry and Exchange Industry: Organization and Value Chain

1. Excellent essays on industrial organization can be found in J. Tirole (1993) *The Theory of Industrial Organization* (Cambridge: Mit Press) and F. M. Scherer and D. Ross (1990) *Industrial Market Structure and Economic Performance* (Boston, MA: Houghton Mifflin).
2. See, for example, A. H. Meltzer (1969) 'On Efficiency and Regulation of the Securities Industry' in H. G. Manne (ed.) *Economic Policy and the Regulation of Corporate Securities* (Washington: American Enterprise Institute for Public Policy Research).
3. The topic of barriers in the financial industry has been investigated from a variety of perspectives, ranging from the market for corporate control to the mechanics of trading. The implications of barriers (in particular of regulatory barriers) for the efficiency of the market for corporate control are analysed by D. R. Fischel (1978) 'Efficient Capital Market Theory, the Market for Corporate Control and the Regulation of Cash Tender Offers', *Texas Law Review*, 57, 1.
4. It may be useful to clarify the meanings of the term *exchange*, since it is used in several ways and to define different, although strictly related, things. In the first instance, when we make reference to the *exchange industry* the term exchange is intended to define the trading process. Otherwise the reference to the *securities exchange* identifies the market place where trading occurs. Quite often, however, the term exchange is referred to the subject who operates the market place. Throughout of the book we will make reference to the term in its different meanings, taking care to make it clear what meaning we are referring to.
5. Although the exchange industry is generally referred to as the industry for the exchange of securities on the secondary market, we maintain that those services involved in primary market operations (i.e. underwriting services) should be comprised within the core services of the exchange industry as well. Since such services are aimed at ameliorating an exchange (in this case, between the issuer and the investors) they perform the same economic function of secondary market services. By contrast all those advisory services for issuers (and which are part of the investment banking) may be comprised within the broader securities industry.
6. The relationship between listing decisions and cost of capital has been widely investigated in the academic literature, in particular with reference to cross-listing decisions. For an in-depth analysis of the topic see M. Pagano, A. A. Röell and J. Zechner (2002) 'The Geography of Equity Listing: Why Do Companies List Abroad?', *Journal of Finance*, 57, 6 (December). According to the authors, the reduction in cost of capital may be achieved thanks to the greater liquidity of the listing market or better forms of disclosure to which

the issuers binds by choosing that market. Other factors that may positively impact on the cost of capital are the visibility deriving from the listing, comprising the analyst coverage. More recently, the issue has been investigated by L. Hail and C. Leuz (2008) 'Cost of Capital Effects and Changes in Growth Expectations Around U.S. Cross-Listings', *Journal of Financial Economics*, 93, 3. They find that firms' cross-listing on US exchanges experience large reductions in the cost of capital, whereas reductions in the cost of capital are smaller for companies from countries with well developed home-country institutions, confirming the bonding hypothesis.

7. Rulebooks generally define the exchange as an organized market where buyers and sellers trade securities. The concept of organization captures the fact that trading takes place according to specific procedures and rules designed to drive the matching between buying and selling orders and discovering the price. Exchanges are also defined as regulated markets in order to capture the fact that they function according to a set of rules and supervisory standards adopted by the law and regulators (supervisory authorities). Sometimes, especially in rulebooks, the marketplace is referred to as a *trading venue*. It means a system, operated according to specific rules and procedures and based on a given technology platform, where trading occurs. It is not just purely a matter of labels. Indeed, in today securities industry, the exchange is only one of the different venues where securities can be traded.
8. It could be possible for the origination phase to be absorbed within the sphere of a supervisory authority due to the evident conflicts of interest entailed by entrusting exchange with admission functions. For example, this is the case of the United Kingdom where the United Kingdom Listing Authority (UKLA) is responsible for admissions to the official list. Obviously, this implies making a distinction between admission to listing and admission to trading that is the decision of the exchange of organizing a market for securities admitted to listing. Although performed by a supervisor, origination continues to fall within the exchange industry. What is relevant is the economic function of facilitating capital market finance for issuers and providing a wide liquidity pool for investors not just the entity managing single functions along the value chain.
9. Actually, they refer to *two-sided markets*. The notion of two-sided platforms has been introduced by Evans and Schmalensee (2007) as synonymous of the Rochet and Tirole's two-sided markets notion.
10. Usage externalities arise *ex post* as trades between end-users occurred. Membership externalities arise when the decision to join the platform generates an agent's positive net surplus from interaction with an additional end-user on the other side.
11. An excellent application of the network externalities' theory to exchange competition can be found in C. Di Noia (1998) *Competition and Integration Among Stock Exchanges in Europe: Network Effects, Implicit Mergers and Remote Access* (Wharton Financial Institutions Center, Working Paper Series, 98–03).
12. Owing to the new institutional approach of the firm we know that firms exist because of the cost entailed by market transactions. However, facilitating market transactions is not only a matter of transaction costs. It entails protecting property rights as well, as widely recognized by many economists.

See, among others, R. Coase (1988)*The Firm, The Market, and the Law*, and R. Coase (1992) 'The Institutional Structure of Production', *American Economic Review*, 82, 4. The property right approach with reference to exchanges has been developed with reference to prices although the body of literature on the topic is scarce.

13. See J. H. Mulherin, J. M. Netter and J. Overdahl (1991). For a critical dissertation see R. I. Webb (2003) 'Transitory Real-Time Property Rights and Exchange Intellectual Property', *The Journal of Futures Markets*, 23, 9. Webb contends that the cost of ensuring accurate process, fully reflecting the relevant information, may be invoked to temporalily protect the real-time prices that an exchange generates from expropriation.
14. For a review of the earliest SEC initiatives alongside the consolidation/fragmentation debate, see Cohen et al. (1986) *The Microstructure of Securities Markets* (Englewood Cliffs, NJ: Prentice Hall) pp. 150–66.
15. Here we should distinguish between physical fragmentation and economic fragmentation, the first being related with the dispersion of the overall order flow among different trading venues, while the latter having to do with the impacts of fragmentation on the quality of prices. To the extent that there is a widespread transparency on prices so as traders have a complete understanding of exchange conditions on different market centres, physical fragmentation would not adversely affect the information content of market prices.
16. For an excellent discussion on the topic and an exhaustive review of possible bias explanations, see K. K. Lewis (1999) 'Trying to Explain Home Bias in Equities and Consumption', *Journal of Economic Literature*, 37, 2.
17. See Pagano, Röell and Zechner, 'Geography of Equity Listing' (cited).
18. Tightening compliance requirements may actually induce relevant spillovers among international financial centres. This was the case of the Sarbanes – Oxley Act in the US, which is deemed as a major factor causing a substantial loss of foreign listings by the New York Stock Exchange (NYSE).
19. Here intended as the choice to identify within the markets that the exchange runs a specified segment functioning according to different admission and trading rules, specially defined to fit the demand of certain issuers.
20. According to best execution duties, a venue quoting inside-the-spread prices, cannot avoid trading with any trader accepting the quoted prices. Therefore, it could not refuse to trade with an informed one.

2 The Exchange Industry: An Overview

1. Eurex was formed in September 1997 when the Deutsche Terminbörse and the Swiss Options and Financial Futures Exchange (SOFFEX) announced their merger. Eurex was operated by a joint venture between Deutsche Börse and the SIX Swiss Exchange until January 2012 when the Swiss Exchange sold its 50% stake to Deutsche Börse.
2. Other relevant exchanges in the region, in terms of attractiveness to foreign companies, are the Canadian TMX Group and the Mexican Exchange.
3. The relationship between market dimension and turnover velocity has been investigated with reference to exchange trading, but trades occurring

off-exchange have not been taken into account. However, the diversion of order flow operated by alternative platforms (or trades occurring over the counter) may have contributed to dampen turnover activity in primary markets. In Europe, following the introduction of the MiFID, trading outside exchanges' platforms have been institutionalized and have started to grow. In 2012 in the US the erosion of the market value of the largest exchanges has also increased.

4. A first step in this direction can be detected in the recent cross-quotation agreement between the LSEG and the Singapore Stock Exchange.
5. Standard & Poor's assigns to securities exchanges and clearing houses assess the viability of the business on the grounds of the demand and supply of listed products. These, in particular, are assessed in terms of the diversity of instruments admitted to trading and their relevance to the financial markets and the real economy.
6. We assume this sector as a reference term since exchanges are usually comprised under the broker–dealer financial sector.
7. We recall, in particular, the mergers between the NYSE and the pan-European exchange Euronext, the aggregation between the London Stock Exchange (LSE) and the Borsa Italiana and the NASDAQ bid for the OMX Exchange. In the same period other relevant deals were promoted but not finalized (mainly because of the opposition of the shareholders of the target exchange); Dubai's bid for the London Stock Exchange is a significant example that comes to mind.
8. See A. Shleifer and R. W. Vishny (1986) 'Large Shareholders and Corporate Control', *Journal of Political Economy*, 94, 3. The authors argue that in corporations with dispersed ownership it may not pay any one of the shareholders to monitor performances. By contrast, they model a setting where large minority shareholders may, at least partially, provide a solution to the free-rider problem. The argument of free riding as a problem lessening incentives to monitor management performances is developed in S. J. Grossman and O. D. Hart (1980) 'Takeover Bids, the Free-Rider Problem and the Theory of the Corporation', *Bell Journal of Economics*, 11.
9. As stated by the WFE, however, mergers and acquisitions in the exchange industry gave rise to somewhat contrasting trends, with some exchanges experiencing cost reductions while others faced cost increases. For example, the NYSE Euronext group enjoyed a 16% cost reduction in 2010 compared to the previous year (with major reductions being concentrated in merger expenses and exit costs) while BM&FBOVESPA faced a 17% increase.
10. NYSE Euronext regulatory costs counts for slightly less that 50% of the overall regulatory costs paid by WFE members. Roughly 60% of the *other costs* borne by exchanges worldwide, are attributable to NYSE Euronext as well.
11. Relevant examples already discussed are the merger between Euronext and the London-based derivatives exchange Liffe and, more recently, the merger between the LSE and Borsa Italiana, which granted, to the former, access to the derivatives business of the Italian Exchange. Another relevant case was the pan-European bond exchange MTS which fell under the control of the LSE at the time of the merger with Borsa Italiana, and was then sold to Euronext which expanded its business model to wholesale trading in government bonds.

12. In particular, the author focuses on the vertical integration policies of stock exchanges. His findings do not provide evidence that a vertically integrated business model leads to greater efficiency.
13. Farrell's notion of technical efficiency refers to the ability of a productive organization to operate on the boundary of its production set (or close to it).
14. As is well known, the relationship between exchanges and other venues is inverted in derivatives trading where, at least for certain underlings, over-the-counter venues have the greatest market share on contracts traded.
15. The EMCF serves as a central counterparty for equities spanning 19 European markets through ten MTFs, among which are BATS, Chi-X Europe, NASDAQ OMX Nordics and Turquoise. Many of these MTFs have designated EuroCCP as a central counterparty as well.
16. In a recent survey the European Commission found that for clearing and settlement services the cost of cross-border securities ranges from 2.5 to three times the cost of domestic trades. The difference is even more pronounced for custody and safe keeping services. For reference, see 'Monitoring prices, costs and volumes of trading and post-trading services', report prepared for the European Commission, DG Internal Market and Services, July 2009.

3 Securities Industry Regulation. Implications for Exchanges' Performances

1. The *bonding hypothesis* was developed by Coffee (2002) and Stulz (1999), and predicts that cross-listed firms experience better corporate governance than non-cross-listed firms from the same country as the former become subject to tighter investor protection. The authors proposed the bonding hypothesis as referring specifically to cross-listing on major US stock exchanges on the assumption that such markets would ensure the best levels of protection. While such a hypothesis has come under scrutiny from a bourgeoning strand of empirical investigations, its implications are powerful and argue for a selection of stock exchanges by disclosure standards. Clearly there would be consequences for investors as well, who would prefer to concentrate on the exchanges that succeed in attracting a large number of issuers.
2. See C. Di Noia (2001)'Competition and Integration Among Stock Exchanges in Europe: Network Effects, Implicit Mergers and Remote Access', *European Financial Management*, 39 (42). Theoretically, it has been argued that, logically, competition should lead to just one surviving exchange unless exchanges form alliances. In that case, competition among exchanges would be converted into a cooperative network. An interesting form of alliance is the network comprising the common ownership of large platforms. The implications for corporate exchange governance are analysed in Chapter 4. However, there are other forms of competition among exchanges whose rationale lies in diverse price discovery mechanisms. See N. Poser (2001) 'The Stock Exchanges of the United States and Europe: Automation, Globalization and Consolidation', *Journal of International Economic Law*, 497.
3. In fragmented markets the risks of negotiating with highly informed agents may give rise to high spreads due to inventory costs (see, among others, Stoll, 1989; Madhavan and Smidt, 1991).

4. Note that the term 'regulatory competition' dates back to C. Tiebout (1956) 'A Pure Theory of Local Expenditures', *Journal of Political Economy*, 64, who applied the term to the provision of public goods.
5. There is no theoretical consensus for the view that less stringent standards are not at all desirable. On the one hand, some complain about over-regulation in the exchange industry, suggesting that increased competition would result in the absorption of certain excesses in regulation; according to this view, regulatory arbitrage would be desirable and the mechanism driving this arbitrage is so-called *issuer choice* (see Romano, 1998; Choi and Guzman, 1998). Against this, some theoreticians suggest that regulatory arbitrage prompts an undesirable race to the bottom.
6. While a sort of home bias persists, we note that issuers may seek a listing abroad as a primary listing or cross-listing in order to be closer to potential capital suppliers, innovation opportunities or customers.
7. As we will see in the following chapter, the morphology of the exchange industry nowadays has some features which resemble networks among the largest exchanges across the world.
8. Innovation in trading practices entails a significant trade-off between increased opportunities to access trading and the risks for market integrity entailed by high-frequency trading.
9. The origins of the Reg. NMS go back to 1975 when amendments to the Securities Exchange Act of 1934 laid the foundations for integrating order execution into a single computerized trading system. In 2005 the SEC adopted Reg. NMS, giving concrete form to the system in US equity markets and reshaping the links between trading venues.
10. We recall, for example, the T2S project enforced by the European Central Bank for overcoming fragmentation in European clearing and settlement procedures.
11. It should also stimulate investment in innovation and thus exert downward pressures on trading costs. With regard to innovation, it might include both technological innovation (fast and reliable trading platforms which reduce latency and failures) and trading opportunities such as smart order routing or high frequency trading solutions.
12. MiFID overcomes one drawback in the previous regulatory framework (the ISD) which applied the mutual recognition passport only to regulated markets, thereby creating significant hurdles to other platforms in terms of competing freely. In contrast, under MiFID all markets are subject to the same market-integrity standards.
13. To ensure fair access to the best-displayed quotations the access rule establishes an upper limit for the cost of accessing those quotations.
14. In order to address the critical aspects involved in strict price priority, the SEC allows fast markets (i.e. electronic markets) to trade-through better prices on slower (manual, floor-based) markets. By contrast, faster markets are not allowed to trade-through better prices displayed on another fast market.
15. A consolidation system is seen as an essential requirement for the efficient functioning of the ITC system.
16. Non-homogeneous protocols and operational standards alongside with interoperability problems were recognized as the major obstacles to full

integration at the post-trading level by the first Giovannini Report (2001) *Cross-Border Clearing and Settlement Arrangements in the European Union*. The Giovannini Group envisaged a comprehensive strategy to overcome barriers to full integration with the priority going to full platform interoperability and homogeneous settlement cycles; see *Second Report on EU Clearing and Settlement Arrangements* (2003).

17. See the European Commission, Commission Staff Working Document (2008) *Improving the Efficiency, Integration and Safety and Soundness of Cross-Border Post-Trading Arrangements in Europe*.
18. See FESE and EACH (2006) *European Code of Conduct for Clearing and Settlement*. In 2007 the same organizations signed an agreement with specific conditions regulating access and interoperability (see the *Access and Interoperability Guideline*).
19. See ESMA Final Report (2012)*Draft Technical Standards under the Regulation (EU) No 648/2012 of the European Parliament and of the Council of 4 July 2012 on OTC Derivatives, CCPs and Trade Repositories*.
20. A tighter approach to access rights here refers to a more restrictive approach to retention policies by platform operators in terms of lower transparency, other access restrictions or the bundling of different services.
21. We may recall, for example, the proposals of the US Dodd–Frank Act, and EMIR, which makes the case for OTC derivatives transactions to be regulated through central counterparties.
22. For an assessment of potential impacts see ESMA(2012)*Annex VIII of the Final report on the draft Regulatory and Implementing Technical Standards on Regulation (EU) 648/2012 for OTC derivatives, central counterparties and trade repositories. Impact Assessment*.
23. For example, CME Clearing Europe is planning to launch open-access clearing for OTC financial derivatives, including CSD. The same path is being followed by the Hong Kong Exchanges and Clearing Houses in Asia. Repurchase agreements (REPOs) are another type of financial transaction that are increasingly subject to central counterparty clearing.
24. A similar solution was followed by the NASDAQ and NYSE that combined their member-regulation functions into a single entity,the Financial Industry Regulatory Authority (FINRA).

4 The Governance Of Securities Exchanges. New Insights

1. The others are the (Spanish) Bolsas y Mercados Españoles (BME), the Brazilian BM&FBOVESPA, the Mexican Exchange, Bolsa de Santiago, Bolsa de Colombia, the Johannesburg Stock Exchange, the Singapore Stock Exchange, the Hong Kong Exchanges and Clearing Houses, the Philippine Stock Exchange, Bolsa de Manila, the Australian Securities Exchange and the Osaka Stock Exchange (the latter now the Japanese Exchange following the merger with the Tokyo Stock Exchange, which was completed in 2012 and became effective from 2013).
2. The largest American exchanges (NYSE and NASDAQ) were incorporated in 2005 and went public following subsequent mergers with already listed exchanges. The BME went public in 2006, and in 2008 it was the turn of CBOE, one of the major derivatives markets.

3. More precisely, the Polish government holds a 38% stake in the Warsaw Stock Exchange and is entrusted with 51% of the voting rights. Despite being a listed exchange, the prevailing vested interests are, arguably, those related to a well-functioning marketplace.
4. Value distribution appears to be relevant to the outcome of merger proposals; the Deutsche Börse bid over the LSEG is a case in point.
5. In most countries publicly traded firms, far from being widely held, actually present only a few controlling shareholders who have the power to designate and monitor managers. See R. La Porta, F. Lopez-de-Silanes and A. Shleifer (1999) 'Corporate Ownership Around the World', *Journal of Finance*, 54.
6. For example, firewalls may consist of Chinese walls that prevent the exchange of information and remuneration policies for regulatory management which are not correlated with other functions undertaken by the exchange.
7. See G. Rooks, W. Raub and F. Tazelaar(2006)'Ex Post Problems in Buyer–Supplier Transactions: Effects of Transactions Characteristics, Social Embeddedness and Contractual Governance', *Journal of Management and Governance*, 10, 3, 239–76.
8. Regulation contributed to this outcome as well by ruling out the concentration of trading, and promoting increasing convergence at post-trading level which aligns costs of cross-border trades to those of domestic trades. Refer to Chapter 3 for an in-depth analysis of the impact of regulation on the economics of exchanges and trading platforms.

5 The Economics of Exchanges

1. For an excellent review of the most relevant contributions to this strand of research, in particular with reference to ownership models and the critical factors affecting efficiency, see R. Lee (2011) *Running the World's Markets: The Governance of Financial Infrastructure* (Princeton University Press).
2. It is worth noting that under MiFID regulation in Europe, institutional investors may directly access the trading system without the intervention of a broker. Investment banks, on the other hand, largely engage in developing alternative platforms for the purpose of enjoying more favourable trading environments to established exchanges.
3. The authors support the notion of the exchange as an institution performing two functions (processing of transactions and evaluation of issuer-specific information) for the purpose of producing two outputs – number and value of trades and number and value of listed companies. The inputs of the production are technology and office expenses and employee costs. This is coherent with what emerges after analysing the main cost items of exchanges, for which see Chapter 2.
4. As we have pointed out, the exchange industry is nowadays even more populated by multi-business exchanges. Notwithstanding this, we believe that focusing on a two-business platform is not too restrictive a hypothesis. Almost all business lines benefit, at least indirectly, from companies admitted to trading and traders admitted to use the trading platforms.
5. Obviously, this holds only to the extent that levels of competition in the industry do not harm the ability of the trading venue to withhold listings in its country.

6. Such a level may be identified with a long-term *Ncr/GDP* ratio in the macro-region where the exchange has its main operations. By assuming a long-term rate we smooth the cyclical fluctuations in macroeconomic conditions. As such, the long-term *Ncr/GDP* rate captures the potential growth rate in the exchange industry.
7. We may think of it as the growth rate in the labour force needed to move along the 1/v curve.
8. The magnitude of change in capital expenses and labour costs, however, is not dependent only on shifts in production but on the industry structure as well. With consolidation in the industry going forward, we expect the rationalization of platform operations making substantial improvements. For example, rationalizations in all of the relevant functions (in particular, admission to listing and monitoring on issuers and operations) of exchanges and other systems may lead to relevant savings in labour and, therefore, to a lower labour/capital ratio.
9. The sale of market data, for example, is dependent on the volumes of trades processed. Post-trading activities grow with trading values as well.
10. The taker–maker model is not particularly widespread. Almost all platforms adopting access fees resort to a maker–taker model.
11. Therefore, a maker–taker pricing model would resemble the widespread practice of payment for order flow.
12. Actually, it means, de facto, the introduction of an order-driven approach within a quote-driven trading environment.
13. In fact, such exchanges didn't charge fees over orders coming from public customers. By contrast, both market makers and broker dealers were charged a per-contract fee on their executions.
14. This implies $\beta_c < \frac{(\beta_{cT}\beta_{Tv} + \beta_{cO}\beta_{Oth})}{\beta_{Tv} + \beta_O\beta_{Oth}} + \frac{[a_{cT} + a_{cO} - a_c]}{TV} \cdot \frac{1}{(\beta_{Tv} + \beta_O\beta_{Oth})}$ where β_c, β_{cT} *and* β_{cO} are the marginal costs of supplying both trading and complementary services, cash trading services only and other services only, respectively.
15. The consolidation process is mainly targeted to pursue rationalizations in the business structure and efficiencies in corporate operations, quite apart from exploiting network externalities by expanding the pool of liquidity. In almost all of the mergers the business plans foresee relevant cuts in costs spreading across all the business functions. By sharing business functions (e.g. the admission to listing) the merging entities plan relevant savings in personnel costs. On the other side, business combinations in the exchange industry support improvements in trading platforms. Therefore, we may expect mergers to result, to some extent, in a rebalancing of the inputs of exchanges with an increase in capital inputs relative to labour.
16. It is worth noting that the phenomena is common at both trading and post-trading level. At each stage of the value chain, in fact, consolidation had led to a substantial consolidation of technical infrastructure.
17. There still remain some small regional exchanges which may be assumed to retain a degree of market power over shares they admit to trading.
18. As we pointed out in Chapter 2 both exchanges and their competitors are largely owned by entities which have interests in trading. Both institutional

investors holding large stakes in exchanges and alternative platforms owned by large investments banks are concerned by the overall costs of trading. Given the profit maximization objective of platforms operators, we assume for the purposes of our model that the objective function of their shareholders is endogenous.

19. Our model resembles somewhat the prevailing models in the literature such as those by Malkamäki and Andersen.
20. Additionally, alternative platforms are emanations from large brokers, or are partnerships between large investment banks with access to advanced technologies and a consolidated network of customer relations.
21. These cost items have, normally, a regulatory origin. The US Intermarket Trading System (ITS) requires orders first routed to an exchange to be sent to other trading platforms when they provide better prices. Obviously, the latter charge a fee per share for routing to their systems. The routing exchange, however, retains the customer relation.
22. The terms are: $\frac{\partial D_T \partial T_{fi}}{\partial T_{fi} \partial T_{fi}}$ and $\frac{\partial D_L \partial L_{fi}}{\partial L_{fi} \partial L_{fi}}$.
23. Cross-network externalities within the same platform are captured by the terms $\frac{\partial D_L}{\partial V_i}\frac{\partial V_i}{\partial T_{fi}}$, $\frac{\partial D_T}{\partial L_i}\frac{\partial L_i}{\partial L_{fi}}$ (which express the impact on the demand on side B={T,L} of changes in quantity on the other side as a result of changes in their own prices) and the terms $\frac{\partial D_T}{\partial L_i}\frac{\partial L_i}{\partial T_{fi}}$, $\frac{\partial D_L}{\partial V_i}\frac{\partial V_i}{\partial L_{fi}}$ (which express the impact on the demand on side B={T,L} of changes in quantity on the other side as a result of changes in the other side's prices).
24. The relevant terms are $\frac{\partial D_L}{\partial L_{fi}}\frac{\partial L_{fi}}{\partial T_{fi}}$, and $\frac{\partial D_T}{\partial T_{fi}}\frac{\partial T_{fi}}{\partial L_{fi}}$.
25. As is well known, of course, the choice of trading platform depends on a variety of factors (costs, speed, execution strategies) and this is what explains the success of certain alternative networks.
26. For example, cross-selling opportunities may arise between cash and derivatives markets. With the exchange expanding its penetration in equity and bond trading the underlings on which to offer derivatives contracts increase as well. Other relevant cross-selling opportunities may develop across trading (either on cash and derivatives markets) and information products. In fact, the greater the liquidity of the markets (with all the relevant implications for the quality of price discovery) the greater the relevance of the price's informative content for market operators. They, therefore, would place a great deal of importance on the information disseminated by market operators.

6 A Risk-Adjusted Model for Peformance Measurement

1. Since the regulations for both banks and insurance companies are grounded, at least in the most advanced approaches, on the use of internal models for calculating regulatory capital, financial institutions are clearly encouraged to

extend the use of such models for purposes that go far beyond mere compliance with capital regulation. Arguably, the calibration of an internal model is strictly dependent on its diffusion throughout the entire range of managerial functions.

2. Their rationale for risk management is, however, closely related to that laid down in the context of non-financial corporations in K. Froot, D. Scharfstein and J. Stein (1993) 'Risk Management: Coordinating Corporate Investment and Financing Policies', *Journal of Finance*, 48, 5.
3. For a formal demonstration of the drawbacks of the VAR for assessing the risk-return trade-off see Artzner et al. (1999) 'Coherent Measures of Risk', *Mathematical Finance*, 9.
4. Despite agreeing that the VAR is a poor measure of risk, the authors implicitly maintain in their study that it is acceptable when assessing the probability of default.
5. More recently the issue has been further investigated in A. Milne and M. Onorato (2012) 'Risk-Adjusted Measures of Value Creation in Financial Institutions', *European Financial Management*, 18, 4.

7 The Economics of the Exchange Industry: An Empirical Overview

1. We refer readers to Chapter 2 for a discussion on the relations between exchanges and other platforms. We document the fact that the relevant markets for fast growing ECNs such as Chi-X and BATS tend to overlap with that of the main exchanges. Arguably, competitive threats spurring from ECNs highly affect the revenue volatility of established exchanges.
2. We recall the linear relation between costs and revenues $(C = \alpha + \beta Rev)$, the relations between trading value and number of companies listed $(Tv = \alpha_1 + \beta_1 L)$, between listing revenues and listed companies $(L_{Rev} = \theta + \vartheta L)$ and between trading revenues and trading value $(CT_{Rev} = \alpha_{TV} + \beta_{TV} TV)$. See Table A.1 in the Appendix for the estimated coefficients across the exchanges in our sample.
3. Our approach is similar to Hasan and Malkamäki (2001) in which the cost function is related to different measures of an exchange's output, in particular the number of trades and trading value for the trading business and number of companies listed and market capitalization for listings.
4. We exclude the Bursa Malaysia, the Warsaw Stock Exchange and the Athens Exchange: the data available are not significant.
5. Chapter 6 discusses at length the notion of capital employed. We adjust total assets in the calculation of the capital employed by excluding certain special current assets related to the conduct of clearing business.
6. However, it should be noted that not all figures are significant. For NYSE Euronext we have data only from 2007 when the merger between NYSE and Euronext was completed. The 48.1x figure for the P/E is, therefore, misleading.
7. We counted 19 deals.
8. According to the terms and conditions of the offer, the implied valuation of LSEG in the bid for TMX is of 10.4 for the EV/EBITDA.

9. Moreover, the implied share value of NYSE Euronext in the Deutsche Börse (25.4$ per share) offer is far below the NYSE Euronext market value at the announcement date (33.4$ per share).
10. As previously noted ECNs operate with far lower margins than established exchanges. For comparative purposes, Chi-X has revenues that are 10% of LSEG revenues.
11. Valuing the company at 610 millions €.
12. CME, despite presenting a high EPS CAGR, experienced poor share performances. NASDAQ OMX itself, while being among the faster growing exchanges as for earnings, presents far lower share performances compared with Asian exchanges.
13. The distribution of skeweness is normal with median 0 and standard deviation of $\sqrt{\frac{6}{N}}$ where N is the number of observations.
14. In those cases where index returns are positively skewed, the skewness is nevertheless lower than that of corresponding exchanges' share returns, with the exception of BME.
15. Here we calculate the ratio of quarterly share performance on index performance. The ratio assumes positive values where the share experienced better performances than the index (both positive and negative) and negative values in the opposite case.
16. Both trading value and market capitalization are taken from WFE statistics.
17. In this we build on the standard governance literature. The idea is that the better investor protection and the lower the power to expropriate by controlling shareholders, the higher the price that outside investors would agree to pay for financial assets. La Porta et al. (2002) examine how ownership structure affects corporate value using the Tobin's q and the price-to-cash-flow ratio to measure corporate valuation.
18. Actually, apart from major financial centres around the world, the attractiveness of other exchanges for foreign issuers is rather limited.
19. As regards the dependent variable, for each quarter we calculate the beta on an annual basis.
20. The figures provided in the Appendix are calculated excluding the outliers. The first quarter of 2008, in particular, presents certain abnormal data.
21. The beta of the assets in place come from the following regression: $ROA_i = \alpha + \beta_{Aip} ROA_M + \varepsilon_i$ where ROA_i is the ROA of exchange i and ROA_M that of the market. We express the latter as the average ROA of our sample. We think that this is acceptable, since listed exchanges approximate the industry in terms of assets and revenues.
22. Calculated discounting the net operative income by a relevant cost of capital obtained from the beta of assets in place, applying the CAPM and considering a 4.23% risk premium (Fama and French, 2002). The risk-free rate is the yield on ten-year government bonds.
23. We measure financial leverage as the ratio of total liabilities, net of clearing funds and margins of clearing participants on total assets, net of the same liabilities.
24. We excluded the Bolsa de Santiago; the beta is not significant due to the virtual absence of movements in the share price. We also excluded those

exchanges for which the time series would be too short (more precisely, those exchanges listed in 2008).

25. Indeed, certain activities which were traditionally regarded as substantially shielded from cyclical dynamics (for example, derivatives trading) are increasingly exposed to competitive pressures.

References

Aggarwal, R. (2002) 'Demutualization and Corporate Governance of Stock Exchanges', *Journal of Applied Corporate Finance*, 15, 1: 105–13.

Aggarwai, R. and Dahiya, S. (2006) 'Demutualization and Public Offerings of Finanicial Exchanges', *Journal of Applied Corporate Finance*, 18, 3: 96–106.

Aite Group report (2009) *European Trading Venues Vie for Victory*, November.

Allen, F., McAndrews, J. and Strahan, P. (2002), 'E-Finance: An Introduction', *Journal of Financial Services Research*, 22, 1–2: 5–27.

Anand, B. N. and Khanna, T. (2000) 'Do Firms Learn to Create Value? The Case of Alliances', *Strategic Management Journal*, 21, 3: 295–315.

Andersen, A. (2005) 'Pricing of Stock Exchange Trading. The Role of Network Externalities', Helsinki School of Economics working paper.

Angel, J., Harris, L. and Spatt, C. S. (2010) *Equity Trading in the 21st Century*, USC Marshall School of Business working paper FBE, 09–10.

Armstrong, M. (2004) *Competition in Two-Sided Markets*, mimeo, University College, London.

Arnold, T., Hersch P., Mulherin, J. H. and Netter, J. (1999) 'Merging Markets', *Journal of Finance*, 52: 655–81: 1083–107.

Artzner, P. et al. (1999) 'Coherent Measures of Risk', *Mathematical Finance*, 9, 3: 203–28.

Bain, J. S. (1956) *Barriers to New Competition* (Cambridge: Harvard University Press).

Beaver, W. and Manegold, J. (1975) 'The Association Between Market-Determined and Accounting-Determined Measures of Systematic Risk: Some Further Evidence', *Journal of Financial and Quantitative Analysis*, 10, 2: 231–84.

Berle, A. and Means, G. (1932) *The Modern Corporation and Private Property* (New York: Macmillan).

Bolton, P., Santos, T. and Scheinkman, J. A. (2011) *Cream Skimming in Financial Markets*, NBER working paper no. 16804.

Brandes, Y., Domowitz, I. (2010) Alternative Trading Systems in Europe. Trading Performance by European Venues post-Mifid. Investment Technology Group, http://www.itg.com.

Brito-Ramos, S. (2006) *Why Do Stock Exchanges Demutualize and Go Public?*, Swiss Finance Institute research paper no. 06-10

Brown-Hruska, S. and Ellig, J. (2000) 'Financial markets as information monopolies?', *Regulation*, 23, 3: 29–35.

Brunnermeier, M. (2005) 'Information Leakage and Market Efficiency', *Review of Financial Studies*, 18, 2: 417–57.

Cantillon, E. and Yin, P. L. (2010) 'Competition Between Exchanges: A Research Agenda', *International Journal of Industrial Organization*, 29, 3: 329–36.

CESR (2010) 'Technical Advice to the European Commission in the Context of the MiFID Review: Equity Markets', 10–394.

Choi, S. and Guzman, A. (1998) 'Portable Reciprocity: Rethinking The International Reach of Securities Regulation', *Southern California Law Review*, 71: 903–51.

Choi, H. S., Clarke, J., Ferris, S. P. and Jayaraman, N. (2009) 'The Effects of Regulation on Industry Structure and Trade Generation in the US Securities Industry', *Journal of Banking and Finance*, 33, 8: 1434–45.

Chung, K. H. and Chuwonganant, C. (2011) 'Regulation NMS and Market Quality', SSRN working paper.

Coase, R. (1998) *The Firm, the Market and the Law* (Chicago: University of Chicago Press).

——— (1992) 'The Institutional Structure of Production', *American Economic Review*, 82, 4: 713–19.

Coffee, J. C. (2002) 'Racing Toward the Top?: The Impact of Cross-Listings and Stock Market Competition on International Corporate Governance', Columbia Law School, The Center for Law and Economic Studies working paper no. 205.

Cohen, K. J., Meyer, S. F., Schwartz, R. A. and Whitcomb, D. K. (1986) *The Microstructure of Securities Markets* (Englewood Cliffs, NJ: Prentice Hall), pp. 150–66.

Cohen, K. J., Conroy, R. and Maier, S. F. (1985) 'Order Flow and the Quality of the Market', in Y. Amihud, T. S. Y. Ho and R. A. Schwartz (eds) *Market Making and the Changing Structure of the Securities Industry* (Maryland: Beard Books).

Coval, J. D. and Moskovitz, T. J. (1999) 'Home Bias at Home: Local Equity Preference in Domestic Portfolios', *Journal of Finance*, 54, 6: 2045–73.

Crouhy, M., Turnbull, S. and Wakeman, L. (1999) 'Measuring Risk-Adjusted Performance', *Journal of Risk*, 2, 1: 5–35.

Cunningham, L. A. (1994) 'Capital Market Theory, Mandatory Disclosure and Price Discovery', *Washington and Lee Law Review*, 51, 3: 843–77.

De Andrés, P., de la Fuente, G., and Pacheco, Leonardo (2008) 'The Impact of Growth Options on Systematic Risk: The Case of European Firms', working paper.

Dessein, W. (2005) 'Information and Control in Ventures and Alliances', *Journal of Finance*, 65, 5: 2513–49.

Di Noia, C. (1998) 'Competition and Integration Among Stock Exchanges in Europe: Network Effects, Implicit Mergers and Remote Access', Wharton working paper series, 98-03.

——— (2001) 'Customer-Controlled Firms: The Case of Financial Exchanges', in Ferrarini, Hopt and Wymeersch (eds) *Capital Markets in the Age of the Euro* (The Hague: Kluwer).

Domowitz, I. (1995) 'Electronic Derivatives Exchanges: Implicit Mergers, Network Externalities and Standardization', *Quarterly Review of Economics and Finance*, 35, 2: 163–75.

——— (1996) 'An Exchange Is a Many-Splendored Thing: The Classification and Regulation of Automated Trading Systems', in A. W. Lo (ed.) *The Industrial Organization and Regulation of the Securities Industry* (Chicago: University of Chicago Press).

Domowitz, I. and Steil, B. (1999) 'Automation, Trading Costs and the Structure of the Securities Trading Industry', in R. Litan and A. Santomero (eds) *Brookings-Wharton Papers on Financial Services*.

——— (2002) 'Innovation in Equity Trading Systems: The Impact on Transactions Costs and Cost of Capital', in B. Steil, D. G. Victor and R. R. Nelson (eds) *Technological Innovation and Economic Performance* (Princeton: Princeton University Press).

Easley, D., Kiefer, N. M. and O'Hara, M. (1996) 'Cream-Skimming or Profit-Sharing? The Curious Role of Purchased Order Flow', *Journal of Finance*, 51, 3: 811–33.

Economides, N. (1993) 'Network Economics with Application to Finance', *Financial Markets Institutions & Instruments*, 2, 5: 89–97.

Economides, N. and Flyer, F. (1997) 'Compatibility and Market Structure for Network Goods', Stern School of Business discussion paper EC-98-02.

ESMA (2012) *Draft Technical Standards Under the Regulation (EU) No 648/2012 of the European Parliament and of the Council of 4 July 2012 on OTC Derivatives, CCPs and Trade Repositories*, Final Report.

——— *Annex VIII of the Final report on draft Regulatory and Implementing Technical Standards on Regulation (EU) 648/2012 on OTC derivatives, central counterparties and trade repositories*, Impact Assessment.

European Commission (2008) 'Improving the Efficiency, Integration and Safety and Soundness of Cross-Border Post-Trading Arrangements in Europe', Commission staff working document.

Evans, D. S. (2003) 'The Antitrust Economics of Multi-Sided Platform Markets', *Yale Journal on Regulation*, 20, 2: 325–81.

Evans, D. S. and Noel, M. (2005) 'Defining Antitrust Markets When Firms Operate Multi-Sided Platforms', *Columbia Business Law Review*, 3: 667–701.

Evans, D. S. and Schmalensee, R. (2007) 'The Industrial Organization of Markets with Two Side Platforms', *Competition Policy International*, 3, 1: 151–79.

Fama, E. F. and French, K. R. (1992) 'The Cross-Section of Expected Stock Returns', *Journal of Finance*, 47: 427–65.

——— (2002) 'The Equity Premium', *Journal of Finance*, 57, 2: 637–59.

Fialkowski, D. and Petersen, M. (1992) 'Posted versus Effective Spreads: Good Prices or Bad Quotes?', University of Chicago Center for Research in Security Prices working paper.

Fischel, D. R. (1978) 'Efficient Capital Market Theory, the Market for Corporate Control and the Regulation of Cash Tender Offers' in K. Scott and R. Posner (eds) *Economic Perspectives on Corporation Law and Securities Regulation* (London: Little Brown).

Fischel, D. R. and Grossman, S. J. (1984) 'Customer Protection in Futures and Securities Markets', *Journal of Futures Markets*, 4, 3: 273–95.

Fleckner, A. M. (2006) 'Stock Exchanges at the Crossroads', *Fordham Law Review*, 74, 5: 2541–620.

French, K. R. and Poterba, J. M. (1991) 'Investor Diversification and International Equity Markets', *American Economic Review*, 81, 2: 222–26.

Froot, K., Scharfstein, D. and Stein, J. (1993) 'Risk Management: Coordinating Corporate Investment and Financing Policies', *Journal of Finance*, 48, 5: 1629–58.

Froot, K. and Stein J. (1995) 'Risk Management, Capital Budgeting and Capital Structure Policy for Financial Institutions: An Integrated Approach', NBR working paper 5403.

——— (1998) 'Risk Management, Capital Budgeting and Capital Structure Policy for Financial Institutions: An Integrated Approach', *Journal of Financial Economics*, 47, 1: 55–82.

Gahlon, J. M. and Gentry, J. A. (1982) 'On the Relationship Between Systematic Risk and the Degrees of Operating and Financial Leverage, *Financial Management*, 11, 2: 15–23.

Galai, D. and Masulis, R. W. (1976) 'The Option Pricing Model and the Risk Factor of Stock', *Journal of Financial Economics*, 3, 1–2: 53–81.

Galper, J. (1999) 'Three Business Models For the Stock Exchange Industry', in International Federation of Exchanges working paper.

Gillan, S. L. (2006) 'Recent Developments in Corporate Governance: An Overview', *Journal of Corporate Finance*, 12, 3: 381–402.

Giovannini Group (2001) 'Cross-Border Clearing and Settlement Arrangements in the European Union, Buxelles', November.
——— (2003) 'Second Report on EU Cross-Border Clearing and Settlement Arrangements, Buxelles', April.
Gomber, P. and Pierron, A. (2010) 'MiFID – Spirit and Reality of a European Financial Markets Directive', report published by Celant.
Gomes-Casseres, B., Hagedoorn, J. and Jaffe, A. B. (2006) 'Do Alliances Promote Knowledge Flows?', *Journal of Financial Economics*, 80, 1: 5–33.
Greenwald, B., Levinson, A. and Stiglitz, J E. (1991) 'Capital Market Imperfections and Regional Economic Development', paper prepared for CEPR conference on Finance and Development in Europe, Santiago, Spain.
Gresse, C. (2010) 'Post-MiFID Developments in Equity Market Liquidity', AMF working paper no. 8.
Grossman, S. J. and Hart, O. D., (1980) 'Takeover Bids, the Free-Rider Problem, and the Theory of the Corporation', *Rand Journal of Economics*, 11, 1: 42–64.
——— (1986) 'The Costs and Benefits of Ownership: A Theory of Vertical Integration', *Journal of Political Economy*, 94, 4: 691–719.
Hail, L. and Leuz, C. (2008) 'Cost of Capital Effects and Changes in Growth Expectations Around U.S. Cross-Listings', *Journal of Financial Economics*, 93, 3: 428–54.
Hamada, R. S. (1972) 'The Effect of the Firm's Capital Structure on the Systematic Risk of Common Stocks', *Journal of Finance*, 27, 2: 435–52.
Hart, O. and Moore, J. (1996) 'The Governance of Exchanges: Members' Cooperatives Versus Outside Ownership', *Oxford Review of Economic Policy*, 12, 4.
Hasan, I. and Malkamäki, M. (2001) 'Are Expansions Cost Effective for Stock Exchanges? A Global Perspective', *Journal of Banking and Finance*, 25, 12: 2339–66.
Hasan, I., Schmiedel, H. and Song, L. (2010) 'Growth Strategies and Value Creation: What Works Best for Stock Exchanges?', ECB working paper no. 1201.
Hautcoeur, P. C., Rezaee, A. M. and Riva A. (2010) *Stock Exchange Industry Regulation. The Paris Bourse, 1893–1898* (Bank of Italy).
Hirst, I. R., Danbolt, J. and Jones, E. (2008) 'Required Rates of Return for Corporate Investment Opportunities in the Presence of Growth Opportunities', *European Financial Management*, 14, 5: 989–1006.
Huberman, G. (2001) 'Familiarity Breeds Investment', *Review of Financial Studies*, 14, 3: 659–80.
Huberman, G. and Sengmuller, P. (2002) 'Company Stock in 401 (k) Plans', working paper, Columbia University.
Huddart, S., Hughes, J. S., and Brunnermeier, M. (1999) 'Disclosure Requirements and Stock Exchange Listing Choice in an International Context', *Journal of Accounting and Economics*, 26, 1–3: 237–69.
IOSCO (2001) *Issues Paper on Exchange Demutualization*, Report of the Technical Committee of the International Organization of Securities Commissions.
Jorgensen, B. N., Kavajecz, K. A. and Swisher, S. N. (2011) 'The Historical Evolution of Financial Exchanges', SSRN working papers.
Kashyap, A., K. and Stein, J. C. (1994) 'The Impact of Monetary Policy on Bank Balance Sheets', National Bureau of Economic Research working paper no. 4821.
Kester, W. C. (1984) 'Today's Options for Tomorrow's Growth', *Harvard Business Review*, March/April: 153–60.

Knipes, G. (2006) 'Competition in the Post-Trade Markets: A Network Economic Analysis of the Securities Business', *Journal of Industry, Competition and Trade,* 6, 1: 45–60.

Kothari, S. P., Shanken, J. and Sloan, R. G. (1995) 'Another Look at the Cross-Section of Expected Stock Returns', *Journal of Finance,* 50, 1: 185–224.

Lannoo, K. and Levine, M. (2001) *The Securities Settlement Industry in the EU: Structure Costs and the Way Forward* (CEPS Publications).

La Porta, R., Lopez-de-Silanes, F. and Shleifer, A. (1999) 'Corporate Ownership Around the World', *Journal of Finance,* 54, 2: 471–517.

La Porta, R., Lopez-de-Silanes, F., Shleifer, A. and Vishny, R. (2002) 'Investor Protection and Corporate Valuation', *Journal of Finance,* 57, 3: 1147–70.

Lee, R. (1988) *What is an Exchange?* (Oxford University Press).

——— (1995) *The Ownership of Price and Quote Information: Law, Regulation, Economics and Business* (Oxford: Oxford Finance Group).

——— (1996) 'Supervising EC Capital Markets: Do We Need a European SEC?', in R. Buxbaum, G. Hertig, A. Hirsch and K. Hopt (eds) *European Economic Business Law: Legal and Economic Analyses on Integration and Harmonization* (Berlin and New York: Walter de Gruyter).

——— (2011) *Running the World's Markets: The Governance of Financial Infrastructure* (Princeton University Press).

Lel, U. and Miller, D. P. (2006) 'International Cross-Listing, Firm Performance and Top Management Turnover: A Test of the Bonding Hypothesis', *Journal of Finance,* 63, 4: 1897–1937.

Lewis, K. K. (1999) 'Trying to Explain Home Bias in Equities and Consumption', *Journal of Economic Literature,* 37, 2: 571–608.

Macey, J. R. and O'Hara, M. (1997) 'The Law and Economics of Best Execution', *Journal of Financial Intermediation,* 6, 3: 188–223.

——— (1999) 'Globalization, Exchange Governance and the Future of Exchanges', in R. Litan and A. Santomero (eds) *Brookings-Wharton Papers on Financial Services.*

Madhavan, A. and Smidt, S. (1991) 'A Bayesian Model of Intraday Specialist Pricing', *Journal of Financial Economics,* 30, 1: 99–134.

McInish, T. H. and Wood, A. R. (1996) 'Competition, Fragmentation, and Market Quality', in A. W. Lo (ed.) *The Industrial Organization and Regulation of the Securities Industry* (Chicago: University of Chicago Press).

Meltzer, A. H. (1969) 'On Efficiency and Regulation of the Securities Industry', in H. G. Manne (ed.) *Economic Policy and the Regulation of Corporate Securities* (Washington: American Enterprise Institute for Public Policy Research).

Mendiola, A. and O'Hara, M. (2004) 'Taking Stock in the Stock Markets: The Changing Governance of Exchanges', SSRN working paper.

Milne, A. and Onorato, M. (2010) 'Apples and Pears: The Relationship Between Risk Capital and Required Returns in Financial Institutions', Bank of Finland discussion paper series.

——— (2012) 'Risk-Adjusted Measures of Value Creation in Financial Institutions', *European Financial Management,* 18, 4: 578–601.

Mishkin, F. S. and Strahan, P. (1999) 'What Will Technology do to Financial Structure?', NBER working paper no. 6892.

Modigliani, F. (1958) 'New Developments on the Oligopoly Front', *Journal of Political Economy,* 66, 3: 215–32.

Morsy, A. M. (2010) 'Understanding the Relationship Between the Demutualization Decision of Stock Exchanges and the Theory of the Firm: A Theoretical Research Note', *European Journal of Economics, Finance and Administrative Sciences*, 23, August: 139–48.

Mulherin, J. H., Netter, J. M. and Overdahl, J. (1991) 'Prices are Property: The Organization of Financial Exchanges from a Transaction Cost Perspective', *Journal of Law and Economics*, 34, 2: 591–644.

Myers, S. C. and Turnbull, S. M. (1977) 'Capital Budgeting and the Capital Asset Pricing Model: Good News and Bad News', *Journal of Finance*, 32, 2: 321–33.

Oesterle, D., Winslow, D. and Anderson, S. (1992) 'The New York Stock Exchange and its Outmoded Specialist System: Can the Exchange Innovate to Survive?', *Journal of Corporate Law*, 17: 223–310.

O'Hara, M. (2005) *Market Microstructure Theory* (Cambridge: Blackwell Publishers).

——— (2004) 'Searching for a New Center: U.S. Securities Markets in Transition', *Federal Reserve Bank of Atlanta, Economic Review*, fourth quarter.

Otchere, I. (2006) 'Stock Exchange Self-Listing and Value Effects', *Journal of Corporate Finance*, 12, 5: 926–53.

Otchere, I. and Oldford, E. (2011) 'Can Commercialization Iimprove the Performance of Stock Exchanges even without Corporatization?', *The Financial Review*, 46, 1: 67–87.

Pagano, M., Röell, A. A. and Zechner, J. (2002) 'The Geography of Equity Listing: Why do Companies List Abroad?', *Journal of Finance*, 57, 6: 2651–94.

Pan, E. J. (2007) 'A European Solution to the Regulation of Cross-Border Markets', *Brooklyn Journal of Corporate, Financial & Commercial Law*, 2, 1: 133–65.

Pirrong, C. (2000) 'A Theory of Financial Exchange Organization', *Journal of Law and Economics*, 43, 2: 437–71.

Polato, M. and Floreani, J. (2010) 'Measuring Value in Stock Exchanges' Mergers, in Consolidation in the European Financial Industry', in R. Bottiglia, E. Gualandri and G. N. Mazzocco (eds) *Consolidation in the European Financial Industry* (Basingstoke: Palgrave Macmillan), pp. 182–206.

——— (2010) 'Value and Governance in the Exchange Industry: The Case of Diversified Conglomerate Exchanges', in F. Fiordelisi, P. Molyneux and D. Previati (eds) *New Issues in Financial Institutions Management* (Basingstoke: Palgrave Macmillan).

——— (2012) 'Stock Exchanges Mergers at the Aftermath of the Crisis. New Insights', in Juan Fernández de Guevara Radoselovics and José Pastor Monsálvez (eds) *Crisis, Risk and Stability in Financial Markets* (Basingstoke: Palgrave Macmillan).

Poser, N. (2001) 'The Stock Exchanges of the United States and Europe: Automation, Globalization and Consolidation', *Journal of International Economic Law*, 497, 22, 3: 497–540.

Pownall, G., Vulcheva, M. and Wang, X. (2012) 'The Post-Merger Segmentation of Euronext. A Solution to the Inadequacy of National Securities Regulators?', working paper.

Redler, S. (2010) 'SEC Should Rethink Reg NMS to Fix HFT Liquidity Problem', *MrSwing*, http://www.mrswing.com/articles/SEC_Should_Rethink_Reg_NMS_to_Fix_HFT_Liquidity_Pr.html.

Rochet, J. C. and Tirole, J. (2001) 'Platform Competition in Two-Sided Markets', *Journal of the European Economic Association*, 1, 4: 990–1029.

——— (2006) 'Two Sided-Markets: A Progress Report', *Rand Journal of Economics*.
Rooks, G., Raub, W. and Tazelaar, F. (2006) 'Ex Post Problems in Buyer–Supplier Transactions: Effects of Transactions Characteristics, Social Embeddedness and Contractual Governance', *Journal of Management and Governance*, 10, 3: 239–76.
Romano, R. (1998) 'Empowering Investors: A Market Approach to Securities Regulation', *Yale Law Journal*, 107, 8: 2359–430.
——— (2001) 'The Need for Competition in International Securities Regulation', Yale ICF working paper no. 00–49.
Scherer, F. M. and Ross, D. (1990) *Industrial Market Structure and Economic Performance* (Boston: Houghton Mifflin).
Schmiedel, H. (2001) 'Technological Development and Concentration of Stock Exchanges in Europe', Bank of Finland working paper no. 21.
——— (2002) 'Total Factor Productivity Growth in European Stock Exchanges: A Non Parametric Frontier Approach', Bank of Finland discussion paper no. 11.
Schmiedel, H. and Schönenberger, A. (2005) 'Integration of Securities Market Infrastructures in the Euro Area', European Central Bank occasional paper no. 33.
Seppi, D. (1997) 'Liquidity Provision with Limit Orders and Strategic Specialist', *Review of Financial Studies*, 10, 1: 103–50.
Serifsoy, B. (2007) 'Stock Exchange Business Models and their Operative Performance', *Journal of Banking and Finance*, 31, 10: 2978–3012.
——— (2010) 'Essays on Stock Exchange Efficiency, Business Models, and Governance: An Economic Analysis on the Stock Exchange Industry', VDM Verlag.
Serifsoy, B. and Tyler, M. (2006) 'Investment Behavior of Stock Exchanges and the Rationale for Demutualization – Theory and Empirical Evidence', Financial Institutions Center working paper no. 17.
Shleifer, A. and Vishny, R. W. (1986) 'Large Shareholders and Corporate Control', *Journal of Political Economy*, 94, 3: 461–88.
Shleifer, A. and Vishny, R. W. (1997) 'A Survey of Corporate Governance', *Journal of Finance*, 52, 2: 737–83.
Shy, O. and Tarkka, J. (2001) 'Stock Exchanges Alliances, Access Fees and Competition', Bank of Finland discussion paper no. 22.
Skjeltorp, J. A., Sojli, E. and Tham, W. W. (2012) *Identifying Cross-Sided Liquidity Externalities* (London: Cass Business School).
Song, L., Schmiedel, H. and Hasan, I. (2010) 'Growth Strategies and Value Creation. What Works Best for Stock Exchanges?', European Central Bank working paper no. 1201.
Steil, B. (2002) 'Changes in the Ownership and Governance of Securities Exchanges: Causes and Consequences', in R. E. Litan and R. Herring (eds) *Brookings-Wharton Papers on Financial Services*.
Stoll, H. R. (1989) 'Inferring the Components of the Bid–Ask Spread: Theory and Empirical Tests', *Journal of Finance*, 44, 1: 115–34.
Stoughton, M. N. and Zechner, J. (2003) 'Optimal Capital Allocation Using RAROC and EVA', working paper.
Stulz, R. (1999) 'Globalization, Corporate Finance and the Cost of Capital', *Journal of Applied Corporate Finance*, 12, 3: 8–25.
Sylos-Labini, P. (1962) *Oligopoly and Technical Progress* (Cambridge: Harvard University Press).
TABB Group (2009) 'Trading in the Dark in Europe: Choice and Complexity on the Cusp of Change', October.

Tafara, E. and Peterson, R. J. (2007) 'A Blueprint for Cross-Border Access to U.S. Investors: A new International Framework', *Harvard International Law Review*, 48, 1: 31–68.

Tesar, L. and Werner, I. (1995) 'Home Bias and High Turnover', *Journal of International Money and Finance*, 14, 4: 467–92.

Tiebout, C. (1956) 'A Pure Theory of Local Expenditures', *Journal of Political Economy*, 64, 5: 416–24.

Tirole, J. (1993) *The Theory of Industrial Organization* (Cambridge: The Mit Press).

Webb, R. I. (2003) 'Transitory Real-Time Property Rights and Exchange Intellectual Property', *Journal of Futures Markets*, 23, 9: 891–913.

Williamson, O. E. (1985) *The Economic Institutions of Capitalism* (New York: The Free Press).

World Federation of Exchanges (2002) 'Member Exchanges' Cost & Revenue Survey 2010', July.

——— (2004) 'Extended Exchange Services. Survey Conducted for the WFE Working Committee by the Taiwan Stock Exchange Corporation', March.

Worthington, A. C. and Higgs, H. (2005) 'Market Risk in Demutualised Self-Listed Stock Exchanges: An International Analysis of Selected Time-Varying Betas', School of Accounting and Finance, University of Wollongong accounting and finance working paper 05/06.

Zaik, E., Walter, J., Kelling, G. and James, C. (1996) 'RAROC at Bank of America: From Theory to Practice', *Journal of Applied Corporate Finance*, 9, 2: 83–93.

Index

Printed and bound in Great Britain by
CPI Group (UK) Ltd, Croydon, CR0 4YY